MODEL

MODEL

BY MARK STEVENS

HARPER & ROW, PUBLISHERS, New York
Cambridge, Hagerstown, Philadelphia, San Francisco,
London, Mexico City, São Paulo, Sydney

1817

FIRST EDITION

Designed by C. Linda Dingler

U.S. Library of Congress Cataloging in Publication Data

Stevens, Mark, birth date
  Model.
  Includes index.
  1. Models, Fashion—United States. 1. Title.
HD6073.M772U57 1981   659.1'52   80–10573
ISBN 0-06-014906-X

---

81 82 83 84 85 10 9 8 7 6 5 4 3 2 1

To Harly David,
My gift from God

CONTENTS

ACKNOWLEDGMENTS

To the many talented and beautiful models who shared their observations and insights with the author and whose names, in many cases, have been changed in this book. And to Arnold Dolin, who as always contributed his talent, skills, and, most important, his constant concern for quality.

MODEL

1

MODELING
A World Built on Dreams

"Being a model was my dream ever since I was five years old. Mom told me that I was beautiful—that I should be a star —and I believed her. And you know what, now that I am a model I'm glad I believed. Because modeling is everything great and wonderful. It's the dream life for every girl. Modeling makes me feel so alive. Playing up to the camera is the ultimate turn-on."
—Dawn, 18, during her first month as a New York model

"Where I am now in modeling is wonderful; it's all I thought it would be. But those early years were awful. Going on go-sees is disheartening. I'd have gaps in my days and just sit in diners waiting for the time to pass. You're a pawn of the system."
—Christina Ferrare, one of the world's highest paid models

We live in the Age of the Model. From the all-American looks of Cheryl Tiegs to the classic imperfection of Lauren Hutton to the artificial mystique of Margaux Hemingway, models now command the international spotlight. It is they, not the Hollywood starlets or beauty queens, who have become our sex objects, our fashion leaders, our glamorous and elusive heroines.

In spite of the great strides made by feminists in reshaping women's attitudes, many young girls today still grow up idolizing not Marie Curie or Gloria Steinem, but the glowing faces on the full-color covers. Witness: in 1979, the Kenner Toy Company of Cincinnati unveiled a doll called D'Arcy, a miniature, make-believe fashion model, calling it the "greatest toy of the century—a replacement for the Barbie Doll." Since her intro-

1

duction by Mattel Inc. more than a decade ago, Barbie has proven to be an extraordinary money machine. Many have tried to imitate Barbie, to dethrone her, to make her look silly and out-of-date, but without success. What made Kenner confident enough to spend millions of dollars on launching its Barbie rival? What secret weapon could the company use to make children abandon their allegiance to Barbie? Simple enough, said the folks at Kenner: a year of exhaustive research by psychiatrists, sociologists, and marketing experts had revealed that of all their wide-eyed dreams and aspirations, today's little girls want nothing more than to be beautiful, smiling cover girls—to be the face in front of the camera. And sales figures so far have borne this out: the D'Arcy doll has, in fact, been a huge success, a virtual sell-out.

Model-watching has become an international phenomenon that influences everything from the design of consumer products to standards of personal appearance and the daydreams of schoolchildren. Although models have for decades epitomized glamour, they have now moved beyond the once-limited sphere of the fashion magazines to become household names. This widespread recognition is, indeed, one of the overriding goals of the new breed of models, for whom glamour, wealth, and success are not enough. Today's top fashion models want recognition as distinct personalities—as three-dimensional human beings. And they get it. The superstars capture the covers of national news magazines, command extensive feature coverage in newspapers and on television, provide unlimited fodder for gossip columns and for hungry rumor rags such as the *National Enquirer* and the *National Star*, are among the mainstays of *People* magazine, and inspire a steady stream of commercial products from perfume to posters. The "Farrah look" prompted millions of women to change their hairstyles, the posters of Cheryl Tiegs have sold more than eight million copies, and the unique appeal of Karen Graham is credited with keeping Estée Lauder at the top of the fragrance industry.

Still, in spite of its pervasive influence and wide visibility, modeling remains a highly secretive business. This is no accident. All that emerges is what the industry powers want to reveal; behind-the-scene machinations are rarely exposed. As a result, the public sees only the glamorous finished products that adorn the covers of *Vogue*, leap from the pages of *Playboy*, or take center stage in a Bloomingdale's ad. Beneath the surface lies a multibillion-dollar business that is integral to the way goods and services are sold in fashion-oriented, free-enterprise societies. Modeling is an industry—a uniquely dazzling industry generating extraordinary profits, paying incredible salaries, and utilizing the skills and talents of an army of beautiful and inventive people. It is an industry in which sixteen-year-olds can routinely pull down $100,000 a year, where twenty-year-old stars can make half a million annually—and in which the product may wind up on the cover of *Mademoiselle*, on the walls of the Museum of Modern Art, or in the wastebasket.

Modeling is an industry built on image. And the most zealous protectors of this image are the big-league modeling agencies. Although hundreds of small and medium-sized agencies exist, all defer to four powerful New York outfits: Ford, Wilhelmina, Zoli, and John Casablancas's Elite. The Big Four account for the lion's share of billings (the amount of money billed to clients for a model's services) and are alone capable of making superstars.

The agency's job is to discover, develop, and represent talent. This is a never-ending task, as a model's productive career lasts only from five to fifteen years. Many aspiring models quit before getting established; others rise to the top only to burn out in a year or two. Under continuous pressure from clients for new faces and new looks, the agencies cast aside once popular models in favor of a different-looking breed. Modeling is a cutthroat and demanding business, but one which attracts an abundance of hopefuls because the rewards can be so great. Of the 3,000 female applicants who send their pictures to the Ford agency annually (many more are told on the phone not to bother applying because their height and weight do not meet the industry standards of 5'7", 110 pounds), only thirty are accepted and only a handful of these make it big.

Although the major agencies all have separate divisions to

handle male modeling, this is a minor part of the business. Men account for less than 20 percent of an agency's billings, and the most successful of the male models barely reach the $100,000-a-year level common among their female counterparts. In terms of money, what constitutes a modest success for a woman is considered superstar class for the males. This side of the industry is growing, however, and there are hopes that it will become more important in the years ahead.

How is a model made? At the Ford agency, the largest in the world, the process conforms to a now classic formula. The thirty young ladies welcomed annually into the Fords' brownstone on Manhattan's East 59th Street come immediately under the tutelage of the most famous and influential figure in the modeling industry: Eileen Ford. Co-founder of the agency, along with her husband Jerry (a former Notre Dame halfback who with his strong masculine appearance looks completely out of place in this ephemeral business), Eileen Ford is the eyes of the agency. Every female model represented by the Fords is approved by Eileen; all must conform to her standards of beauty. In fact, for the first two decades of the agency's existence (it was founded in 1947), Eileen Ford singlehandedly established what came to be regarded as the ideal in American beauty. "I have the only say on every new girl we take on," says Eileen, with a confident air typical of the modeling power brokers, "and this is certainly an important part of my job. But even more crucial than the initial selection process is the development of a model. I have to take raw material and mold it into something I can sell. I get thousands of beautiful applicants who aren't worth much in front of a camera. They are blobs. Some always will be, to be sure, but others can be trained to be models—to have personality as well as looks. So when I get a really gorgeous girl, I'll often work with her to make her great."

Eileen's technique is reflected in a Mueller's Macaroni commercial, in which she portrays a kind of mother-figure surrounded by a group of models seated around a dinner table. Her real-life character is remarkably similar to her television persona, for a key part of model development, in her view, is the selection of two or three hopefuls to live with her and her husband for a period of from three to six months. Immersed in the Fords' luxurious life-style, the girls get a taste of what may be theirs if they can get through the early months of hard work, disappointment, and rejection. Even more important, the Ford home serves as a finishing school for raw talent, the last bit of polishing up before the girls go out on their own.

"Eileen is like a mother hen," says Dawn, a bony, flat-chested eighteen-year-old with long blond hair and a pixie face. "I lived with her during my first three months in New York and it was wonderful. But I also learned. Eileen constantly works with you, teaching you how to smile, how to stand, and how to dress. She's not being picky, she's teaching, and she's usually right in her suggestions. Eileen's loudest warning is not to gain weight. Here she can be especially tough if she has to, even threatening to drop you from the agency if you don't shape up."

Young models such as Dawn dare not say a negative word about their mentor or about the modeling business in general. The rules of the game are that you never complain, never voice a negative opinion—not in the early days of your career. Agents want newcomers to behave like Girl Scouts, all virginal and sweet. Only established models can talk about the nasty side of the business and get away with it. The others must disguise their hostile feelings. They must be discreet.

Dawn's route to the world of big-agency modeling was a classic one. Exceptionally attractive from childhood, she was groomed and pushed by a mother who "always told me I was beautiful, that I should be a star." Entering the business at the age of thirteen in her native Los Angeles, Dawn was accepted by Nina Blanchard's prominent West Coast agency. Her talents immediately evident, she won bookings with local department stores and with *Teen* magazine (magazines offer notoriously poor pay to all models but they provide an excellent showcase and are therefore considered important throughout a model's career). Blanchard thought enough of her young star to present her, several years later, to Eileen during one of Ford's California talent hunts. The introduction to "the great lady from Manhattan" is part of the system: to make it to the top in modeling, a girl must work in New York. Virtually everyone in the industry agrees that there is no other way to do it. New York has the powerful magazines, the leading agencies, and the world-class photographers. It is in the Big Apple that young talent comes to public attention before being catapulted to national fame. Agencies like Blanchard's therefore reserve their brightest stars for the so-called New York connection: getting girls signed with a big-league agency such as Ford and then taking part of the standard 20 percent agency fee collected by the New York outfit. When a rookie comes to New York and makes it big, her agent in L.A. shares in the profits. A similar procedure is followed by agencies throughout the world, the smaller shops serving as a sort of farm system for New York's Big Four.

Dawn's first year in New York proved to be the kind of success story the agencies love to tell—one that keeps new hopefuls coming to the city in droves. Seemingly a perfect model for the fashion look of the times, she gained rapid acceptance with a host of clients, including *Harper's Bazaar* magazine. After only three months at Ford, she was promoted to the "high board"—where the pictures of the agency's full-fledged working models are posted (newcomers start at the "testing board" and move to the greater heights only if they show promise of success). Dawn traveled the world—sunning in South America and in Puerto Rico in the winter months—moved out of the Fords' home and into an apartment of her own, and started earning at the rate of $50,000 a year.

Dawn's success, rapid as it was, nevertheless followed the traditional route: doing the rounds with photographers and advertising agencies, making connections, getting known, putting her face on the map. Sometimes a newcomer can leapfrog this whole process, arriving in the Big Apple and taking the town by storm in a matter of days. This is the kind of heady stuff dreams are made of. It happens just often enough (rarely more than once a year) to keep legends alive. It happened to Kathy Spiers.

A native of Washington State, Kathy is typical of many models in that she experienced, in her early teens, an overpowering drive to burst out of her small-town existence. Unlike her friends, who daydreamed about local boys and were content to plan a quiet life in the community much as their mothers had, Kathy heard the call of the big city. Somehow, someway, she knew that eventually she would make her home in New York. This starry-eyed fantasy of a better life far away—the compelling need to seek excitement and glamour—motivates many would-be models to abandon school, friends, and family to launch their careers. "I felt from the earliest days of my life that I needed to be a model," Kathy recalls. "More than anything else, I needed glamour. Dreams of coming to New York and being a cover girl were the grist for my fantasy mills. The dreams kept me going."

What distinguished Kathy from millions of young girls with similar fantasies is that she was blessed with the physical attributes—a chiseled nose, high cheekbones, slender frame, and above-average height—to make her dream a reality. Early evidence that she had what it takes came by pure accident: walking to school, shopping with her parents, or dining out, she would be approached by local agents and photographers, told she had the right features to be a model, and asked to pose for them. A good many successful models enjoy this kind of early, spontaneous discovery, beginning before puberty and frequently leading to a first assignment modeling for a department store or a local apparel firm. The recognition that the girl has real potential—that she is different from others and should be encouraged to pursue her dream—builds confidence in both the child and her parents. For Kathy, this led to her first beauty contest—for the title of Miss Teen Northwest—which she won hands down. From that day on, any doubts she had about her chances for a career as a model vanished.

After an early marriage (at age seventeen) and relocation to Colorado, Kathy signed on with a local franchise of the John Powers agency.* Her timing was perfect. Barbara Stone, then a powerful New York agent, came through Colorado on a talent hunt and asked the Powers office to introduce her to their three

*Once a great New York modeling agency, now a group of beauty training schools.

best girls. One look at the blond, lanky, all-American with Washington apple cheeks and Stone knew that Kathy had great promise.

"She asked me to come back to New York with her that day," Kathy notes. "I was floored that anything could happen so fast and so I hesitated. . . . I didn't go at first, but I was chafing at the bit. I couldn't decide what to do."

This fear of taking the first step is a common problem experienced agents deal with all the time. Regardless of how much the girls want to be models, the fears of leaving home, of coming to New York, and of living alone are real and understandable—especially since many are still so young when they are discovered. Some never overcome these fears, never test their potential. But others simply need a push, and when that's the case, the agents know just how to handle it. To pry Spiers loose from the Rockies—and from her short-lived marriage—Stone used an old ploy that Eileen Ford is said to have developed years ago when she first started looking for talent in Europe.

"About a month after she met me, and after all the telephone pleadings failed, Barbara just sent me an airline ticket to New York," Kathy recalls. "Just her card and an airline ticket. It was so simple, so inviting, so clear-cut that I just packed up and flew out."

The rest, as they say, is history. On her very first day in Manhattan, Kathy was ushered into the offices of *Cosmopolitan* magazine. The only way for a new face to get that far so quickly is for the agent to make it clear that the discovery is something special, an extraordinary find. Agents don't do this casually. Credibility is crucial to their success, and so the best agents never promote second-rate girls. The hoopla is reserved for those with undeniable appeal—with all the assets to make it to the top. Stone believed Kathy Spiers was such a find. *Cosmopolitan* agreed. "I thought she was a rough-cut diamond," says Gretchen Parks, *Cosmo*'s picture editor. "I see a lot of girls with promise, but every once in a while one comes in here and bowls me over. Kathy did that."

The *Cosmo* editors rushed Spiers to one of the most powerful forces in all of modeling, photographer Francesco Scavullo. A great talent—a man who makes ordinary women look exceptional and great women look breathtaking—Scavullo is the most sought after fashion photographer in the world. He can have virtually any assignment he bids for. His fees and his personality match his reputation: he gets $10,000 a day, appears to be deeply in love with himself, and comes off as haughty and arrogant.

The great man agreed that Kathy Spiers was indeed something special, and after a bit of testing under the lights, he did what only Scavullo can do: he reserved an upcoming issue of *Cosmopolitan* for Kathy's debut as a cover girl.

The session with Scavullo was only the first miracle to occur in Kathy's two incredible days in New York. The best was yet to come. Day two featured a tour of the big William Esty advertising agency under Barbara Stone's tutelage. Here Kathy was spotted, quite accidentally, by an executive responsible for the Noxema account. "That's my Noxema girl!" was the cry Kathy heard as she walked past executive row—just the way a starlet is discovered in a Hollywood musical. But this was for real.

As it happened, Noxema's top brass was readying a new advertising campaign designed to shed that venerable old skin cream/face cleanser's stodgy image and add a little sex appeal to their product. The emerging campaign hinged on finding *the* model to represent the client—to be the perfect embodiment of the new Noxema image. The search ended when the small-town girl from Nowhere U.S.A. walked into the Esty agency. Kathy Spiers, who two days earlier was just another dreamer marking time in the Rockies, found herself signed to co-star in a television commercial with the then red-hot Joe Namath. Her first line as a television actress: "Men, watch Joe Namath get creamed." The year was 1972. The experience paved the way for a highly successful career that has included five *Cosmopolitan* covers, TV guest shots, and major spreads in all the top fashion magazines. Still a leading model, Kathy is now with the Wilhelmina agency and is said to earn in excess of $250,000 a year. Since her fateful first two days in New York, she has produced almost $1 million in billings. That's the kind of dream-come-true the modeling establishment loves to package and sell to the public.

Many models who go to New York seem to be cut from the identical mold: born and raised in small southern, western, and midwestern states, they usually have middle-class parents employed in local businesses, agriculture, or ranching; are one of many offspring (six or more siblings is quite common); and are the products of stern parental discipline and of religious households. Most are white, Protestant, and blond or light brunette. Face to face, the average model is often disappointing in appearance, with a sterile, artificial, mannequin-like look that is almost one-dimensional (which, however, suits the medium of photography). Many have boyish mannerisms and figures. Their breasts are small, torsos lean and tapered, arms and legs long and often gangly. Their eyes are typically large, noses perfectly shaped and slightly sloped, mouths fragile. To the experts—the trained eyes of photographers and agents—a model's cheekbones and chin are crucial: the former must be high and prominent; the latter, small and delicate.

"Models look exactly like what they are," says agent John Casablancas, the "bad boy" of the industry and modeling's most controversial figure.

The sex appeal that many models exude in their photos rarely comes across in person. Instead, most have a fresh-scrubbed, peaches-and-cream look that is more readily found in a 4-H Club than in the uninhibited discos of New York. The truth is that the camera does lie: what appears in print to be a dazzling and vibrant woman is often, in person, no more than a skinny kid. The model's appeal on film frequently has less to do with her physical attributes than with the photographer's transforming touch. Good photographers know that modeling is based on illusion: viewers focus not on the total woman but on the moist lips, windswept hair, or suggestive pose.

"We know how to take a plain Jane—which so many of the girls are—and give her an exciting look," says a top fashion photographer. "That's how we earn our money. A skilled photographer can look a girl over and immediately size up her strengths and weaknesses and can then use the camera to accentuate the former and camouflage the latter. I do it every day of the week. People who idolize some of these models should see what they really look like when they walk in here. Some have so many faults in their appearance, you wouldn't look at them twice on the street. But because film is different than real life and because we can play tricks with the camera, these same girls can be striking on paper. The person looking at a cover girl may think he's looking at a face but what he's really seeing are angles, shadows, makeup, and hair."

Cosmo's Gretchen Parks, one of the heavyweights in selecting models for the magazine's famous covers, says: "When it comes to judging a model's beauty, it is one of those rare cases in life where seeing someone in the flesh is not as good as seeing them in pictures. Models troop into my office just about every day to be examined for cover potential, but I'm not really interested in looking at them. I want to see their books [the trade term for a portfolio of photos and tearsheets]. That's the only way I can evaluate them. In this business we are rarely interested in how a girl looks in real life. We want to see her on film. And very often, there's a world of difference between the two."

Most models are similar in their level of intelligence as well as in appearance. Here again, their common backgrounds are probably responsible. Although few, if any, are intellectual giants, most are several IQ levels above one agent's appraisal that "there are few models who look great and can spell cat." The cliché of the "dumb model" in all likelihood stems not from lack of mental ability but from singlemindedness: most successful models are intelligent women, knowledgeable about the business in which they work, and quick to learn the ropes; they are serious, ambitious, and driven to get to the top. But the business is so competitive and demanding—the girls' dreams and objectives are so grand—that success requires total devotion to modeling. Most are willing to make this sacrifice: shop talk is their only conversation, stardom their only dream. Top physical appearance is so crucial to working that it must, by its very importance, become an obsession. What's more, the pressure of the business prompts many aspiring models to seek escapist entertainment in their free time. Discos, TV game shows, and drugs are big favorites.

The very industry that labels models as "stupid and brainless clothes hangers" fosters this image by demanding that models shut up and look pretty. Photographers, who as a group tend to be the models' severest critics, all have their favorite "dumb blond" stories. But should a model express an intelligent opinion about her work or the photographer's technique she soon acquires a reputation as a know-it-all who needs to be put in her place. Professional standards call for the ideal model to look attractive and nothing more. Models who have real intellectual substance are willing to take orders and do what is expected (at least until they are big enough stars to begin voicing their opinions openly) because most have an unbridled ambition and know that if they toe the mark their chances of succeeding are increased. Inferior intelligence? No, they are just playing by the rules of the game.

Serena, an eighteen-year-old newcomer to the Ford agency, has had a typical career scenario. A delightful and charming young woman, Serena said: "I have no doubts about where I want to go. First, I hope to make it big in print work, lots of cover shots and prestige magazine spreads. This should get me good exposure in the business, enough to bring on the offers to do television commercials. Then once I'm on the air, I'll become a household name and that will lead to my next big step: acting parts. I want to be a major actress, starring in very good, quality films. Stardom will then get me what I really want. That is to run a major entertainment complex. I'd like to be a top entertainment executive, the owner of a company that packages and produces films. I want to be on the business as well as the talent end. Not to say I'll get this far, but it is what I would like."

Similar dreams are cherished by most of the young women who win admission to the exclusive Big Four agencies in New York. Modeling is a convenient stepping-stone to even greater things: they want more, much more—millions of dollars, exclusive contracts with one or more advertisers, choice movie roles, international recognition.

These are the dreams that today's modeling industry holds out. The promise of such rewards provides the motivation for thousands of teenage beauties from Durham to Denver, who walk with books piled on their heads, brush their hair 100 strokes a night, exercise two hours a day, gaze into mirrors, ignore boys and junior proms and homework; who live in fear of pimples, starve themselves thin, close their eyes to the world around them and dream only of New York; who surrender themselves to local agencies and then wait for Zoli, Casablancas, or Eileen Ford to ride into town in a white Rolls-Royce, take one breathless look at the hometown beauty, and jet her off to New York and the big time.

For most it's a long, long wait—and that happy ending never happens. For what the model industry fails to tell its hopefuls is that the odds of making it to the top are less than one in a half million. And that only one face a year makes it to the superstar set.

"It's like a human auction," says one New York attorney involved in the modeling business. "All of these naive kids, pushed by stage mothers, throw themselves at the feet of the all-powerful agents. Few realize how tiny their chances are of being selected by the big shots and how much harder it is to go on from there. But they don't know, partly because they don't want to hear and partly because no one wants to tell them. The whole thing is pathetic; it truly makes me sick."

Up to now, the modeling establishment has been largely successful in keeping its sordid aspects from the public spotlight. Rather than trying to actually cover up an unpleasant incident or to evade the press entirely, the agencies keep up a steady flow of glamour stories that command attention and become the basis for the industry's coverage. Fashion reporters prefer to pick up on gossipy, inconsequential rumors rather than undertake lengthy investigations. Why focus on the industry's outrageous contracts or on the models who suffer nervous breakdowns before they get a single job when they can write a great story about Cheryl Tiegs's cleavage or Lauren Hutton's false tooth?

But it is the underside of modeling that is rarely exposed

to outsiders—where naive teenagers are psychologically brutalized, arrogant power brokers casually destroy delicate egos, and petty jealousies force famous and successful people into juvenile and vindictive behavior. The truth is that many of the people who come in contact with the modeling business are damaged by it in one way or another.

2

THE POWERS THAT BE
The Model Agencies

"It's no coincidence that the first model agent was named
Powers. No coincidence at all. It just had to be that way. It's
impossible to describe agents without using the word 'power.'
They're the only people in the business who have lots of it, bask
in it, use it freely, want much more of it, dream of it, worship
it, and pray like hell that they don't wake up one morning and
find that it's gone."
—A prominent New York fashion photographer

The Big Four agencies are the self-appointed guardians of modeling's image. They are the bedrock of the industry, the closest thing modeling has to institutions. The agencies overshadow, by their size and resources, all of the other elements in the field.

Modeling is, for the most part, a business composed of sole proprietors. Photographers, makeup artists, hairstylists, and models—all are in business for themselves. They are the tiniest of commercial entities. When a proprietor dies, retires, or falls out of favor, the business collapses. There is no continuity. Only the agencies are multidimensional organizations managed by professionals and supported by a broad cross-section of regular clients. They have lines of credit, cooperative bankers, powerful law firms, high-priced executives, and a management hierarchy that is not totally dependent on a single individual. As they have proven time and again, they can outspend, outfight, and outlast everyone else in modeling. They have power.

"Fighting city hall and winning has to be a good deal easier than fighting the agents and winning," says an angry model who jumped from one agency to another and has encountered legal problems because of it. "Even if you are right in principle,

15

and even if the courts decide in your favor, the time and money you have to spend to get that far can take a heavy toll. For me, it's been a personal and financial nightmare but to the bitches at the agency it's just another case. Costs for this kind of thing are built into their budgets, they're tax deductible, and what's more their lawyers handle all of their dirty work anyway. They can afford to go to court just to be vindictive—to be pushy. They love to throw their weight around. It keeps everyone else in line."

Adds an editor at *Harper's Bazaar*: "Challenging the agencies is a no-win proposition. They are the most powerful forces in the business, they know it, and they're not at all humble about it. Try to fight them and you learn the hard way what the agencies already know: that they are the only game in town. They have a lock on all the top models in the world. Mess with them and you may not get some of the best girls to work with. Complain to an agent that her bookers are arrogant or discourteous and your words fall on deaf ears. There's no attempt to change. The attitude is that if you don't like us, don't use us. Those clients who think that they can get satisfaction by switching agencies are sorely mistaken. Except for John Casablancas—who I think runs the best shop in New York—they're all the same. What you hate at one agency you'll find at the others."

Badmouthing the agencies is a popular pastime. Their enemies are legion, their friends few and far between. In spite of their preeminent position, their overwhelming power, and wide influence in the industry, some of the executives at the large agencies behave like spoiled children who must have everything their way—when they want it, as they want it. The uncivilized nature of the business is evidenced by the way the agencies relate to one another: they are mortal enemies, vicious competitors, tangled up in webs of hatred, bitterness, and legal feuding that are all-consuming. "This is a small rumor-ridden industry," says John Casablancas. "We call it the Arab telephone. You want to spread a rumor and you tell two people; two weeks later everyone knows." So deep does the animosity run that there is little room for the kind of off-hours professional courtesies competitors in other industries extend to each other. Law firms may wrangle for clients, manufacturers may outbid one another, and advertising agencies may disparage each other's work, but most can drop their guard, share cocktails, and make small talk at conventions, trade shows, or luncheons. They are associates as well as competitors. Not so in modeling. New York's model wars are so intense, the wounds so deep, that the parties involved rarely lay down their arms. Gracious conduct is not admired. In fact, some agency principals ask to be quoted saying vile things about their counterparts as a way of venting their anger. They love to describe each other in foul terms, to pass innuendos, to start vicious rumors, and to trade ruthless barbs. They don't ask for anonymity because they are so openly antagonistic and so deeply involved in lawsuits that they imagine there's nothing more to lose. But they are wrong: by succumbing to their basic instincts and by refusing to act like professionals, they all lose. By joining in the battle, regardless of who is at fault or who threw the first punch, they are forced to roll in the mud with the others. As a result, the entire industry suffers.

Why can't there be peaceful coexistence? Why such bitter fighting? What are the issues? To comprehend this behavior, one must understand the nature of modeling agencies, how they came about, how they developed, and where they stand today.

First visits to the Big Four agencies are disappointing if you expect them to exemplify the glamorous business they represent. Generally, they are poorly furnished and less attractive than most of Manhattan's business offices. The Fords occupy a run-down brownstone on the wrong side of Third Avenue; Casablancas has a sterile suite of rooms in an anonymous office tower; Zoli's shop is downright ugly; and the Wilhelmina agency runs its show from a decrepit-looking building that's about as chic as a warehouse. The modeling industry—which boasts beauty, glamour, and dazzle—makes its home in unimaginative quarters.

At the front line of every agency sits a receptionist at a

massive switchboard. These women are the palace guards. They keep out the sugar daddies, the stargazers, and the scores of would-be models who are too old, ugly, or fat to ever win a place on the agency's headsheet. Their mission is to screen out undesirables—to prevent them from clogging up the works, wasting agents' or bookers' time. Although they are not permitted to make policy decisions, they can dismiss callers or in-person applicants according to broad guidelines established by management.

In a scene recalled by the author that took place at Casablancas's tiny reception area, a young woman, sporting skintight Bonjour jeans and a flowing crepe de chine blouson, confidently approached the Bazooka-chewing receptionist and requested an appointment with the top man.

Visitor: "I'd like to see John Casablancas."
Receptionist: "For what, may I ask?" the receptionist chirped.
Visitor: "I want to be a model. I'm here for an audition."
Receptionist: "Sorry, you're too old."
Visitor: "What?"
Receptionist: "Sorry, we're not accepting older models any-more."
Visitor: "You must be joking! How old do you think I am?"
Receptionist: "Over sixteen."
Visitor: "That's old? I'm only eighteen."
Receptionist: "Too old for us—sixteen's the cut-off. Try the other agencies."

A major part of the receptionists' screening is done by telephone. Each of the Big Four receives up to 500 calls a day, many from eager youngsters trying to get a foot in the door. Receptionists hear the same stories over and over again: "Hi. I'm Mary Jane. I live in Toledo and I want to be a model. How do I apply? Do I need a portfolio? How tall do I have to be? Should I fly to New York now?"

The receptionists bark back the standard answers: "Send five or ten pictures; they don't have to be professional, a portfolio is not necessary. The ideal is 5'9" and 110 pounds. If you're shorter or fatter, don't bother. If we want you, we'll call. Bye."

The heavy flow of calls makes it extremely difficult to reach the agencies during any part of the working day. It is not unusual to wait twenty or thirty rings for an answer, and this is only the first of many frustrations. Callers are routinely put on hold, only to be informed later that the party they want is out or too busy to speak to them. People throughout the modeling industry, including important agency clients, complain bitterly about the telephone problem but to no avail.

Says Cathy Spellman, the president of her own small but well-respected advertising agency, Spellman & Co.: "The agencies have a lock on the market so they don't care what you think. At some, the service is not at all responsive, not even polite. Tell an agent that you had to wait an hour to get through to a booker and he says, 'That's life.'"

Much of the communications bottleneck could be untangled if each agency hired one additional receptionist to handle the flow of calls. But the principals stubbornly refuse to do so.

"We carry a huge overhead as it is," snaps Dan Deeley, director of Wilhelmina Men. "We can't just put on more help every time someone has a complaint. Sure, people bitch about us, but that's because we're an easy target. Getting through to photographers or art directors is just as hard—but they don't see that, heavens no. It's always the agency's fault. Well, I'll tell you this, if we put on five more receptionists and callers had to wait three seconds to get through, they'd still curse us out."

At the heart of every agency is a large open office that is the nerve center for most business activities. Formally known as the "female booking department," it is actually a telephone boiler room where the models' daily activities are assigned, recorded, and processed. Desks line the outer walls, each equipped with a telephone and a hanging file of cards listing models' names, a brief description of each, and weekly appointment calendars. Here sit the bookers, the agency professionals most responsible for seeing to it that the maximum number of models are out working every single day of the week.

The booker's life is a hectic one. The day begins at 8 A.M., ends at 6 P.M., and knows no letup. Each booker handles a set number of models, usually an alphabetical grouping. Virtually all of the bookers' work is done by telephone. The first order of the day is to check the models' calendars and to ring those girls slated for wakeup calls. This valet service is a courtesy to the model but is also the agent's way of making sure that late sleepers get up and out on time. Considering the widespread use of drugs and the late-night socializing, many of the girls do have a hard time getting up in the morning. Those who need help, whether they ask for it or not, get their daily wakeup call.

Shortly before 9 A.M. the first trickle of orders begins. This is the major business of the day: matching up client requests with the appropriate models, and getting both the girls and their books to the right place at the right time. It is a tough juggling act but one the bookers handle well.

"The nature of client requests ranges across the board," says a Big Four booker with three years of experience. "They can be very general, asking for a sexy-looking brunette, or very specific, demanding a particular model by name. With the former, my judgment comes into play. I have to decide which of the girls will best fit the bill. With the latter, I have to be certain the girl is available, that the client will pay her hourly minimum, and that it is the kind of work she'll agree to do. Once the girls get to the request stage of their careers, they tend to get rather picky. They won't take all the bookings offered to them. One may not like a certain photographer, one may not want to travel, one may be on vacation. I have to know all of this; if I slip, the girls and the clients get pissed off and you can guess who takes the heat."

Models and their bookers communicate daily, and often several times a day. The booker deals with clients, sets assignments, fills the model's calendar; the girls call in to check up on all of this, to see how their workload is shaping up, to get the details of their next appointment. Good rapport with a booker is always important, but never more so than in the early stages of a model's career.

"You have to get it on with your booker—that's so, so important," says a young Casablancas model. "If they like you, they'll send you out on the better go-sees. Let's say a photographer wants to see a tall blond. The booker may have twenty-five girls who fit that description and who are eager as hell to go. You'll get the call, however, if you're the booker's pet. The others will lose out."

Bookers are undoubtedly the hardest working and the most efficient pros in the model agencies. They are besieged with calls and complaints and are challenged by the sheer logistics of this demanding business. Theirs is a no-nonsense workday that leaves little time for haughty airs, idle gossip, or catty put-downs. They must massage delicate egos, placate demanding prima donnas, keep a mental inventory of each model's strengths and weaknesses, and get everyone going in the right direction without tripping over one another. For this, they earn about $500 a week—fair compensation by objective standards, but an amount agents constantly complain about, despite the fact that theirs is an industry where sixteen-year-olds can earn four times as much for a three-day week. The bookers, for their part, appear to be satisfied.

In spite of the bookers' hard work and professionalism, foul-ups are commonplace. With so many models and assignments to coordinate, with touchy personalities and tight advertising deadlines to meet, the opportunities for error are great. Models routinely forget their assignments or arrive at the wrong location at the wrong time; bookers assign models to jobs they will not take; bookings frequently run beyond the scheduled time, playing havoc with the models' tightly packed schedules for the rest of the day. With each blunder there are angry calls, hot tempers, alternative plans to be made. It is a chain reaction—one that complicates the bookers' work and fuels the hostilities among agents, models, and clients.

The Big Four, although the giants of their industry and the predominant forces in it, are not themselves large-scale businesses. The Fortune 500 would find them too small to eat for breakfast. In terms of billings (after the models' shares are subtracted), Ford, the biggest agency by income, brings in about the same as four successful McDonald's restaurants.

(The agency does, however, enjoy a much higher profit margin.) Still, they enjoy the kind of national reputation and wide influence that is normally reserved for huge corporations, and for this reason they appear to be much bigger than their balance sheets would indicate. Most have only one office, fewer than twenty employees, and no appreciable assets. Equally important, they are owned, managed, and controlled by founding entrepreneurs who view the agencies as personal statements and as symbols of their most significant achievements. Proud of what they have accomplished, they exhibit traits common to self-made capitalists: cocky self-confidence, the fear that things could suddenly turn bad, and the determination never to let that happen. Most have tasted failure at one time or another and have come back to muscle and claw their way back to the top. Now that they've made it, they don't intend to step aside.

For all their arrogance and pride, most agents betray a great deal of insecurity. Perhaps this is because they are still uncertain about their place in the world and are uneasy about the future. They are keenly aware that the model agency business is still a relatively new one, with little in the way of history or traditions to give a semblance of stability to the industry.

Before the advent of agencies, models had no meaningful representation, no central clearinghouse. They found their work through informal contacts, mostly with photographers, who called them when assignments were available. They had no contracts, were paid a modest per diem fee, and found that bookings were few and far between. They had little in common with today's wealthy and famous cover girls.

Things changed when the very first agency, founded by John Robert Powers, opened its doors in New York in 1923. A country boy from rural Phillipsburg, New Jersey, Powers at first wanted to be a farmer. But his grandparents, who played a major role in his upbringing, were determined to "edjicate" their handsome, black-haired grandson. Powers was schooled at the Easton Academy, Lafayette College, and the University of Pennsylvania before coming to New York to seek a teaching position. Then, in a classic turn of events—the kind that seems to happen only in show business—he found himself headed for the stage rather than the classroom. He had promised, upon his arrival in Manhattan, to deliver a note sent by a college chum to Sir Herbert Beerbohm, the famed British actor, who was then in rehearsal to play King Henry VIII at the New Amsterdam Theatre on 42nd Street. While waiting in the wings to see Sir Herbert, Powers was beckoned to take a place on stage. For two hours he stood motionless, note in hand, watching the characters bring the play to life. When the curtain closed and it was finally time to deliver the note, Powers got much more than he'd bargained for: a $9 per week acting role as a halberdier. Thus was launched a stage career, albeit a brief one. The Beerbohm troupe, which was only visiting the States, packed up after the play's scheduled run and returned to England.

Once again Powers turned to teaching, only to be drawn back to show business through another twist of fate. This time it was silent movies. Walking along Broadway, the young man was approached by a stranger, who inquired whether he'd like to earn $10 for a day's work—a whopping wage in 1920. Powers consented without even knowing what he was required to do. As it turned out, the assignment was to pose for publicity stills featuring film star Mary Pickford. Although Powers got paid for three days' work, he was never called on to do anything but sit in a dingy studio and await the photographer's call, should he be needed. The call never came, Pickford never appeared, and Powers went away somewhat disappointed but $30 richer. More important, he made contact with an influential PR agent who liked Powers's rugged good looks and called on him for subsequent bookings. Without really trying, the former farm boy backed into a career as a full-time professional model.

That too was short-lived. But his big break was right around the corner. Booked as a model for a dazzling fashion show being produced by Hart, Schaffner, and Marx, Powers was asked by photographer Baron de Meyer if he could round up some women to work in the show. The young model-about-town was quite familiar with many of New York's budding actresses and had no trouble at all lining up a sizable crew. Baron de Meyer, duly impressed, called on Powers to do the same on subsequent occasions. Powers—a cordial, easygoing, and likable man—obliged, found his fame as a go-between spreading, and his workload growing. Still, it was a gratuitous service, performed without a fee or compensation. Powers would simply provide photographers with models' phone numbers or, if asked, would make the calls himself. It was a casual, seat-of-the-pants operation.

Until a woman entered the scene. Powers's fiancée was irritated both by her beau's wasting time providing free services and by his meager income as a male model. Determined to solve both problems simultaneously, she prodded Powers to collect fees for his work in lining up models. "Why not get into business and cash in on this?" she suggested. Powers thought it over, agreed it was worth a try, and opened an office at 19 West 46th Street. Thus was born the world's first modeling agency. And a precocious infant it was. Although there were numerous obstacles to overcome (simply getting a license to operate this kind of business required a special act of the state legislature), the agency enjoyed phenomenal success from the start. A look at Powers's early headsheets shows why. The list included some of the most beautiful and talented women in America's emerging generation of stars: Barbara Stanwyck, Kay Francis, Paulette Goddard, Joan Blondell, Jennifer Jones, Gene Tierney, Marsha Hunt. They were dubbed by illustrator Arthur William Brown as "Powers' long-stemmed, American beauties." Among the actors who got their start as male models with the Powers agency were Henry Fonda, Brian Donlevy, and Fredric March.

Much of Powers's concept of the business (primarily of the agent representing models in return for a commission on their earnings) remains in force today. Even his system for listing bookings on models' charts hung above a battery of telephones is still the predominant practice. Success breeds imitation, and Powers was very successful: he grew rich and famous through his burgeoning agency. A magazine reporter, Edward Miller, visiting his relocated and much enlarged office at 247 Park Avenue in 1948 (about twenty-five years after the agency's founding) described it this way: "You get off at the sixth floor, turn left, and enter a quiet, spacious, orderly group of rooms. There are seven in all, but they may as well be one, considering the sun-lit atmosphere pervading them throughout. To the right is the glass-partitioned nerve center of this world-famous agency. A battery of thirty-five glistening black telephones line the long desk. At least six of them ring constantly. On the back wall are hung the faithful charts, daily work schedules of the nation's loveliest women. And on every other wall are pictures —some framed, others pasted together in jig-saw fashion—of the hundreds of girls over the past twenty-five years who can pridefully boast of their Powers affiliation."

Personally, Powers lived the dual life of an urbane entre- preneur in a highly cosmopolitan industry and of a wealthy country gentleman at his home in Locust Valley, New York, where as a devoted equestrian, he kept a stable of thorough- breds and hackney coaches. He demonstrated that modeling could be a legitimate, organized, and profitable business—that agents would not only be accepted in the field but that they could become the driving force in it. Once his fledgling venture was firmly established, Powers took the lead in setting the models' professional standards, fees, and working conditions. This was his greatest contribution to the industry.

Still, Powers was markedly different from today's crop of tough, aggressive agents. He was a softer, more casual individ- ual who took himself and his business less seriously than most of his present-day counterparts. "We're just a clearing house here, that's all we are," Powers said in a 1948 interview with *Hold-It* magazine, a now defunct publication for fashion mod- els. "I began accidentally as a one-man clearing house for mod- els in the old days before agencies existed. Now I've gotten to the point where I need a little assistance from twenty-odd phone girls or secretaries, but that's the only difference."

On the process of model selection and representation, which today's agents like to describe as a highly complex func- tion requiring the aesthetics of Michelangelo and the legal in- stincts of Thomas Jefferson, Powers had this to say: "I just look them [model candidates] over, and if I think they'll do, I have a secretary make a note of her name and address. None of my girls are ever required to sign a contract. Why should they? It's not healthy. If a girl enjoys working for me, she'll stick, and if she doesn't . . . well, then, who wants her to stay against her will? After all, my job is simply to make people happy and keep them happy."

Powers, who died in 1977 at eighty-four, dominated the model industry (his only serious competitor was the Conover agency) from its founding until the late 1940s, when he turned his attention to related ventures, including modeling schools, a cosmetics business, books on modeling, and a syndicated column. It was in this post-World War II period that a new force emerged in the industry—one who would dominate the business far longer than Powers, bring a tough new discipline to its workings, and achieve a greater level of public recognition. That force was Eileen Ford.

"I got married in 1944," Eileen recalls. "Jerry was a midshipman in the Navy and went overseas on duty. While he was gone, I worked in New York's apparel industry as I'd done throughout the war. I had a number of jobs, mostly in the promotion end of the business, and I did some modeling too. I got to meet a lot of fashion models—knew them personally and professionally. They liked me, confided in me, and, because of my knack for promotion, started asking me to do some bookings for them. Although I was reluctant at first, because I didn't know if I had the time to get involved, I finally agreed and handled my first booking on October 1, 1946. I started with two models and by the end of the year, I had eight. From there, one thing just led to another."

Much like Powers's first efforts, Eileen's early agency began as a seat-of-the-pants operation. But that didn't last for long: she was blessed with a keener business sense than her predecessor. "This was inherited partly from my father," Eileen says. "He ran a successful New York credit firm and I was always interested in his work." In addition, husband Jerry was trained in management and had the tough, aggressive streak one would expect from a former Notre Dame football player and school boxing champion. This competitive husband-and-wife team was not about to dabble in the agency business like amateurs. They decided to devote themselves to it full time and opened the first Ford office in 1947, the year Eileen gave birth to their first child.

Although plagued with early cash flow problems (it takes some time before commissions begin to cover an agency's costs) and the need to gain recognition in what had been a Powers-dominated business, the Ford agency managed to establish itself rather quickly. Eileen's uncanny ability to select and groom highly desirable models and Jerry's solid work on the financial end earned the couple the respect of models, photographers, and art directors. There were a handful of competitors in the field, but Ford soon became *the* agency. By 1951, it was billing more than any of its competitors. Today, their agency—the biggest in the world—bills more than $13 million annually. Since about 20 percent of this represents the agency's commission, gross income is estimated at roughly $3 million including fees.

From the very beginning, Eileen focused on the personnel side and Jerry handled the finances. Both established standards that are still in evidence today. Eileen's preference for tall, blond, wholesome, midwestern-looking women with chiseled features, fair skin, and lanky bodies is still the classic look. The biggest group of models at all of the agencies today fit this mold. That Zoli and Casablancas have earned reputations for having more exotic, sexier models is mostly PR hype. Although these agents may have a slightly greater variety of girls, the bulk of their models fit the Ford standards. Says Zoli about an *Esquire* magazine piece ("Holy Zoli's Empire") which declared his agency to be a haven for sex goddesses: "That was all a reflection of *Esquire*'s imagination. They thought it would sell magazines to portray a sexy image, so they played it up like that. The experience with that story really gave me an insight into how things can be distorted. My models aren't any sexier than anyone else's. They can't be. All agencies are in business to serve virtually the same clients and those clients want good-looking, girl-next-door beauties. Most want the wholesome blond look."

Asked if they've been influenced by the Ford vision, the other agents respond with a vehement "no." But this is simply not true. Eileen is a much disliked woman in the modeling industry, and most refuse to credit her with anything.

"Eileen Ford is full of shit," says Bruce Cooper. "She never used the all-American girl until we started using American girls. She always imported all of her girls from Europe." Adds John Casablancas, "The only standards Eileen ever set are how Jerry should behave. She's his boss, his leader, and no one else's. Eileen's a copier, an imitator, not an innovator."

Regardless of Eileen's low popularity among her colleagues, most knowledgeable and objective observers agree that her standards of beauty, her system of grooming models and closely supervising their development, and her insistence on tough standards of professional conduct are now followed by her competitors. Eileen herself is justly proud of her imprint on the industry, not only because imitation is the sincerest form of flattery or because her methods of operation have led to extraordinary success, but also because she believes that she has brought simple good taste and old-fashioned morality to the business.

"I don't like exotic looks," she says, "and I don't like unorthodox behavior. The most exotic I get is Cheryl Tiegs and that's pretty close to the all-American ideal, don't you think? I think beauty should be simple; no devices are necessary. I'm usually right but I have made some mistakes. I thought Farrah Fawcett's hair was a device, so it's good for her sake that she didn't have me as an agent. I would have made her cut it off; she would have gone nowhere. But in most cases my standards of beauty are applauded by the public. They love our girls."

Surprisingly (because he is not well known to the general public), Jerry Ford is widely credited with having made equally important contributions to this field. Even his fiercest competitors praise Jerry for his innovations, his persistence, his dogged determination to get the most for agents and for their models. Almost as soon as he entered the business, Jerry recognized that models and agents alike were held in low esteem by those who used their services. This was evidenced by one glaring fact:

many clients never paid their bills or were horrendously delinquent. It was not uncommon for agencies to have a 50 percent receivables problem. This disgraceful practice flourished because no one had the nerve to seriously challenge it or the business acumen to recognize that freeloading clients are worse than no clients at all. Powers and others who ran the early agencies were not confident that their novel service could withstand controversy. They believed that the world could easily survive without model agents, so they were afraid to make waves. No one dared upset the apple cart. Not until Jerry Ford came on the scene.

Jerry had two secret weapons: first, he personally believed that the service he was providing was a profession, as legitimate as law or accounting. Second, he was not at all timid about taking legal action to put teeth into agency demands. Over the years, he shifted the balance of power away from advertisers and photographers to the agents. The following are just some of the major reforms he initiated:

- Weather-permitting cancellation fees: In the old days, clients would book models on a weather-permitting basis. If inclement conditions caused a postponement in an outdoor shooting, the model was not paid. Now she is entitled to 50 percent of her standard fee whether or not the shooting is held.
- Prompt payments: Clients must submit payments for models' services promptly. Chronically late payers are not serviced; seriously delinquent accounts are taken to court.
- Contracts for cosmetics: Models who are used extensively by a single cosmetics firm, so much so that they become closely identified with that brand alone (thus making it difficult to work for other clients), can get a contract with the firm they work for that guarantees them a minimum level of income over a set period of time. Ford established this precedent in his negotiations with Yardley over the use of former superstar model Jean Shrimpton. In another famous case, he did the same for Cheryl Tiegs, winning her a contract with Cover Girl cosmetics.
- Residuals for print: Models in the broadcast media have long earned residual payments for every airing of commercials in which they appear. Ford demanded a similar provision for print ads as well, assuring models of residuals for frequent use

of their pictures in newspapers and magazines, on billboards and the like. This has made it possible for a model—and her agent—to earn several times the basic per diem rate for appearing in an ad.

"A part of every dollar every agent and model earns must be credited to Jerry Ford," says commercial agent Cye Perkins. "We've all benefited from his guts and initiative."

Admits rival Bruce Cooper: "I won't even try to take it away from Jerry. He's done a lot for this business. In terms of the respect agents and models get, in terms of how and when we get paid, Jerry deserves some of the credit."

The Fords are an interesting couple, with feet planted firmly in two contrasting worlds. One is the bitchy, glittering, and hotly competitive arena of New York's modeling business. Here they throw elegant parties at their sumptuous townhouse, lunch at Orsini's, make headlines, appear on talk shows, and hobnob with the rich and powerful. There's more to this than just having a good time: Eileen has a keen sense of public relations. As the most famous woman in the modeling establishment, she knows she has a role to play and plays it to the hilt. At first impression, it seems as if she does this effortlessly—as if the real Eileen Ford is a cool, savvy Manhattanite. But both Jerry and Eileen seem to be more at ease, more comfortable when they escape to their private, woodsy retreat in privileged Fairfield County, Connecticut. Here, the couple's all-American, midwestern values are expressed.

The house itself reflects the other side of their personalities. A huge center-hall colonial, it features quaint shutters, a grand staircase with polished oak banisters, high ceilings, and spacious rooms. The furnishings are early American, with nubby fabrics, lots of maple and pine, fireplaces, and log bins. There is a relaxed, cluttered but cozy look about the place and the Fords enjoy it immensely. Here Eileen—who reports to her New York office stylishly dressed and carefully manicured— loafs around like a Kansas farm wife on a quiet Sunday. She chooses simple clothing, including double-knits and cardigans, and wears no makeup. Jerry, still very much the jock, sports athletic outfits and plays seemingly endless sets of tennis on the estate's private court. Late afternoons and evenings are often spent in the den; the couple and their dogs gather in front of the color television, usually to watch a sporting event. Both are football fans, and will not even talk when a play is in progress. Eileen goes even further, refusing to make weekend appointments when a big game is scheduled.

On the surface, the Fords appear flip about their success, their station in life. Asked what motivates her now that she's achieved all that she set out to do—now that she has considerable wealth, power, status, and fame—Eileen answers, "I'll tell you what motivates me. I'll tell you what makes me still want to jump out of bed in the morning. Where we live in New York there is an opposite-side-of-the-street parking rule. Every day, we have to move the car from one side to the other so the sweepers can come through. That's why I get up: to move the car before 7 A.M."

Although certainly meant in jest, this remark is probably even further from the truth than Eileen would like to admit. What truly motivates Eileen to keep plugging, to rise before the competition, and to work harder than anyone else is an overpowering determination to stay number one.

In reality, she is not at all casual about success, power, or money. Interviews with scores of people, some of whom have known the Fords for decades, reveal Eileen to be a shrewd businesswoman and a superb manipulator. When there is something to be gained—signing up a hot model, winning the loyalty of a major client, or gaining flattering treatment by a journalist —Eileen can graciously disarm even the most hardened skeptics. But cross the lady, fall out of her favor for any reason, and it is said that she will come at you like a combination of a cobra and a street fighter. Says a longtime Ford observer, now an editor at a top fashion magazine: "Eileen thinks you are an enemy if you compete against her, get friendly with one of her competitors, say something even slightly negative about her agency, question her billings, or criticize one of her models."

Some of this bad feeling about her is obviously based on jealousy. Eileen is undoubtedly the most talented and successful person in the business. Still, if she is authoritarian—as her critics contend—it may be because things went too much her way for too long. From the founding of her agency in 1947 to the opening of Wilhelmina's shop in 1967, Eileen enjoyed unquestioned leadership of the increasingly lucrative modeling industry. Although a handful of other agencies (most notably Plaza Five, launched by her onetime partner Natalie Paine) achieved some prominence during this period, the Fords were the monarchs of modeling for more than two decades. They had the best models and the best clients at a time when the industry was really taking hold, earning a place for itself as a legitimate and highly profitable service.

Because they themselves built much of the industry virtually from scratch, it seems that the Fords believed, subconsciously at least, that the field should be theirs alone. "You know the old saying about how power corrupts and absolute power corrupts absolutely," says the above-quoted fashion magazine editor. "Well, something like that happened to Eileen and Jerry. They got more powerful—so used to calling all the shots in modeling—that they started to think of the industry as their personal fiefdom. They didn't look kindly on those who would dare challenge their authority. . . . Also, they both enjoy making big money and the agency they built turned out to be better than a key to the mint. Would you want anyone tampering with that? Would you react kindly to competition?"

Like it or not, the Fords did get competition—a new wave of competition, starting with the opening of Wilhelmina's agency and continuing with the arrival of Zoli and John Casablancas. These rivals were different from previous intruders on the Ford turf because they enjoyed tremendous publicity hypes and were positioned as the agents of the future. It is said that Eileen never regarded them simply as other agents trying to make a living in the same industry but as usurpers to the throne.

Wilhelmina, Eileen's most successful challenger, was herself a onetime Ford model. It was partly for this reason and partly because she had had a dazzling career as such that the Fords allegedly viewed the opening of Willy's agency as a major threat.* "In my experience as a Ford model, I learned the inside workings of the agency business," Willy noted. "I always had my eye on the business end as well as on the camera, so I picked up a tremendous amount of information. Most important of all, I learned what should not be done. I saw the faults in the Ford operation and I believed that success would come to me if I could do a better job. That's what gave me the confidence to open my agency and what led me to believe it would be the best of all."

A striking Dutch beauty raised in Chicago, Wilhelmina rose to the pinnacle of modeling in a story that reads like the script for a Rocky-type movie—the kind where hard work, determination, and the American way triumph over the odds. That's the Wilhelmina story in a nutshell: poor working family girl dreams of glamour, yearns to be a model, saves her pennies, takes lessons, gets her break, achieves success, becomes the toast of the world. To Willy, it was the Cinderella story of the century. She loved to recount it over and over again—in her official bio, her book, and her agency's promotional kits.

"I was the greatest model who ever worked in this business," she declared, shortly before her death. "In just about any way you want to measure success, from the number of covers to international recognition, I was tops. Now I'm deeply involved in another career and I'm equally proud to say that I'm the best model's agent in the world too."

Chimed in ever-supporting husband Bruce Cooper, "She's right on both counts. You can bet your ass on that."

Raised in the small town of Culemborg, Holland, the daughter of a local butcher, Willy engaged in the rich fantasy life so common to many would-be models. At age eleven she fancied herself an international counterspy living a life of glamour, intrigue, and foreign travel. Quite unexpectedly, the travel part came true: Willy's father decided to leave Holland and to seek a better life in the United States. The family moved to

---

*She died of lung cancer on March 1, 1980, at the age of forty. Husband Bruce Cooper relinquished his interest in the agency soon after, turning over ownership and control to two longtime executives of the agency, William Weinberg and Francis Rothchild. No major changes were planned in agency operation.

Chicago, where Willy entered high school, studied English, and latched onto something that would change the course of her fantasies, and her real life, for many years. That something was fashion magazines.

"Quickly they became my favorite English reading material. I even went to second-hand stores to buy all the old issues I could afford on my rather meager allowance. As I grew up, I read them from cover to cover, devouring every word of the text and every picture of my new idols, the beautiful models who reached so glamorously from the pages—out to me.

"Of course, I had no idea of how one went about becoming a beautiful model. Before me lay a mysterious world replete with thousands of unanswered questions.

"Then one day a friend asked me to go with her to a local modeling school for an interview. She was frightened and needed my moral support. As it worked out, my friend was too short for a modeling career, but the director of the school assured me that I was exactly right. My head began to spin as I realized my own life could prove to be an American dream transformed into reality."*

The seed was planted. Willy, now eighteen, convinced her father to advance her the modeling school tuition with the stipulation that she would repay it. To do so, she worked after school in a five-and-dime store, earning sixty cents an hour. But it was a good investment. Willy, who had temporarily renamed herself Winnie Hart, fell into the right hands in the modeling community. Most important, she was coached by noted photographer Skrebenski. Her early test shots and first promotional composite, completed in 1960, showed a dazzling, elegant woman with a classic European flair just right for the fashion of the day. Willy's career took off, and she was soon the highest paid model in Chicago. She made enough to reward her parents with a paid up mortgage on the family residence and a gift of a new car. Then, following a route that is often taken to inflate a new model's reputation and to build up her book before the all-important introduction to New York, Willy was off to Paris to

---

*The New You by Wilhelmina (Simon & Schuster, 1978).

make a name in her native Europe. Within months she was featured in a slew of prominent fashion magazines, with one devoting an entire issue to her.

After fourteen hectic months of European image-building, Willy was ready to tackle Manhattan. "I knew that to be recognized as *the* star of the industry, New York would have to be captured," she said. "It's the modeling mecca of the world. You can't claim to be number one unless you make it here." And make it she did. The year was 1961: soon after she arrived in New York, Willy's first *Vogue* cover hit the newsstands. Twenty-five more would follow. The Cinderella Dutch girl became the hottest model in the world, racking up an unprecedented 390 magazine covers in the course of her career. In 1967, after having achieved every measure of success a model can hope for, Willy hung up her smile, moved out of the camera's eye, and opened her agency.

By her side was husband and partner, Bruce Cooper. A former production executive for "The Tonight Show," Bruce arranged Willy's first television appearance with Johnny Carson. It was there that they met. "Willy had been named one of the ten best coiffured women in the world," Bruce recalls. "I had to get somebody from the list for the show and I couldn't get Grace Kelly and I couldn't get Jackie O., so I got Willy." That was in 1965; they were married a year later.

The setup at Wilhelmina Models was similar to that at the Ford agency. At both an outspoken woman commanded the spotlight and selected the models, while the husband-partner took care of the financial end of the business. Cooper appeared to have based his role on the one established by Jerry Ford— the tough, behind-the-scenes mover and shaker who's as macho as they come and who guards the place against competitors, irresponsible accounts, and disloyal models. For the most part he's never succeeded in becoming an industry leader. Unlike Jerry Ford, he has made few major innovations in the business and is not widely praised outside of his agency. The picture that emerges from several interviews with the author and from conversations with acquaintances and competitors is that of a man of only average intelligence and ability.

From the day they opened shop, Bruce and Willy focused on one primary objective: to surpass Ford in annual billings and to become the world's largest modeling agency. In this, the agency still has some way to go. Although Cooper claims to have edged out his rivals by as much as $1 million a year in billings, some objective sources deny this, claiming it is an exaggeration designed both to irritate the Fords and to establish Wilhelmina Models as preeminent in the industry.

This is not to say that Wilhelmina Models has not been tremendously successful. The agency is a certified winner. In the thirteen years since its founding, Willy's shop has approached the volume of business it took the Fords three decades to generate. And the race is not over: with the opening of a new talent division on the West Coast—set up to handle show business personalities—the Wilhelmina agency has entered another lush market that may yet give it unchallenged possession of the number-one rank.

The Ford/Wilhelmina rivalry is more than just the usual game of business oneupmanship. It provided the first sparks for the launching of Willy's shop and fueled Wilhelmina's determination thereafter. According to Willy, it was firsthand observation of the Fords' tactics that prompted her to strike out on her own: "Their attitude was that they were gods and that everyone represented by the agency was at their mercy. You couldn't express yourself, voice an opinion, or even ask an intelligent question about your career. They were the absolute rulers. . . . That's why I started Wilhelmina Models. Bruce and I believed there was a real void in the market for a new type of agency—one that would treat its models with respect and would really service them as professionals. We believed that agent and model should be joined in a partnership of sorts, where both worked to help each other. We still believe that. We don't accept the notion that agents are supreme and models are second-class citizens. To us, both sides are equally important.

"The Fords' attitude that models should jump for joy at being represented by an agency doesn't sit well here. Not at all. We consider ourselves fortunate to represent these girls. And we don't take them for granted. Never! It's our belief that we work for the models; we service them. Every girl here gets the full measure of this agency's talent and resources to make her career a success. There are no exceptions. As a former model, I know what the girls need, and I see to it that they get it."

There is no doubt that Wilhelmina's phenomenal modeling career played a major part in the growth and development of her agency. Her glowing reputation as a model gave her a great head start in terms of publicity. Like a film star who enters politics, Willy was a known commodity the day she opened shop. Models and advertisers knew and admired her greatly. Aspiring models idolized the woman; art directors respected her grace, elegance, and professionalism. From the very start, Willy had the talent and the clients to make the venture a going concern. There were hurdles, to be sure, but she had a much easier road to success than others who had preceded her in the modeling business.

What's more, Willy was an intelligent woman who well understood the psychology of the business: how to motivate the girls and how to make them give 100 percent to achieve status, recognition, and wealth. Herself a product of this manipulative process, Willy knew precisely how to pull the strings to make the puppets dance. In one technique—still used today—she encouraged intense competition among the girls themselves. A modeling agency is, in ways, similar to a harem in that a collection of beautiful women all vie for the attention, admiration, and even the love of the masters who manage them. Many of the girls are young, far from home, frightened by the enormous pressures and demands of modeling. They look to their agency heads as parent-figures to guide, supervise, and care for them. Willy held out the promise of this treatment to those who performed well for the agency. She built a star system that rewarded the achievers not only with wealth and fame but also with recognition inside the agency as Bruce and Willy's pet.

"Willy knew that most models are nothing more than star-struck little girls," says a noted photographer who worked with Wilhelmina throughout her career. "So she played the kind of little games that really turn them on. She made it clear that anyone who turned a couple of hundred grand a year would be loved—would be held out as examples for the others to follow. You have no idea how much the girls want this. They all pretend to be sophisticated, independent, and totally supportive of their sister models, but that's pure bullshit. They are competitive cats who want top billing and want their colleagues to know it.

"That's why Willy set up her so-called 'Hollywood Blvd.' This is a special little corner of the agency where two bookers handle the affairs of the agency's small and select group of stars. It's as close as this or any other agency comes to giving personalized attention. Here, every five or so stars share a booker; with the bulk of the models, it's one booker for every forty or fifty girls. 'Hollywood Blvd.' is corny and silly but the girls do eat it up. Willy knows how to give them what they crave."

Willy's side of the story was, of course, totally different. She boasted that her modeling experience made her more sympathetic to the girls, that she alone knew the trials and tribulations they face, and it must be said that many of Willy's models adored and respected her.

For the most part, there is little substantive difference among any of the Big Four. To be sure, each has its own personality—its own strengths, weaknesses, styles, and quirks—but all operate according to similar procedures. For young models first breaking into the business, they can be frighteningly similar.

3

THE BIG BREAK
Making It in New York

"They come with an innocence that reflects good clean
living and traditional midwestern values. Their frame of
reference is a one-horse town with a diner, a movie theater, and
a church. Most have never done much more than babysit, kiss
the local boys, or maybe model for some nickel-and-dime
clothing store. But then suddenly, sometimes in a matter of
months after coming to the Big Apple, they are deeply
immersed in the New York scene: hanging around with fast,
sophisticated people, trying to get noticed, making $750 a day.
It's a shock to their systems. Many can't cope. They become
nervous, edgy, and irritable. They live life in a pressure
cooker."
—A prominent fashion photographer

The youngsters who flock to New York and try out for the Big
Four are a different breed from their peers back home. Most
know they will be models at a time in their lives when other kids
are still absorbed in doctor/nurse/Indian chief fantasies. The
hunger for glamour develops early on and intensifies throughout their teens. They start preparing themselves before puberty. They don't know yet that modeling has a dark side. All
they see is the glitter, and they want to be part of it. They want
to be models.

"The first spark comes from picking up a copy of *Seventeen* and seeing their first beautiful cover girl," said Wilhelmina. "Like youngsters who go to the movies and dream of
being actresses, future models can dream only of those magazine covers. From that day on, they can think of little else.
That's what happened to me. It really grips you.

"You start your regimen right away. You read books and

39

articles on what it takes to be a model and you begin preparing
yourself. The accent is on the physical. As the teen years go by
and you begin to mature, you learn the right hairstyles, skin
care, and posture. Basic things, like walking, have to be re-
learned. Walking not like a child—but like a model."

In many ways, childhood ends as soon as the training begins; the two just can't mix. By age thirteen, there are strict
bans against the fun things kids indulge in: no more junk food,
no more slumping in chairs or staying up late.

"The youngster makes a startling discovery at a very tender age," Willy added. "She learns that she'll eventually have
to leave her hometown, to say good-bye to her parents. She is
forced to look beyond her local community. To make it big in
modeling, she must come to New York. The day may seem far
away when she first learns it, but it comes to pass very, very
quickly."

Success demands that before the age of twenty—prefera-
bly by seventeen—the budding model must be accepted by a
prominent New York agency. The fact that all other cities are
the bush leagues is universally accepted, not only by the New
York modeling establishment, but by its counterparts in Chicago, Atlanta, and Los Angeles as well. Manhattan is the undis-
puted center of modeling: hundreds of top photographers are
located within walking distance of one another (mostly in the
downtown lofts of Soho, Broadway, and lower Fifth Avenue),
and virtually all of the leading fashion magazines and advertising and model agencies dot a mile-long strip of urban landscape
from 37th Street to 59th Street.

How models make it to New York varies. Most go the farm
system route, signing up with local agencies in their home-
towns. The hope is to make a name for themselves in Podunk
and then to be whisked away by a visiting New York agent.
Others take a more daring step—although to some it is simply
seen as the more glamorous choice—and head straight for the
big city as soon as they can cut the family cords. For many, this
is the culmination of years of waiting, and leaving their home-
town is like releasing steam from a pressure cooker.

But those who come to New York without a sponsoring

agent soon find that they are very much alone. They face life in a city that is fast, tough, impersonal—and expensive. The $1,000 kitties the girls expect to live on for months is barely enough for advance rent and security on a modest studio apartment.

Darlene, a leggy six-footer from Ann Arbor, Michigan, is typical of New York's model immigrants: she believed that her stake of $1,500 would be enough to support her royally for the first months in the Big Apple. "I feel like such a fool when I think about it now but I had these visions of being the fashionable would-be model about town," Darlene says. "I imagined myself with a terrific apartment—a fireplace, great Bloomingdale's furniture, friends coming and going. My days would be spent interviewing at the agencies, getting a booking here and there, shopping on Fifth Avenue, and doing the disco scene at night. That's the way they always showed it in the fashion magazines and I believed it."

Darlene's experience had little in common with her fantasies. After only two nights in New York, the tab for her room at the Hilton, cabs, food, and tips came to $310—more than 20 percent of her stake. Economics dictated a change of address, but where to?

"I had to get out of the Hilton fast, there was no doubt about that," Darlene recalls. "I had no idea New York would be so expensive. One thing you learn quickly is that the high cost of living dictates compromises, the first of the many compromises you have to make, compromises that test your ethics, morality, and pride. It means abandoning the dream of the super apartment and instead squeezing into a modest box with three roommates. I wound up with an awful setup: two girls in the bedroom, two in the living room, $200 a month each. No glamour, no style, no privacy. It was an expedient arrangement pure and simple. It allowed me to afford to live in a fashionable neighborhood even if it was not in the way I'd always imagined it. It was a matter of survival. That's a model's top priority."

The vision of an elegant life-style is not the only thing that has to be revised: dreams of taking New York by storm are usually shot to hell in a matter of weeks. Getting even the slightest bit of recognition in the city's tough and blasé modeling community is exceedingly difficult. Agencies, photographers, editors, and art directors are a hardened bunch, all too familiar with the tactics of the hopeful newcomers. They've all been subject to hundreds of desperate phone calls, urgent telegrams, messages slipped under the door. They are bored and annoyed by the tedious and seemingly endless process of examining faces, 99 percent of which are rejects. They are tired of hearing the familiar sob stories about grand ambitions, tired of the beauty contest anecdotes. But of course they put up with it all because the newcomers are the raw materials of the industry: only by sifting through thousands of faces and photos can they hope to turn up a diamond in the rough. Nevertheless, despite their own dependency on these aspiring models, they give them a difficult time. The newcomers learn the hard way that being a hot number in Duluth doesn't mean a thing in New York.

"You get cut down a few notches the very first time you approach the famous agencies—they really put you in your place fast," Darlene recalls. "I did it by telephone. Thought I'd call up and make a nice formal appointment to show off my beauty to Eileen Ford. Well, it just doesn't work that way—nowhere near it. First, the girl who answered the phone at Ford Models put me on hold for about eight minutes, came on the line, asked what I wanted, and before I could answer put me on hold again. Finally, I got a second to blurt out my request and was told that open auditions are held the following morning. If I wanted a chance, I'd have to show up then, just like all the others. No private interviews granted; no personal calls or chitchats with Mrs. Ford."

The open auditions, held by most of the big agencies, are what one attorney prominent in the industry calls "the slave markets." Here is where the hopefuls line up for a review by modeling's starmakers. The procedure at the Wilhelmina agency's cramped offices on East 37th Street is typical. Three mornings a week, from 9 A.M. to 11 A.M., any girl with a passion for modeling can come up for a personal evaluation by the staff. No special dress, photographs, or resumé are required. For the

vast majority of applicants, interviews last less than five minutes, and many are rejected at first sight.

"Don't laugh when you see who's sitting out there," Wilhelmina's PR woman warned an agency visitor about to view
his first open audition. "Some of them are so ugly you won't
believe they have the gall to apply as models."

And she was not exaggerating. The menagerie of hopefuls
includes the fat, the pimply faced, the sloppily dressed, and the
just plain homely. One especially obese young woman, interviewed in the agency's crowded reception area, was asked why
she was pursuing a modeling career. At roughly 5'7", 170
pounds, it was obvious to everyone else in the room that she
could sooner become a nightclub bouncer than a model.

"I hate to sound stuck-up or anything, but Mom always
told me I was one of the prettiest girls in Austin [Texas], and
that I should be a model when I grew up," she said in a sparrow-
like chirp that belied her stocky build. "Mom herself wanted to
be a model, but her face got burned in an accident and that was
that. But there was never any doubt that I'd go into the field.
So here I am."

The presence of these modeling misfits gives the more
attractive applicants a false sense of confidence and of superior-
ity. Yet comparing themselves to the "freaks" is a meaningless
vanity, since being more attractive than the outright losers
doesn't bring the majority of applicants any closer to agency
acceptance. Even those blessed with all the right physical attributes—slender body, chiseled nose, high cheekbones—are
shocked by the experience of their first audition at a top New
York agency. For most, it involves hours of waiting, a speedy
interview, and then out the door and onto the streets. It is a
hard, cold, slap-in-the-face rejection. Just what form the rejection takes depends on the agency and the interviewer. Most
agents believe in leveling with rejects on the spot, since leaving
them with any glint of hope often subjects the agents to follow-
up visits, incessant phone calls, and a steady stream of letters
and reminder cards.

"You have to cut the cord right then and there," says Joan
Howse, head of Wilhelmina's talent division, which books mod-

els for commercials and soap operas. "If you don't, they'll haunt you. They'll keep coming back day after day, year after year, until you make it plain they don't have a chance. Getting it over quickly, at the start, is better for them and for us."

The industry grapevine has it that some agencies show absolutely no sympathy for the rejects; they make no attempt to soften the blow. Eileen Ford is said to be particularly rough. She is especially intolerant of obesity. She crusades against fat.

For a budding model, the first audition is rarely the last. Most aspiring models make their first stop at Ford. Those who strike out at their first interview usually make the rounds at the rest of the Big Four. This kind of persistence often pays off, since it is well known that the selection of models is highly subjective. An applicant denied entry on the Ford roster may be welcomed with open arms by Zoli. This can happen for two reasons. First, agents differ slightly in their personal aesthetics. Two blond, blue-eyed products of Wisconsin who seem to a layman to be cut from the same cloth may appear worlds apart to an agent's trained eye simply because their mouths or cheeks are shaped differently. Second, the agencies like to balance out their stables with a smattering of models who do not conform to the classic WASP mold; they like to have on hand a token assortment of blacks and maybe an Oriental or two. No social message is implied here—it is simply a carefully calculated strategy designed to have the right candidates available when the orders come in for "special" models. That is why a stunning, ebony-skinned beauty quickly rejected by Ford may gain entry at Zoli's agency on the same day. Zoli may have a gap in his roster for a black; Ford may not. It is purely a marketing decision, much the way a merchant balances inventory.

But even persistence does not always pay off. Sometimes there are no convenient openings, no vacant slots to fill. Many of New York's model immigrants, in fact, get rejected at all of the Big Four. It is a serious personal setback, in many cases a traumatic experience. Those least able to cope typically return home at once. Suddenly, their native town may not seem so bad after all.

"It's not as if they've been in the Big Apple for years," says Bob Stone. "They can go from great hope to severe disappointment in a matter of weeks. Those who can't stand it and have to flee home immediately don't have all that hard a time readjusting to the small town. If they haven't been in the city long enough to get it in their blood, they can go back to the farm."

Most of the applicants, even those who get nowhere at the Big Four, stay in New York, working on their style and appearance so they can try again to get a foot in the door. For these troopers, there is little time for self-pity: they have planted their flags in Manhattan. They must eat and pay rent, earn a living, and do something to tide themselves over until there's reason to take another shot at the Big Four. Many aim for a place on the fringes of big-time modeling. They turn to the so-called commercial agencies, the biggest of which is run by Cye Perkins.

"The same girls rejected by the high fashion agents are often accepted by our agency because our standards are different," says Perkins, a soft-spoken, likable man who started out in the business some forty years ago as a male model. Although his business is housed in run-down offices, it is said to be healthy and quite lucrative. "We are not into high fashion. We provide models for advertisers selling a wide range of products from industrial machines to food. We don't need girls who are perfect looking; they just have to be the kind of face the client wants. That can range from a thirteen-year-old pixie selling breakfast cereal to a grandmother for a denture ad. Advertisers don't want beautiful faces for those kinds of products, so they call on us. It is, therefore, easier to get into our agency and a good number of the girls who don't qualify as high fashion models come here. The catch is we offer much less in the way of money. A top commercial model makes only about $40,000 a year; that's peanuts in high fashion."

As disillusioning as this may be, acceptance by a commercial agency is still several notches above selling sweaters at Saks. Most of the first-round rejects wind up in occupations far removed from modeling, and indeed a high proportion of them can be found behind the sales counters at New York's top department stores.

"It never happens this way, but here's how a little star-struck would-be model from Minnesota should leave home," says a top executive at one of New York's Big Four. "The sweet little violet goes down to the sleepy junction to catch the train to New York. She's a high school queen, just graduated, and is ready now for the career everyone always knew she'd pursue. Her family, neighbors, boyfriend, pastor, and teacher are there to say farewell. The train pulls in, she mounts the steps, and as she turns and waves her hankie she says, 'Wish me luck; I'm off to work for Macy's.'"

For the winners in the find-an-agency game, victory is sweet. The girl with agency backing is free to pursue her career, to do what she left home, friends, and family for. She can devote herself to making it as a model. The fantasy of a lifetime is about to begin. But exciting as it is, there are still major hurdles ahead.

"The girls get so euphoric when an agency has accepted them that they lose track of where they really are—and that's pretty close to nowhere," says Bob Stone, who has photographed hundreds of budding models. "First, they still have to make ends meet financially until the bookings come in, which can take many months; second, they have to work on their looks and camera poise; and third, they have to develop some recognition in the industry. Just getting accepted by an agency is no guarantee of success."

Making ends meet financially can require help from home, working part-time, or finding a rich patron. That patron can be the model's own agency, which will from time to time hand out temporary rent and food subsidies. But this Cinderella treatment is reserved for only the most promising models. Agents don't dole out subsidies routinely. And they don't do it to be kind. They pay up when it is the only way to keep a promising prospect fed, sheltered, and building her career in New York. Put in business terms, it is strictly an investment in future revenues—one that is carefully calculated before a dime is spent.

"The best young model is a hungry young model," says Bruce Cooper, brushing the sleeve of his superbly tailored English pin-striped suit. "While we will help out from time to time, we don't do it for long and we try not to pay all the costs. It's our experience that the girl who has to get up and out of bed to get the career going and to get the rent paid will hustle much more than her pampered counterpart."

The Fords think differently. They are well known for their parental approach, and Eileen's pet prospects are virtually adopted into the family. They eat, sleep, and socialize in the Fords' elegant New York townhouse and weekend in their splendid country estate. This togetherness keeps the agency's brightest hopes under Eileen's watchful eye. In the process of providing support, she coaches them and keeps them living clean and working hard.

"It was great living with the Fords," says Ford protégée Serena. "They have a butler and a cook and oh, it's so easy to get spoiled. But Eileen is always coaching and is always helpful. She notices the kinds of things only an expert sees. Like once I was wearing a bow tie and Eileen got mad at me. 'Take that damn thing off,' she said. When I asked why, she said, 'Because girls with beautiful necks should never conceal them.' It's a lesson I'll never forget." This anecdote is revealing: Although Eileen Ford is the most controversial woman in the modeling industry, she is more devoted to the business than anyone else. Although her competitors will not admit it, her drive, her instincts, and her talent are unequalled. When it comes to competing against Eileen, getting up with the roosters isn't good enough: Eileen Ford, it is said, never sleeps.

"Many of the girls are raw material when they first come to me," Eileen notes. "They may be beautiful, yes, but they need to be more than that. They need to have talent in front of the camera. Any agent can pick a pretty face. What separates the leaders from the also-rans in this business is the ability to make models out of pretty girls. I think I do this very well, and part of my success at it is attributable to the fact that some of the girls live with us. I have the time to work with them around the clock."

Also offering the girls financial aid in their lean days is the old-fashioned "sugar daddy." Although they are frowned upon by the modeling establishment, sugar daddies are believed to support more of the would-be models than the agencies. They are usually paunchy, balding, middle-aged men who like to be surrounded by beautiful young models thirty or more years their junior. Most run successful businesses and have a penchant for hand-tailored suits, elegant automobiles, and fine dining. Many are married, have a townhouse in the city, a home in the suburbs, and three or more cars. For these men who have everything, two prizes still turn them on: youth and beauty. Models offer both.

"I love my wife, my poker partners, my nice comfortable life-style," says Buddy,* a men's pajama manufacturer from Great Neck, New York. "But . . . I'm the kind of guy who needs a little action, a little excitement now and then to keep me going. Being with models does that for me. I have a co-op on 63rd Street that I tell Uncle Sam is for entertaining out-of-town buyers, but there's always one model in residence there at all times. The deal is simple: the girl is my escort for dinner one or two nights a week at Maxwell's Plum or Sign of the Dove. Then it's a fast hop into bed together, a quick shower, and I drive home to Great Neck. For this, the girl gets to live in a beautiful place, eats the best foods, and drives around the city in a $25,000 Gucci Seville. She doesn't love me but I don't care. For me, it's an exciting diversion, something to keep me young and alive; for her, it's a way to get the bills paid so she can concentrate on modeling and enjoy the New York scene at the same time. Once she starts making big money, she goes off on her own and I've got a new arrival ready to move right in. It's a beautiful deal. If you know how to go about it, finding models is easy."

Not really. Men like Buddy go out of their way to lure the youngsters as soon as they arrive in New York. The best hunting ground is outside the model agencies, where sugar daddies love to cruise their gleaming Cadillacs and Mercedes-Benzes or simply offer free rides to the girls' next appointments. Others

*Name and address are fictitious. The details of his story are true.

show up at the discos, bistros, and restaurants popular with the modeling crowd.

"These guys have one-track minds—all they want is models, models, models," says a waiter at Yellowfingers Restaurant, just blocks from the Ford agency. "If they see you waiting on a model that you seem to know socially, the vultures will offer big money for her phone number. A hundred bucks is the going rate, but I've been offered as much as $400. I think it's disgusting; I turn them all down. I'm no pimp and, what's more, I have no way of knowing what sick things these guys may have in mind. But there are waiters and maître d's who take the money and tell all. They don't care what happens to the babes."

Agents detest the sugar daddies and make every effort to protect the girls from them because they can give modeling just the kind of sordid image the industry leaders are trying to avoid. For this reason, it is virtually impossible to get agents to reveal models' telephone numbers. All messages must be left at the agency switchboards. Home numbers are top secret.

There is no denying that the models' sugar daddies are a pathetic and repulsive group. To be around them is to sense their desperation, the need to prove themselves powerful and attractive at any price. Some sugar daddies refer to the models as whores, but the truth is that in these relationships both parties are the prostitutes. What's more, it is the men who are rejected over and over again. Most models decline their invitations, but there is always that one young model in fifty who is dazzled by a show of wealth and enticed by the opportunity to sample New York's high life. The wolves keep sniffing until they track their lamb.

"They are always out there," says Dawn. "Wherever you go, it seems as if they're never far behind. They just get off on being around us—they really do. I've never had anything to do with them; it's not my style, but there are other girls who do play along. I think it's raunchy."

Actually, there is little time for a new model to worry much about sugar daddies, food bills, or where her next buck is coming from. Her life immediately after agency acceptance is a

whirlwind of long days, hectic schedules, and intense preparation. Still high from her triumphant welcome into the winner's
circle, she unknowingly enters a stage of her career in which
others call all the shots. In this period she is readied for market,
much the way any other commercial product is designed, packaged, and promoted. She is viewed by the agency as raw material to be polished, perfected, and presented to the industry as
salable merchandise. This is done in two stages, which we'll call
research and development (R&D) and marketing.

R&D begins with a study of the model's strengths and
weaknesses. At the Wilhelmina agency—which has one of the
more elaborate R&D programs—analysis of the new recruit is
conducted by the the agency's Development Board (composed
of bookers and top executives). Typically, the analysis may find
that a new model has two glaring weaknesses: poor use of
makeup (many use too much and accentuate the wrong features) and a lack of poise. This is noted on a chart and the girl
is then assigned to the agency's own classes in makeup and
camera presence. Here, photography sessions are simulated to
show the girls exactly what they will be facing on the job. The
classes, which used to be taught by Willy herself, are successful in that they demonstrate in professional surroundings just
how damaging poor makeup, the wrong hairstyle, or bad posture can be to a model's on-camera appearance.

Facing Wilhelmina's Development Board—or its counterpart at other agencies—is an unnerving experience. A fledgling model feels as if she is stripped bare before a jury: every
feature of her face, body, and personality is subject to professional scrutiny. What's more—and this is indicative of the new
recruit's powerlessness—she is obliged to alter herself according to the agent's whims. A change from natural curls to a
meticulously coiffed body wave may be ordered; red-dyed hair
may have to be blond again; and a pleasant, simple smile may
have to be replaced by an ear to ear Hollywood flasher. This is
the bottom line in modeling: the girl changes herself to conform
to the agency's standards; agencies, in turn, develop standards
they believe will be suitable to advertisers; and advertisers
establish standards designed to attract the great masses of
middle-class consumers. The result is a safe, sterile look as

exciting, predictable, and controversial as vanilla ice cream.

The girls give in to this homogenizing process partly because they have no choice and partly because they want very much to please. The message goes out to them very early that to make it in modeling you have to play by the rules. In general, there is no place in the business for individualists. It is widely accepted that the agencies know better than anyone else what kind of looks a girl needs to be successful in the marketplace. Agencies simply dump those who refuse to cooperate. For this reason, the vast majority of girls submit without a fight, avoiding any struggle with the agency that will put them out on the streets again or, worse yet, on a bus back to Minneapolis.

"When you are accepted by a big New York agency, you feel on top of the world, but also pretty nervous," says Myra, a farmer's daughter from Plainview, Texas, who was accepted by the Wilhelmina agency after brief stints as a prelaw student and a Lord & Taylor's salesgirl. "I got sidetracked a bit, but I always knew I wanted to be a model more than anything else. . . . I had a pretty big head. But when you come to New York and you go to the auditions and see all the other beautiful girls, you lose a lot of self-confidence. The competition here is tremendous; you tell yourself that you'll do just about anything to make it. Your agent's wishes are your commands. When I went into Kay Mitchell's office [the manager of Wilhelmina's women's division], I was actually trembling. Whatever Kay suggested that I do to prepare for my career, I accepted at face value. I don't remember if there was anything I disagreed with but, if there was, I didn't argue. After all, the agency people know best."

The making of a professional model involves more than simply polishing the rough edges. A good deal of effort also goes into creating an image. Should the model have a slightly sexy look? Should she be the wholesome girl next door? How about the outdoorsy type? Just how the girl is packaged depends on her natural attributes, the fashion of the times, and the personal tastes of her agent. Quite often, a model will adopt a daring and voluptuous look, only to have it drastically toned down by her mentor.

This "repackaging" process helped one top model parlay her overnight success into a lasting career. Positioned by her first New York agent as a sexy *Cosmo* girl, she made a big splash but was in danger of having the wrong look as the mid-70s ideal of wholesome natural beauty came into vogue. Fortunately, she then signed up with Wilhelmina, who steered her away from the sexy image to a more classic, high-fashion look. As a result, the model is sought after today by leading apparel and cosmetics advertisers, who traditionally shy away from exotic models.

"We have to give our girls images that conform to current tastes," says Bruce Cooper. "If wide-eyed country types are in style, we'll have lots of them. If a more sultry look is in, we'll try to give the new girls that image. Very often the same model can be made to have several different kinds of looks. She should always be flexible so that she can get the most jobs. Models need a central image, yes, but they can't be chained to it."

Take the case of the highly regarded model Roseanne Vela, wife of artist Peter Max. A native of Galveston, Texas, Rosie has achieved extraordinary success because she has that all-important asset that comes from within—a natural camera personality. She can be, on film, whatever the client wants her to be: sexy, sporty, sophisticated, innocent, daring, vibrant, sweet, or slightly wicked. This great flexibility translates into constant work because advertisers and photographers—the powers responsible for most of the bookings—appreciate this quality above all else. As a result, Rosie lists among her many credits more than two hundred appearances in *Vogue,* a slew of Revlon ads, and television commercials as the L'Air du Temps perfume girl.

The marketing of a model begins shortly after the R&D analysis. Properly packaged, the girl is now publicized and presented to the industry's movers and shakers.

"At this point, attention shifts away from the girl herself and on to her book," says Zoli, referring to the portfolio of pictures every model uses to sell herself to clients. "We have to teach her to compile a really super book because that can make or break her career, especially in the early stages."

A model's book is similar to the sales brochure or catalogs used in other industries. Resembling an oversized family album, this zippered portfolio is filled with photographs, slides, and magazine tearsheets featuring the model in various poses, types of apparel, and settings. The book is designed to reveal the model's beauty, flexibility, and camera personality. Since these traits can be pivotal elements in the selling of a model, extraordinary preparation and care go into assembling a first-rate book. For some models, this becomes an obsession that haunts them throughout their careers.

"I'm constantly second-guessing myself," says a lovely commercial model with the Perkins agency. "My book will be all set, arranged precisely the way I want it. Then it goes out to be seen by an advertiser and I don't get the job. I blame the outcome on my book. I tell myself that one picture or another blew my chances and should be torn to pieces. Suddenly, I'm sure that this shot or that makes me look too old, too fat, or too plain. So I hastily remove the culprits, replace them with other, more suitable shots, and feel confident as hell that the book is okay. That lasts until the next time I lose a job. Then the crazy second-guessing starts all over again. It's an occupational hazard you have to accept."

Models are known to wake up in the middle of the night to check and rearrange their books. Some ask every friend, lover, and associate for their opinions on which pictures should be included, which should be dropped. Their books are never the same for two days in a row. There is good reason for this madness. In nine cases out of ten, the book, not the model, wins or loses a booking. When a client calls for models, the applicants must come with books in hand. Many times, model selection is done entirely by the book; the girl herself isn't even asked to show up. Agency messengers bring the book from client to client for review, analysis, and discussion. It is safe to say that at any one time, 500 books are circulating by messenger among New York model agencies, art directors, and photographers.

Assembling a good book is especially tough in the early days of a model's career. Here, she runs smack into a classic Catch-22 situation: to get the best photos—the kinds of dramatic and artistic shots that can propel a budding career—a girl needs the services of a top photographer who will help the novice to discover and accentuate her strengths, to put herself together well, and to relate with confidence to the camera rather than simply standing before it. The problem is that few youngsters can afford to pay from $1,500 to $10,000 a day for their services.

Established models don't have this problem, since they come before the great photographers routinely, in the course of their work. When Christina Ferrare poses for a magazine cover, the session with Scavullo is paid for by the client and Christina gets free copies of the cover photo for her book. These tearsheets are considered the most prized entries in a book—even better than good photographs—because they give evidence that the model is already working and in demand. Nothing does more for a model's book than having in it a cover from *Vogue, Harper's Bazaar,* or *Glamour,* or a slick ad for Revlon, Max Factor, or Ralph Lauren. Like the rich, who keep getting richer, the star model's books keep getting better—and a good book leads to good jobs, working with talented photographers, and super tearsheets.

"There's a way to start this cycle—to get it working in your favor—but you must enter on the ground floor," says Dawn, her brilliant eyes fired with ambition. "That means going to testings with just about any photographer willing to shoot you. These are practice sessions, used by the photographers to test out new cameras, lighting, or models. There's no money in it, not a dime, but it provides those all-important pictures. Your first priority after getting into an agency is to build up a great book. That's what gets the ball rolling."

"You are deliriously happy to get testings in the early days of your career," adds Christina Ferrare. "Even though the work is for free, the girls compete for it tooth and nail. This is especially true if the testing is with a well-known photographer. You have to audition for the opportunity: a hundred girls may apply for the chance. So when you land one and the shots turn out good, you are in seventh heaven. It means your book is on the way; things are starting to come together."

Once a book has at least ten or twelve good photos, the

model is ready to compete for work on a paying basis. But is the industry ready for her? Is there a market for her special blend of looks, camera personality, and personal appeal? Does she have the right image to sell fashion? To move products? If the model is going to make it as a professional, the answers to all these questions have to be "yes."

Models learn early on that the search for work begins anew every day. They must sell themselves over and over again. Life is an endless round of "go-sees" (that's modeling shorthand for "go see if they want you"). It works like this: Art director John Doe at Grey Advertising puts together a Revlon nail polish ad with a disco theme. He calls his casting director, Jane Smith, to come up with a seventeen-to-nineteen-year-old model with a New York look. Jane takes the order and relays it to her favorite bookers at the Zoli, Ford, and Casablancas agencies. Bookers there scan their files for likely prospects and send every available girl who fits the bill to a go-see with John Doe. When the models arrive at Grey, they are led to a waiting room where all the other go-see girls are corralled until John Doe can look them over.

Every threatened creature—models included—has its own defense mechanisms. To get through the go-sees with their sanity intact, most of the girls adopt a standard rationalization that deadens the pain of constant rejection. You hear it, virtually word for word, from model after model.

"When I leave a go-see empty-handed, I know it's not me they're rejecting," says Dawn. "No one girl is better than the others. The people making the selection have a specific look in mind before anyone even enters the place. It's more a matter of them picking what they want, rather than rejecting what they don't."

There is some truth to this line of reasoning, but the identical, robotlike response one hears from so many models makes the statement seem more practiced than believed.

Do go-sees breed jealousy among the models? Although most of the girls say "no" (they seem to be vying for the Miss Congeniality award), deeper probing reveals that all is not sweetness and light.

"When you are waiting at a go-see you daydream," says

young model Barbara. "There's nothing else to do. Sometimes, I scan all the other girls sitting around the room and I fantasize that I'm a lady wrestler. I pick out the girl most likely to get the job and I see us both in an arena, maybe Madison Square Garden. I rush toward her, twist her arms, pull her hair, tear off her blouse and bra, squeeze her nipples, and then make her stand up and show the crowd how small her boobies are. She cries, the crowd cheers like crazy, and I feel great. I know it's a weird dream, but it makes me feel good when I have it."

Although physical violence among competing models is rare, verbal disputes are quite common. Just what form this takes depends on the models' ranking. The superstars, many of whom despise each other for petty competitive reasons, argue through intermediaries like reporters or gossip columnists. The jab is made to a go-between likely to pass it on. This is how it's done among the stars—no rolling in the mud. Barbs are traded across a DMZ.

Things are different, however, in the lower ranks. When the fledgling models fight, feathers fly. The hair comes down; the gloves come off. There's real verbal combat here. That's because there's more at stake—careers, not just vanities. When the tensions the girls bring to the go-sees do boil over, they can produce vicious arguments. Typical was a recent scene in the lobby of 717 Fifth Avenue, home of *Harper's Bazaar* magazine. A tall, lanky white model accused an elegant looking black girl of bad-mouthing her to a well-known photographer both had worked with in testing sessions. The dispute started quietly enough at *Bazaar*'s offices, heated up while they were waiting for the elevators, and was going at full force in the lobby.

"You told Ron not to bother calling me because I was supposedly peeling from a sunburn," the white model screamed, pointing a threatening finger inches away from the black girl's nose. "And you knew it was a total lie. I haven't been in the sun since the summer—that's seven months ago. Everybody knows there's nothing you won't do to put others down and to put yourself ahead. You're a cunning bitch."

"You just can't take it that Ron likes me better," the black girl answered, hands firmly on her hips. "If you weren't so busy fucking him you wouldn't be so sensitive about anyone else."

"You lying bitch. You've made yourself a pest—a social cause—not a model. He's afraid not to use you."

"Drop dead."

"You too."

Fear, frustration, intense jealousy and competition, daydreams, fantasies—all are part of the young model's life. It's hard to cope. On top of it all, the pace is grueling.

Take a typical day in the life of Patti, a promising beginner whose exotic, sexy looks belie her simple farm background:

April 18, 1979
6:30 A.M.
   Wakes to clock radio, disco station WKTU.
6:40–7:40 A.M.
   Does calisthenics, sit-ups, leg raises, meditation.
7:40–8:00 A.M.
   Washes accumulated dirty dishes that fill the sink of her 21st Street studio apartment.
8:00–8:30 A.M.
   Showers, shampoos and blow-dries hair, carefully makes up eyes and lips, dresses in designer jeans and red velour top.
9:00 A.M.
   Rides bus to lower Fifth Avenue for important testing at a photographer's loft studio.
9:30 A.M.
   Chats with photographer's assistant. Photographer will be forty-five minutes late. First disappointment of the day. If she waits, Patti will miss an 11:30 go-see at *Glamour* magazine. The session with the photographer is too important to pass up, so she waits.
9:40–11:05 A.M.
   Stares out the windows of the studio at the dirty streets below.

11:05 A.M.

Photographer arrives, apologizes, and quickly sets up the testing. It will have to be rushed.

11:15 A.M.–12:30 P.M.

Photo session.

12:30–2:00 P.M.

Patti buys a banana ice cream cone (the only lunch she can afford) and walks sixty blocks uptown to a go-see with another photographer, one she's met before and detested. But the assignment up for grabs is an important one: two weeks with a *Harper's Bazaar* crew in Puerto Rico shooting summer fashions.

2:10–3:15 P.M.

Waits her turn at the photographer's studio.

3:15–3:22 P.M.

Spends five minutes with the photographer, who silently looks over every picture in her book and then dismisses her. His lack of overt cruelty this time is a pleasant surprise but of little consolation.

3:30–4:00 P.M.

Takes bus downtown to a go-see at Macy's.

4:00 P.M.

Arrives at Macy's exhausted. Is told the go-see is postponed because the art director is detained at a shooting in New Jersey.

4:15–5:05 P.M.

Makes the slow trudge home. Buys a box of Good and Plenty to cheer herself up. Has $2.17 left in her wallet. Worries about money.

5:06 P.M.

Arrives home. Feels guilty about her weight. Throws out the Good and Plenty.

5:15–6:45 P.M.

Undresses and falls asleep nude.

6:45–10:30 P.M.

Showers, puts on same clothes, smokes two joints, eats an apple and two Ritz crackers. Watches "The Dating Game," plays records, files her fingernails, catches part of a TV movie.

10:30 P.M.–2:10 A.M.

Goes to Xenon discotheque (gets in free because she dates one of the managers). Dances, smokes two more joints, and drinks two vodkas with grapefruit juice (on the house). Makes weekend social plans. Invited by a friend of a friend to a condo in Sugarbush, Vermont.

3:00 A.M.

Arrives home and falls asleep fully dressed.

9:20 A.M. (the following morning)

Oversleeps. Awakened by ringing of the telephone. Her booker calling: Surprise! She's landed the *Harper's Bazaar* job! Off to Puerto Rico Sunday night. Her very first job, her first booking.

"The first break makes you feel wonderful—you're lighter than air," Patti says. "The feeling that makes you so high is that someone really wants to pay for your services. Not a small town department store or anything, but a famous magazine or ad agency. You think that there's nowhere to go but up.

"Unfortunately, the high doesn't last long. Before you know it, the booking's over and you're back on the go-see trail again. The fear that haunts you is that it was a fluke and you'll never work again. A month after the greatest high in your life you are back down in the dumps. Worrying again. You drink and you smoke and you try to get through it all."

It's a seesaw life.

4

THE RISE
AND THE FALL
A Model's Career

"Modeling is the last business in which you can make it
big, very big—over $100,000—in the very first year. You can't
readily do that on stage or television anymore."
—Merv Griffin

The fear of failure that grips most models in the early stages
of their careers is fueled both by the overpowering need to
make it big and the realization that there are no guarantees.
For most, success is not viewed as a desired objective but as an
absolute necessity. This demanding of oneself, the refusal to
accept second best, is the reason for much of the neurotic behavior common to models: the obsession with physical appearance, the fear of aging, the compulsive lying.

But failure is very much a part of the modeling business.
As in all the glamour fields, there are thousands who knock on
modeling's door for years but never gain entry. Stories of pathetic souls who devote a lifetime to climbing and falling off the
modeling ladder are legion, and they haunt the newcomers.
"Will that be me?" they ask themselves. "Will I fail too? Will
I delude myself year after year after year? Will I then look in
the mirror and see an older woman who never knew when to
stop?" For young models, this fear intensifies whenever the
phone doesn't ring, when there is no work in sight.

Take the case of Lana. A lovely and delightful woman
approaching her fiftieth birthday, Lana is the mother of five
grown children, the wife of a successful attorney. Standing
outside her ranch-style home on a manicured, tree-lined street
in Greenwich, Connecticut, she appears outwardly like any

other good-looking, smartly dressed lawyer's wife in a pleasant suburban community. But there is a difference. Lana lives for modeling—and has for most of her life. Her time, talents, energies, and even part of her home are devoted to a career that has eluded her in spite of heroic efforts.

Raised in Staten Island, New York, Lana was the kind of little girl they write songs about. Her beauty grew even more striking in her preteen years; wherever she went, there was talk about "that gorgeous little girl."

"I was always considered a beautiful child," Lana recalls. "Mom knew it and thought I should make the most of it by being a model. It certainly sounded exciting to me too. I always loved fashion, celebrities, show business—anything with some style and glamour to it. Also, I liked being admired for my looks."

Lana's modeling career began in earnest at the age of twelve when she was taken, proud mama at her side, to the then fledgling model agency run by John Robert Powers. Powers thought the youngster had exceptional looks and great potential, and he signed her up on the spot. Still a child, Lana seemed to have been given a ground-floor opportunity in a burgeoning industry.

"It was exciting, but it turned out to be somewhat of an empty victory," Lana explains. "I was a Powers model, but I didn't get many modeling jobs. I mean—it was bleak. Years went by and I hardly worked at all. No one knew why, but I just wasn't getting any offers. Powers was busy managing so many models that he didn't have the time to give my career the attention it needed. I was depressed; my mother was disappointed; it was quite a letdown for all of us."

By the time Powers finally paid attention to his young discovery, he realized that her career was going nowhere fast. Lana was sixteen at the time, and she had blossomed into a beautiful young woman with an exceptional face and near-perfect physical proportions. Her career problems, it seemed, were due to a lack of finesse rather than to physical drawbacks. A successful model must know how to hold herself with a sort of casual elegance—to have what is known as camera poise. The ideal is a combination of Grace Kelly and Lauren Bacall. Some girls achieve this instinctively, much the way a born boxer moves in the ring. But Lana lacked the grace, the natural talent to stand in front of the camera. Powers recognized this and laid down the law: Lana would have to take his course in modeling dynamics (posture, camera presence, makeup) or leave the business. He could not afford to retain an unmarketable commodity. The choice was hers.

Lana enrolled. "It was really helpful," she recalls. "Powers gave instructions right at his offices, so it was very convenient. We learned the proper technique for good posture, how to walk with head high and shoulders square, how to move with the right amount of poise and control. As soon as the classes started, I realized just how much I really needed this polishing up. The proof was in the pudding: as soon as the course was over, I had some new photos taken for my book and they looked very professional. After that, I started getting work. It was an entirely different ballgame. I would go out on go-sees and I'd go home with a booking under my belt. The pay was only $5 an hour, but in 1946 that was considered a lot of money."

Nevertheless, Lana's taste of success was short-lived. The trickle of work that came her way never really developed into steady bookings. Just as some models click in the market and go on to extraordinary success, others can never break through. Some invisible barrier seems to hold them back. Just why they don't catch on is even a mystery to their agents. This was Lana's plight, but she did not give up. She has never given up.

Although Lana has achieved the traditional life-style sought after by most of her upper-middle-class Jewish peers, modeling has always been there like a powerful magnet drawing her back time and time again. She waited two years after completing the Powers course for her career to take flight, and then did the next best thing for a bright and beautiful Jewish girl: she enrolled in a college located in New York, majored in elementary education, became the campus queen, and graduated with a teaching degree. But after a year of work as a grade school substitute, it was back to modeling.

"Once again I came up against a brick wall. I worked a bit here and there, but I didn't achieve any real success." Foiled again, and now much older, Lana was forced to accept the fact that she was out of the running as a high fashion model. "I saw myself applying for bookings with seventeen-year-olds who were having more success than I. In high fashion, once you pass a certain point, you're over the hill."

So Lana put modeling on the shelf, married, and devoted herself to raising a family. "I was dormant as an active model then," Lana says, "but I kept up with the industry. I knew the looks that were in style, which agencies were hot, the kinds of fashion that were in vogue, and who were the big models everyone was talking about. I even tried to get my daughter started as a model, but she had no real interest. What a shame; she could have been so good at it."

Once the children were old enough to fend for themselves, Lana turned back to modeling, this time as an instructor at a modeling school in Connecticut. Here Lana taught the basics of hairstyling, cosmetics, and posture that she herself had learned twenty-five years earlier at the Powers agency. The school was never more than a minor enterprise—but it kept Lana involved in the business she loved most. Still, she wanted more. Fifteen years after her last go-see, she wanted to give it one more try.

"I was itching to make it as a model again," Lana notes. "Not in high fashion—I knew I was too old for that—but as a commercial model. There's no age ceiling for commercial work. I had gotten kind of housewifey—you know, lumpy in the wrong places—so the first thing I did was diet, exercise, and get myself back into top shape. It was like training for combat: I was determined. Once my weight was down to the old college level of 118, I went to see a commercial agency about resuming my career. I hit it off right away with the owner. He accepted me and I was off and running."

But to where? In spite of the fact that she has held up extremely well and is an attractive, intelligent, and ambitious woman, Lana's career as a commercial model has been similarly disappointing. She has been plugging away at her comeback attempt for a decade now, but the jobs have been few and far between. Still, her days revolve around modeling. The hope, the dream that the big break is around the next corner keeps Lana working at it with all the energy and the naiveté of a teenager. The further she gets from her lifelong goal, the more elusive it becomes—and the harder she works.

"Sometimes I think Lana's problem is that she just tries too hard," says her agent, who is fond of Lana and wants her to succeed. "You have to come across as a winner in this business, as the one everyone wants. Unless you can develop that kind of positive image, you're not likely to get many bookings. Lana goes out on all the go-sees we get for her, but they usually come to naught. Maybe Lana's fault is that she wants success *too* much."

Lana's agent is known in the business as a gentle and sensitive man. He is willing to hold on to those he likes regardless of their performance in the marketplace. Big Four agents will not do that. But whether his more liberal policy is kinder to models in the long run is a matter of debate. Do you force the unsuccessful models to confront their failure early on or do you leave them clinging to false hopes, even if it's hope alone that keeps them alive?

Lana—and there are tens of thousands like her—has never been able to bridge the all-important gap that puts a model solidly on the path to success: that is, graduation from the rat-race go-see circuit to a steady flow of bookings known in the trade as "requests." A model is said to be on the rise when more and more of her days are booked out to clients who have requested her by name. It means fewer idle days and wasted hours at ill-fated go-sees. Once the girl generates a substantial number of requests, she is more than a commodity: she is considered "talent"—someone special and unique—and, most important, she has gained personal power. The more requests she generates, the more power she has. Her agents can demand more money for her, they can insist on minimum half- or full-day bookings, and they can snare the lucrative contracts that make both models and agents rich. This is the launching of a famous face.

Getting requests is the classy way to work in this business.

As a major model, Kathy Spiers enjoys this privilege routinely. With requests, clients call the agency and ask for Kathy and Kathy only. They don't want to see twenty girls with a California look. They call and ask for Kathy Spiers by name.

"What this means is that I don't have to twiddle my thumbs at go-sees. There are few cattle calls or open auditions in my life. When I show up, it's to work and get paid, not to wait to be inspected."

Only a handful of models ever reach this position, where bookings are by request only. How and why it happens is often hard to say. Everything just seems to come together, much the way a dancer moves from the chorus line to center stage. There are no guarantees, of course—as the case of Lana woefully demonstrates—but being in all the right places at the right times vastly improves a model's odds. Lightning has to strike only once: just one major booking, one big break can start the cycle moving in her favor.

"If that happens, everything's different than before," says Zoli. "Suddenly, she's a professional model with a tearsheet or two to prove it. Her book is slightly better and her confidence climbs a notch. The face that only recently was lost in a crowd is now, thanks to a single ad or fashion feature, pasted on the pages of countless publications across the nation. That's the power and the immediacy of the business: a single photograph can be seen by millions of people only months or sometimes weeks after it is shot. To the general public it is just another pretty face; to the modeling establishment it is a new presence. The powers that be make a mental note. The next time the model shows up for a go-see, her face may ring a bell with the photographer or casting director calling the shots. She has that slight edge over the others who have never worked, never appeared anywhere except in a family album or a small-town store catalog. So she gets her second job. And then her third, fourth, and fifth. Gradually the recognition factor accelerates. More and more people in the industry know her by sight, others want to know who she is. Suddenly the face has a name. She is on the rise.

"That's when it starts clicking. This is the kind of business where everyone wants to be completely on top of things. Yesterday's news is considered old news. You have to try to predict what will happen tomorrow and latch on to it today. People are terribly afraid of being second to anyone else. This is especially true when a new model comes on the scene. If she gets some good exposure, those who don't know her will start inquiring. They'll track down her agent. They'll ask me for a booking. She's in demand."

This burgeoning career path has an added boost if the model gets cozy with an important client. Let's say the booking is with Revlon. If the timing is right, Revlon—one of the most sophisticated fragrance and cosmetics marketers—may have a new perfume on the drawing board. Chances are the company needs a model to represent their product. A great deal of effort goes into selecting the right girl.

"Revlon is very positioning oriented in its selection of models," says Cathy Spellman. "That means they figure out precisely which groups of women will likely buy the product— what position in the market it will occupy—and then design a promotion to appeal to these groups. The model selected for this purpose must be a perfect embodiment of the positioning concept. Her looks must reflect the product's mystique and image. This can be the most crucial part of the sales effort. There's no denying that Karen Graham, the Estée Lauder girl, has played an enormous role in that company's success."

For a model fortunate enough to click with a product's positioning, the rewards can be great. If she's chosen to be the new "Babe" or "Charlie" girl, she is assured of months or even years of steady work. She'll be called back again and again to shoot dozens of advertisements and commercials. A hot product is promoted to death. There are summer ads, winter ads, holiday ads—different themes for different times of the year. Every time a new ad is produced, the model's services are required. What's more, the client usually demands an exclusive contract with the model, preventing her from representing other fragrances but assuring her of perhaps $100,000 a year (she is still free to earn more by modeling for other product categories). Winning an "exclusive" with a major advertiser really puts a model in the winner's circle. She is established financially, and her reputation and professional status are greatly enhanced.

She may start the contract as an unknown but is likely to end it as a famous face.

That's exactly what a fat contract and a super hype did for a skinny, 6'1" kid from Idaho—who just happened to have an illustrious last name. The granddaughter of writer Ernest Hemingway, Margaux Hemingway spent her early teens living up to the Hemingway legend as a gutsy ski bum in her native Ketchum. Her specialty: women's freestyle hotdogging. Although she seemed to be at home in Idaho's rugged ski region, Margaux had dreams of bigger and better things. Christened Margot, she changed the spelling of her first name when she learned that her parents had been drinking Château Margaux wine nine months before her birth.

On the occasion of her fourteenth birthday, Margaux decided that she would someday go to New York to seek fame and fortune. She then put the idea on the back burner and waited until the timing seemed to be right. In the typical damn-the-fates style of a daredevil skier, she chose Friday the 13th (September, 1974) for this auspicious event. It proved to be an enormously lucky move. Soon after arriving in New York, nineteen-year-old Margaux turned to modeling and quickly found herself at the top of the heap. Thanks to her unique combination of a famous name and a brand of good looks that is especially striking and sensual, Margaux got far more than the traditional newcomer's welcome. She landed a photo spread in *Vogue*, feature treatment in *Women's Wear Daily*, and was called "a model about town" by *People* magazine. This set the stage for the big break, which came when she was brought to the attention of Richard Barrie, executive vice-president and chief operating officer of Fabergé, Inc., the maker of Fabergé and Brut products.

"I saw her pictures and thought she was beautiful," Barrie says, "but the time was wrong—we had nothing for her at the moment. About a week later, I realized she might be perfect for this exciting brand new fragrance line we were working on— Babe. Three or four weeks later we had a deal."

At $1 million for five years, the contract was the biggest of its kind in the industry. In a country where money talks, that kind of price tag makes news in itself. The public took notice and Margaux—now the "Babe" girl—quickly became a household name. Hemingway detractors believe that in Margaux's case it was the contract and the million-dollar hype that went with it that made the model. "People just naturally think something's great if it costs a lot," says one critic. "Top models get top contracts, yes, but when it comes to the making of a star, the reverse can also be true: top contracts can also make top models."

Most successful models, even those who become stars, ride a much slower track than Margaux Hemingway. The transition from go-sees to requests is a gradual, day-by-day process. If things go well, the emphasis shifts from auditions to appointments. At the first signs of success, requests may increase from 5 percent of the model's bookings to 10 percent. Then, if she catches on, they may continue to grow steadily, up to as much as 60 percent. Some models, unknown to the general public but considered stellar performers in the industry, are virtually booked out by appointment. They work practically every day, by request, and generate a minimum of a quarter million dollars a year.

A successful model can easily pull down a total of $1 million before her twenty-first birthday. Weekly checks of from $1,000 to $2,000 start flowing in with her very first bookings, rewarding her for her early achievements and fueling her ambitions to go on. She gets a taste of the good life, and she loves it. Even the new model who is booked for only one or two days a week can be earning at the rate of $50,000 or more a year. Once the money starts coming in, spending patterns are predictable. Most models on the rise use their first earnings to establish independence, moving out of the roommate or sugar daddy setup and landing a one-bedroom apartment in an East Side high rise. Then it's off to Bloomingdale's for furniture, Bendel's for clothing, and Tiffany's for jewelry. Most of the girls seem to adore jewelry, especially fine gold pieces, and they spend lavishly, often more than they can afford. Clothing is another matter. Contrary to popular opinion, models have limited wardrobes. Like others in the high fashion business, including most apparel designers, models prefer a simple basic look. Many insist that the secret to good dressing is to purchase only a limited number of classic outfits and to embellish them with a wide assortment of accessories. So they spend big on hats, belts, and shoes.

"When they first start working, it seems to the girls as if there's a hole in the ceiling and money is pouring through," says Frances Grill, a well-known agent representing fashion photographers. "I had the feeling too in my first lucrative years, so I know exactly what goes through their minds. It's as if someone is going to find out about that hole and cover it up before you have a chance to spend it all. Just to make sure that doesn't happen, the girls go out and buy everything in sight. They don't know what they want first, so they take a little of this and a little of that. Some can't control themselves."

The luxuries are even greater for those models in the upper echelons. Here income levels can reach as high as $6,000 or perhaps $8,000 a week, and the caliber of purchases rises accordingly. Star models can indulge their tastes for extravagant automobiles (classic sports cars are very popular), prestige co-ops (Sutton Place is considered best), and stunning vacation homes in Amagansett, Aspen, or Vail. The fact that these dazzling luxuries are also good investments is no accident: top models have accountants, financial consultants, brokers, and lawyers advising them every step of the way. Many models are even incorporated to take advantage of sophisticated tax strategies.

"You have to figure all the angles when you're dealing with the great money-makers," says a New York attorney connected with the modeling industry. "Unless she has a savvy tax guy, that girl's going to give a big part of the best money she'll ever make to Uncle Sam. Take a hot property like Cheryl Tiegs. I'd say she's making more than a half million a year now. I don't know who handles her finances, but with numbers like that, he'd better be good."

Tiegs is certainly a superstar. She is probably the most famous model in the world and is certainly one of the richest. A native of Alhambra, California (the daughter of a former mortician), she was discovered by Nina Blanchard in 1964, came to New York in 1966, and was photographed for an astounding seventy magazine covers in the next three years. One of the very few women who have been able to move on from high fashion modeling to even greater status as a beauty "personality," Cheryl has enjoyed an unusually long and lucrative career. She has lived the high life for more than a decade, and the sums she earns today surpass the hefty amounts she raked in as a full-time model. Simon & Schuster gave her a $75,000 advance for her book *How To Be Naturally Beautiful,* her posters sell in the millions, and she has a long-term television contract with ABC.

Beneath the all-American good looks (she has, according to Eileen Ford, "the best face in the world") and the innocent demeanor, Tiegs is said to be a tough, ambitious, and competitive woman. She is driven to achieve ever-greater success and money. She adores the public spotlight and savors her hard-fought victory over Farrah Fawcett as America's number-one sweetheart. She likes the freedom and the elegance that money can buy—the noontime tennis dates, lavish dining, international travel, and a Spanish-style mansion. Recently returned to New York after an abortive attempt to live in California and commute to Manhattan by jet ("There's no escaping it; most of my work is still in New York"), Tiegs has taken up residence in a sumptuous co-op near Central Park. Chauffeured around town in a limousine, she is—again according to Eileen Ford—"an inspiration to every young model in this city. Living proof that it pays to apply themselves, to work at it, to give all they have to make it."

Whether young models who are on the rise and who show great promise will ever make it anywhere near the level of success Tiegs has achieved is impossible to predict. Models often show great promise in the early stages, only to peter out as rapidly. Some just tire of the business and stop hustling; others get deeply involved with drugs and partying and simply run themselves into the ground. They begin to look worn out, fail to show up for appointments, and start throwing temper tantrums on the job. Soon they may have earned a reputation for bitchiness and irresponsibility that spells disaster for a new-comer.

"The last thing I'm going to put up with is some freaked out little girl who gets high as a kite at night and then strolls into a booking an hour late 'cause she can't get her head to-gether," says a top photographer. "Some of the girls who do this know they are wrong and try to apologize, but others act as if we're supposed to put up with whatever they do. They get a few modeling jobs and suddenly it goes to their heads. Sweet-hearts like that I write off fast. I like models, and I get along well with most of them. But when it comes to those who behave unprofessionally, I just tell the agency not to bother sending them because they can't work here."

Incidents of this type are damaging not only to the model but to her agency as well. Agents share the rap when their girls' behavior is unprofessional. That's why a consistent goof-off is cut from the agency headsheet (a printed list of the agency's models) and is literally thrown out of the business. No responsible agency will jeopardize its reputation for the sake of a single model on the rise.

Some promising careers fail to materialize even though the model is likable and hardworking: often, the girl just isn't good enough to go all the way. Perhaps there is something lacking in her looks, personality, or poise. The models whose careers take off with a bang and who keep going all the way to the top are usually blessed with great camera personality. If the model has this most valuable asset, she is more than good-looking: she can turn on a special glow, charm, or style that brings a dy-namic quality to her work. One look at her pictures and that quality is apparent. She is more than a girl in a dress, bikini, or lingerie. She is the epitome of glamour, affluence, and worldli-ness. When a girl can create this effect—when she can bring to a shooting more than her physical attributes—she is adored by the pros in the business, especially the great photographers. They love her because she is wonderful material to work with. She makes them look good.

Clean-living, self-assured models who have style, play by the rules, and plug away at success day-in-day-out are the girls agents dream about. Nothing pleases them more than to have a young discovery break out from the pack and "on the rise." Her success is cause for jubilation at the Ford brownstone or the Zoli townhouse. The reasons are clear: first, the girl's rise brings status to the agency as well as to the model. This is million-dollar publicity that positions the agency as a trend setter, a hot shop, and an astute manager of professional careers—and puts it high on the list with clients and with the new wave of would-be models knocking on New York's door. Equally important, of course, is the fact that the model on the rise assures the agency of a healthy return on its investment. The expenses incurred in coaching the girl, preparing her for the marketplace, and perhaps paying her rent in the early days turn from red ink to black as heavy billings start flowing through the agency's coffers. As the model's account moves solidly into the plus column, she earns money for the agency almost every day. A single successful model can generate more than $75,000 a year in agent's commissions. If she's extraordinary, that kind of cash flow will continue for ten years. To the agent, this living, breathing asset can be worth upwards of three quarters of a million dollars in the course of her career.

Numbers like that talk loud and clear to agents. But for the model on the rise, there is more than just her newfound wealth. She is suddenly treated like a VIP, showered with all the rights and privileges of stardom. She gets little perks like the direct-dial numbers that circumvent the busy switchboards and go directly to the brass. She's also routinely wined and dined at New York's fashionable restaurants (most notably Orsini's and Sign of the Dove) and is a frequent weekend guest at her agent's winter ski retreat or Hampton summer home. All this is designed to make key models happy; to keep them pleased with their agents; to suppress any thought of agency hopping.

The tables have been turned: the frightened bag of bones that tiptoed into New York a year before has come a long way and now she's in a position to call the shots. The agent needs her more than she needs the agent—and both know it. Although most of the agencies now use legal contracts to bind their models, experience has shown that the only thing that keeps top talent from jumping ship is good service. Top models expect to be treated like precious gems—and they are.

The darlings of the agencies—the prima donnas—enjoy the kind of attentive service even a pasha would envy. Typical was a scene at the Wilhelmina agency. A journalist arrived at the agency to interview talent chief Joan Howse and star model Kathy Spiers. When Kathy arrived ahead of schedule, the first interview, with Howse, was abruptly cut short in order to accommodate the star. In spite of the reporter's preference to adhere to the original plan and complete the Howse interview before moving on to Spiers, the agency brass would have none of it. They would not keep Kathy Spiers waiting.

"Kathy has come around a bit early," said Joan Howse, putting down the phone after an urgent inter-office call from Bruce Cooper, "so why don't you see her now and then come back here and finish up with me."

"That's impossible," the reporter snapped, "because some of the information I get from you will serve as the basis for Kathy's interview. Anyway, she'll have to wait another ten minutes or so because . . ."

"Ten minutes? Forget it! This is Kathy Spiers we're talking about. I'll tell her you're on your way."

In modeling, the star's crown is always borrowed, never owned. The nasty thing about model/agency relationships is that they are fickle and short-lived. Even if the girl's every whim is satisfied while the agency is raking in bushels of money, the bond between them is superficial and not destined to endure. As soon as either side is angered or disappointed, the relationship is jeopardized, if not doomed. When models walk away on their own, it is usually because of emotional considerations. They may complain of poor treatment or of a lack of attention by Eileen, Zoli, or Casablancas. To agents, however, the status of a relationship is determined by a calculator. Is the girl producing an adequate income? Is she yielding a return large enough to keep her place on the headsheet? If the answer is "no," the model will likely be dropped. This can happen at any time in a girl's career.

To a young model who starts off with great promise, rises, but then falters unexpectedly, the end of star treatment and the sudden question mark surrounding her status as a model can be devastating. "The girls never take it well when we have to sever our relationship with them or just warn them that they are in troubled waters," says Bruce Cooper. "But as much as we hate to tell them this, we must do it for two reasons. First, the rising model who suddenly slumps may have grown too cocky, may have stopped working hard and simply needs a good jolt to put her back on track. If that is the case, our warning that she's in jeopardy may do just the trick. Second, we're not here to hold people's hands or to protect sensitive egos. This is a business. A girl who is not producing weighs heavily on my overhead. Bookers are spending time with her; the accounting department services her, and she's utilizing executive talent that could be better employed elsewhere. So we have to watch a girl's performance very closely and dismiss her if the results are unsatisfactory."

Agents refuse to say just how much models have to earn to keep their place on the headsheet. It's a touchy matter because none want to divulge their secrets to the others. Still, knowledgeable sources say that the standards are similar at the Big Four:

- New models are allowed one year to start generating substantial billings.
- Models are expected to produce a minimum of $50,000 in annual billings by the second year.
- Any model earning $100,000 the first year or more than $200,000 annually thereafter gets the full measure of star treatment.
- A major decline in billings is considered a warning sign. A reprimand is in order.
- A prolonged decline will often lead to dismissal.

Even the best, most highly motivated models must, sooner or later, face that period of drastic and irreversible decline. The sad thing is that the cycle completes itself so quickly in the modeling business. In what is considered a good and successful career, a model may rise to the top by the second year, plant her flag at the summit for five more, and then rapidly fall from stardom to virtual oblivion within six months.

Once the handwriting is on the wall, when it is clear that the girl is no longer in demand, the agent will sever the cord. It is more than the old pink-slip treatment: it is telling someone still quite young that she is no longer useful, that she can no longer perform the only kind of work she's ever wanted to do. And even more devastating, it says to women who have always judged themselves by their looks alone that they are no longer attractive.

"It's my job to tell a model when her career is over," said Wilhelmina, who, seated in her modern, trendy office, looked like central casting's version of the confident, intelligent, and beautifully radiant woman executive. "It's always an awful scene. When I first break the news, their faces are expressionless—like they don't even hear me. Then they start to tremble slightly and you can tell that they're terribly pained. There's deep agony in their eyes. When the crying starts it goes on and on for what seems like hours. All I do is try to calm them and provide reassurance. . . . It's very tough."

Those who went through the experience never forget it.

"It has left a permanent scar on me," says a former New York model whose career included a cover of *Mademoiselle* magazine and two television commercials. "I had six good years in the business, rising from zero a year to a high of $170,000, but it all fell apart in the seventh year. I just started looking a little worn. The side effects of age, pressure, and crazy hours took their toll. I knew I wasn't looking as sharp, and that I was getting less work, but I thought I could hold on. I mean I was such a star at the agency at one time that they hired a limousine just to take me to a party. So when they lowered the boom and told me I was out, it was too sudden, too terrible to take. I reeled as if I'd just been slammed in the stomach. The crying lasted for weeks, the self-pity for months. There were days when I didn't even get dressed and just stayed in my pajamas. I was headed for a nervous breakdown. Luckily, a friend forced me to go to the Institute for Rational Behavior, a no-nonsense therapy clinic, and they put me back on track. I now have a moderately successful career as a nude model for B-grade men's magazines. There's no big money in it, but I still support myself modeling. I'm not young enough for high fashion anymore, but I still look super in the buff."

Modeling is often equated with show business. Both are high-profile industries associated with glamour, beautiful people, and big money. But there the similarities end. The young entertainer has years to practice and learn his or her craft. In fact, those who achieve overnight success are often suspect, their talents questioned. Not so in modeling. Here, the faster the rise, the better. There's no time for long apprenticeships. What's more, while an entertainer's career can span generations and thrive as long as the talent lives, models never achieve lasting recognition. The greats of the business are known for but a fleeting moment, replaced quickly in the public's consciousness by another pretty face. People still adore Crosby, Gable, Valentino, Crawford, Bogart; few remember Candy Jones or Jean Shrimpton.

Modeling is a "What have you done today?" world. Yesterday is ancient history. The only ones who recognize just how devastating that attitude is are the bright-eyed young girls themselves, who enter the business filled with hope and then find how quickly they reach the top and are replaced. The end of the line is reached with appalling swiftness.

5

THE MODEL WARS
Reports from the Front

"They're all jealous of us—all the other agencies—because
we have the best girls, the best clients, the best of everything.
Some of the others are poor excuses; they're a disgrace."
—Eileen Ford

The names and the faces of big-time models come and go like
records on the Top Ten charts. Today's hit is tomorrow's oldie,
for the business demands youth and novelty, and even the
best models cannot remain popular for long. Careers rise and
fall.

But present through this rise and fall—season after season, year after year, career after career—are the top New York
model agencies, giving some permanence to the business. As
tastes change, with new fashions coming into vogue and a new
breed of models in demand, the agencies are on the scene,
promoting the new looks, grooming new faces, discarding the
old. And they are there deciding how a model should behave,
how her career should be built, how much she should earn, and
how long she should work. This staying power—the ability to
weather the fads and trends rather than being destroyed by
them—makes the agencies the most potent force in modeling.
Agencies succeed not by being young and beautiful, but by
having savvy, guts, strength, and connections.

Today, more than ever, they need it all.

In recent years, the Big Four have been trying to use their
power as a selling tool, as a way of convincing models that they
are the best career-builders in the business. They have positioned themselves as allies in the models' quest for wealth and

agency clients as well. Why waste precious time sifting through the mix of models at standard agencies when one shop could provide an array of proven stars? What's more, advertising agencies could win Brownie points with their clients by claiming that they dealt only with the best—with Elite.

Casablancas recounts that most important of all, agencies always did some discounting for their model rates, especially for stars. If they had a star and wanted to charge higher than standard rates for her, the ad agencies would threaten not to use the agency's lesser models. So sometimes they would have to back off and charge less. But with only stars on the headsheets, he believed he'd never have to compromise. What's more he wouldn't have to tolerate slow payers. Clients that didn't pay on time wouldn't get girls—and by losing out on the Elite girls, they would be shutting the door to some of the best models in the world. That meant that most of the cash flow problems he'd had with Élysée Trois would not be a factor with Elite.

Putting his concept to the ultimate test, Casablancas opened Elite in Paris in 1971. Quickly, it proved to be a success. In less than two years, many of France's top models were lured away from other agencies and became Elite girls. But John soon spotted a flaw in his concept. He'd overlooked one major problem: as his models aged and fell from popularity, he would need a new crop of girls to replace them. With the other agencies now more prepared to defend against his tactics, he could not rely forever on raiding talent. He needed a sort of farm system—a place to groom and develop models good enough to eventually win a place on the Elite headsheet. To do this, John launched a sister agency to complement Elite. Called L'Agence, its objective was to concentrate solely on new talent, to breed up-and-comers, to develop future "Elitists."

The system has worked well, but in doing so it has created a bitter feud between Casablancas and the modeling establishment, most notably the Ford and Wilhelmina agencies. This success story makes for a classic tale of greed and power, a David-and-Goliath battle, with the young upstart challenging the established giants—and winning a resounding victory.

What impels Casablancas to outmaneuver rivals who themselves are shrewd, driving competitors? It all starts with Casablancas's personal vision of international economics: one that holds American business interests as big bad bullies who have dominated Europe and forced local entrepreneurs to take orders from New York. John's outlook has always been Continental—one mad European eager to beat the Americans at their own game and to reverse the traditional flow of power across the Atlantic.

"There has always been American domination of the business world," Casablancas says. "U.S. companies set the standards. This was true in the model industry too." He believes that they dominated the activities not only of the American agencies, but the European ones as well. They called the shots and felt it was their right to do so.

Casablancas's reference here is to the system by which American agencies use Europe to discover and to cultivate top models. This works in two ways: because it is easier to crash the market in Europe than in the U.S., an inexperienced teenager will be sent to Paris or Italy to build up a book of prestigious tearsheets that will aid immeasurably once she is put up for sale in New York. In effect, Europe is used as a finishing school. In an equally common practice, American agents routinely scout Europe for hot local models on the rise and ship them to Manhattan for the big time. In either case, European agents stand to benefit by working with the New York biggies. Whether providing models or accepting them, they share in the talent's success. Virtually every European agent wants a piece of this action, and the Big Four use a network of agencies in principal cities to conduct these transactions. Casablancas was no different. At the very beginning of his modeling ventures he claims to have tried hard to make the New York connection.

"Ford and Willy ignored me," he says. "They thought I didn't fit into the picture, and I was considered a rich playboy. Every once in a while they'd let me take them to dinner and show them pictures of my models. I was hoping that I would get a good relationship with Ford and Willy, but I got nowhere with them. Ford and Willy thought I was just a rich playboy who fucked all the girls."

The opening of L'Agence forced Casablancas into head-to-head combat with the New York establishment. Once he was in the business of developing raw talent, rather than simply raiding other French agencies for Elite, John too had to comb Europe for hot prospects. When he started scouting in Scandinavia, considered by New York agents to be prime territory for young blond beauties, Casablancas says that Eileen viewed his entry into this market as poaching on her private preserve.

Casablancas and Eileen would bump into each other in different cities, and Eileen would be livid. At first, Casablancas believes, she tried to force him out of the market by stating to local agents that if they worked with him, they could not work with her. When that didn't work, Casablancas says, she tried to con him into a business deal. In 1975, Eileen and Jerry came to visit Casablancas in Paris. They had a proposition: they would use each other's models. Casablancas would use their models in France; they would use his in New York, and if either of them made a discovery in Scandinavia, they would also share this talent the same way. The year before, when Casablancas approached the Fords they called him a "loser" and refused any deal. "Now that I was successful, they wanted to work together."

Casablancas at the time thought that the deal with Eileen sounded pretty good. He went ahead with the deal and now in his estimation made a big mistake. Casablancas stated "I got too lackadaisical, I trusted her.

"The Fords have an acting role: Eileen acts mean and tough and Jerry walks in and acts like a peacemaker. People fall for it, but it is very rehearsed."

Eileen Ford—as well as Bruce Cooper and Zoli—refuse to comment specifically on Casablancas's allegations. All say that he has benefited tremendously from an inordinate amount of press coverage and they do not want to give him more exposure by discussing his charges. But John is not at all shy about recounting his side of the story. According to Casablancas (who tends to describe everything in simplistic terms of all good or all evil), a swift-moving series of events shattered his truce with the Fords, started a pitched battle with the rest of the top agents, and led to the opening of an Elite office in New York.

As he sees it, the Fords reneged on the model-sharing deal by backing the start of a new Paris agency to be run by a longtime Ford model and friend of the family, Karen Mosberg. To Casablancas, this was tantamount to the Fords opening an agency of their own in his territory, and he made a public announcement stating so. In addition, he threatened to pull off a merger of the big French agencies and to use their combined resources to open a division in New York. Concerned about this, the Fords allegedly invited Casablancas to New York for another powwow.

According to Casablancas, they were supposed to have a private business dinner, but when he arrived in New York, Eileen called and said the plans were changed. Instead, there was going to be a meeting at the 21 Club with Eileen, Jerry, Willy, Cooper, Zoli, and John. They were going to thrash everything out, once and for all, and come to an agreement everyone could live with.

As soon as he got there, Casablancas knew it wouldn't work out that way. The tension was so thick you could cut it with a knife. Rather than rationally discussing the situation, Casablancas claims that everyone just wanted to point a finger and attack him viciously—threaten to wipe him out if he opened a French office in New York. After what seemed like a verbal free-for-all, calmer tempers did prevail. When the shouting died down, Casablancas insists they were able to make at least one key decision: "I wouldn't open in New York if Eileen would behave herself in Paris. Eileen would not give financial or spiritual support to Mosberg, whose agency had already opened. Eileen promised to do this."

Casablancas was wiser this time than he had been in his previous dealings with Eileen. He did not this time take a Ford promise at face value. Soon after the New York meeting he followed Eileen on a trip through Scandinavia. "Where she went, I went a few days later to test her. I asked people [local agents] she'd met 'So I hear Eileen is backing the Mosberg agency and wants your models to go to them.' They all fell into the trap and said that's exactly what she said." When Casablancas heard this, he believed that Eileen had broken her part of the "21" agreement. From that day on, he was determined to open an agency in New York. Nothing could stop him.

Nothing did. After some false starts with other French agencies, Casablancas opened Elite in New York in June of 1977 and shortly thereafter launched Model Management, the U.S. equivalent of L'Agence. Then the fireworks really began.

The arrival of Señor Casablancas proved not to be the threat the New York agents had envisioned—it was actually much worse. From day one, he exhibited an uncanny ability to lure away top talent, snaring their executives as well as their models, and to command the publicity spotlight. Casablancas was portrayed by the press as an exciting new presence in the Big Apple. He had the aura of a winner—an irresistible combination of style, money, and success. Models, clients, and the media flocked to his side. It was chic to be with Casablancas, chic to know him and work with him.

From his first days in New York Casablancas showed that he meant business. He proved this with a quick strike at Ford's midsection. In a blitz that reached deep into the Ford empire, John hired two of that agency's top bookers, Monique Corey and Monique Pillard. Angered by Casablancas's tactics and fearing that the two women would help him lure their models to Elite, the Fords retaliated with a whopping $7.5 million lawsuit. This barely a month after Elite had opened its doors. Casablancas regarded the suit as a way to bleed his new agency at a time when it could least afford huge legal bills.

"But it backfired and actually worked in my favor," Casablancas boasts, leaning back in his swivel chair. "The suit generated a publicity bonanza—more than I could have bought for a million dollars. Although I was well known upon my arrival here, the Fords saw to it that I was a household name in New York. Without knowing it, they played right into my hands."

No one was angrier than Eileen Ford. Casablancas says this was made evident by a now famous incident which he maintains revealed her arrogance and her obsession with power. Shortly after their move to Elite, Monique Corey and Monique Pillard received packages which they believed were, although there was no proof of the identity of the sender, sent from Ford. The contents: Bibles, with numerous pages paper-clipped and specific sections underlined in red. All of the under-lined passages related to Judas Iscariot. Typical was the following: "And as they sat and did eat, Jesus said, 'Verily I say unto you, one of you which eateth with me shall betray me.' " There was no cover letter enclosed, no note from the sender. Was it to appear as a sign from Heaven, via the Ford agency?

One thing is clear. Eileen is still burning mad at Casablan-cas's success in snatching up some of her top models. "There has been a real bitchy atmosphere here since Casablancas ar-rived," says one photographer who is on a first-name basis with most of the Big Four. "There is outright hostility and backstab-bing. Casablancas is hated by the others because he does not take direction from them. He doesn't look to the older agencies to set the industry's fees, contract terms, or anything else. They resent his independence."

The booker raids were only a small part of the frustrations experienced by the Fords. Casablancas struck again and again, claiming star models from the top agencies—Maaret Halinen, Christie Brinkley, Janice Dickinson, Lisa Cooper, and Beverly Johnson (the world's top black model). Soon Casablancas was known as the kidnapper, the raider, the pirate. But why did these models jump ship, foregoing the power and the prestige of established shops like Ford, Wilhelmina, and Zoli for an untested, fledgling agency? What made them trust their ca-reers to Casablancas?

Everyone in the model business has different opinions. Some credit it all to John's charms, his way with women, his exciting mystery-man image. Rumor has it that he wines and dines his models, serves as part agent, part friend, and gener-ally affords them the attentive, tender loving care most models crave. Casablancas's competitors are not so generous. The Fords claim that he used the two Moniques to lure away their top models. Jerry Ford, who does counter much of Casablan-cas's story, adds that John won over models "by agreeing to accept any commission terms they demanded—as low as five percent. What's more, if there was ever any double-crossing in this business, it was done by him. He assured us that he wouldn't open an agency in New York and on that basis we were sending him models to use in Paris. All the while, he was planning to snatch those girls away when he came to New York. His story about our supporting Karen Mosberg is nonsense. We went out of our way to discourage her from opening. The truth is that he planned on opening in New York for many years and was simply looking for an excuse to do so. And when he arrived, whatever success he had he got by offering models ridiculous terms."

John himself credits his success to two factors. First, he says his reputation as a leading French agency followed him to New York and prompted many of the girls to want to work with him. Second, he mouths the now familiar line about offering superior customer service and treating the girls as stars rather than as employees. His statements in this regard are almost identical to the ones made by Wilhelmina at the opening of her shop more than a decade earlier.

"When I arrived here, things were ripe for change," Casablancas says. "Ford and Willy had an unholy alliance. Before I came, all models were afraid of their agents. They were pawns of them. We said it should not be that way. We said we are here to serve you."

Casablancas's most appealing qualities are his freshness, his candor, his informality. "I'm the best agent in the world," he says, "but that's no brag. Look, this business is bullshit. Compared to important professions, we are just a bunch of jerks. We just manage people who are being photographed. . . . My secret is that I make friends with people. I have a charismatic approach."

Janice Dickinson, an early Ford defector, agreed, saying on the occasion of her switch to Casablancas: "She [Eileen] told me I looked ethnic. I never once in four years went to Ford and sat there for two seconds. Johnny gives you a Coke."

Today, Casablancas is a successful agent both in the U.S. and in Europe. His New York operation bills about $6 million a year, and he still has a major share in the Paris agencies (which are managed by his partner, Christine Lundgren). His talent raiding days are pretty much over; about 80 percent of the Elite girls are now graduates of his own Model Management division. Still, there are two lingering effects of the Casablancas invasion. The big lawsuit that greeted John soon after his New York debut is still simmering and has been countered by further actions on both sides. Casablancas has won the opening rounds, but the war is not over.

"In the first suit, the one for $7.5 million, the Fords claimed 'tortious inducement,' which is legal terminology for breach of faith," says Ira Levinson, Casablancas's attorney. "This stemmed from a preexisting relationship the Fords claimed that John had when he was in Paris conducting his French agency. We learned of this suit, by the way, by reading the paper rather than hearing it from the Fords. In addition, there were two other suits commenced by Ford against the two Moniques, in which the Fords claimed a breach of restrictive covenants contained in both of their contracts. The restrictive covenants in the Ford employment contracts prohibited the Moniques from working for competitors within two years of leaving the Ford agency. We claimed that these restrictive covenants were against the laws of New York. Most courts frown on these covenants because they take people out of the job market in the field they are most familiar with.

"The Fords alleged that the Moniques had gone to Elite in order to lure away models from them. For this reason, the Fords demanded a percentage of the commissions of the models who went to John. But we brought these models to court and they testified that they went to Elite simply because they knew John, had worked with him in France, and liked him. Their actions had nothing to do with the Moniques. Both of the Fords' suits against the Moniques were dismissed by the American Arbitration Association."

In another issue, more crucial to the future of the modeling business, the Fords sought a preliminary injunction to stop their former models from working with Casablancas. But this too was denied. The courts do not like to issue injunctions unless the plaintiff (in this case Ford) can show that it is being irreparably damaged. Since the Fords were continuing to do business as usual, and were still the world's biggest agency,

Levinson says they were hard put to prove that their very survival was in jeopardy. Levinson based Elite's defense on the fact that the movement of models from agency to agency has always been a common practice, one considered part and parcel of the business even before Casablancas came on the scene. To prove his point, Levinson pointed out that most pre-Casablancas model contracts had thirty-day termination clauses. Levinson argued this meant the contracts were terminable at will.

"We were elated when the injunction was denied," Levinson says, admitting that he was concerned about the suits. "John's resources and his reputation were on the line. The victory couldn't have pleased us more. But we weren't out of the woods. Ordinarily, when an injunction is denied, that's the end of the suit. It usually takes the wind out of the plaintiff's sails. Not in this case. The Fords continued a tremendous amount of legal activity. The case is still pending. When, if ever, it will go on the calendar for trial is not certain."

"Although it may be true that we lost some issues in court, there is still no doubt that Casablancas committed a despicable act," says Jerry Ford. "He's the one who violated our confidences."

Another suit which is still pending (and one which Levinson terms as "remarkably similar" to the Ford action) was filed by Wilhelmina against Elite model Iman. A beautiful black woman discovered in Kenya by photographer Peter Beard, Iman left Willy in the summer of 1978 to join Casablancas. At the time of her move, there were still a few months remaining on her contract with Wilhelmina Models. Wilhelmina asked for a preliminary injunction to halt the departure. This was granted but then denied when Levinson convinced the Appellate Division to reverse the initial decision. The injunction was dismissed.

"In ruling in our favor, the court made a very important statement," Levinson notes. "It said that models are not employees of the agencies but that agencies work for the models. That's been John's philosophy: if a girl's not satisfied with her agent, she should go wherever she wants. He has never asked his girls to sign a contract binding them to him and he has no plans to institute such action. But the rest of the industry has

moved in just the opposite direction, tightening up their contracts rather than allowing for the free movement of girls. The
Fords, for example, have come up with an incredibly tough
five-year contract calling for exclusive representation. They
came up with this new contract after failing to get the injunction they wanted in the $7.5 million Casablancas suit."

"I am first starting to have my models sign contracts,"
says Zoli. "I've been in business for about nine years but never
felt I needed to use contracts until now. That's because others
have shown how easily they can claim a girl in whom you've
invested your time and money in developing from scratch. You
have to protect yourself in this business."

But to date, the more restrictive contracts haven't stopped
anyone from moving anywhere. Many models regard them as
pieces of paper their lawyers can handle—documents to be
casually disregarded should the need arise. "They confront you
with these very lawyerish-sounding papers to sign," says a
perky redhead from Minneapolis. "I didn't know which end was
up then, so I called my dad to see what I should do. He had me
call his attorney, who asked that I read the contract over the
phone. When I was finished reading there was silence at the
other end. About a minute later he asked what my options were.
I said either to sign or give up my invitation to join the agency.
Silence again. Then he said the agents were bastards but that
I should sign and we'd bust the contract later if we ever had to.
As far as I'm concerned, the contract doesn't mean a thing. I've
stayed at the same agency because I know they all suck. I have
friends at the other agencies and we share stories. The gripes
are the same everywhere. When it comes to money, I'm doing
as well as can be expected—about $140,000 last year—so I have
no real motivation to leave. But if things changed and I got
dumped on badly here, I'd leave in a minute. The contracts are
fish wrapping."

Casablancas's legal victories have fostered this kind of
attitude. The battle to keep models has turned into a cold war
—a war of hype, promises, and public relations. Agents hope
that by establishing an image as the "model's best friend," as
the most sympathetic and service-oriented agency in New York,

they will snare the most promising newcomers and hold on to the best of the established models without having to resort to long and expensive legal battles. The desire to portray the friendly image has made all of the agencies extremely PR-conscious and concerned about negative publicity. The Wilhelmina agency keeps a full-time professional publicist on the payroll to float flattering comments about the boss and to show the press "the wonderful world of big-time modeling." The Fords woo reporters at their offices or their Connecticut country home; Casablancas devotes hours to interviews about himself and the marvels of the Elite concept; and even Zoli now comes out of his shell to meet the press.

When first approached to be interviewed for this book, Eileen Ford asked: "You're not writing an exposé, are you?" The reaction from the Wilhelmina agency's PR person—when she was asked to set up a second interview—was similar:

"What kind of book will it be?"

"An in-depth book about the modeling business."

"What do you mean by in-depth?" she asked.

"A look at the finances, the personalities, the rivalries, the good and the bad."

"You don't want to include the lawsuit stuff, do you?"

"Yes."

"Why do that? Don't be stupid. This is a glamorous business. You'll just bore people with that stuff."

"Let me decide that. Please tell Bruce what I want to discuss and set up another interview."

"He'll be out of town."

"When will he be back?"

"Hard to say."

The past decade has been an exceptional one for the modeling industry in that new agencies have arrived on the scene, have earned a place for themselves in the market, have survived and indeed prospered. With the arrival of each new kid on the block—Willy, Zoli, and then Johnny—the pressures have intensified and the business has changed somewhat to reflect the best attributes of the newcomer.

"Of course, you must bear in mind that there's been even more competition than the general public is aware of," says Zoli. "That's because most of the agencies that open up in New York don't last long, so they don't get widely known. But they've been competitors for as long as they lasted. I'd say there have been fifteen of these unsuccessful agencies in the last ten years alone."

To his way of thinking, experience is the essential ingredient for success in the agency business. Zoli himself (born Zoltan Rendessy in Hungary) worked for more than a decade with the small Wagner agency before striking out on his own. This long apprenticeship, he believes, enabled him to learn the ropes and to establish a reputation.

"Most agencies fail because the people who start them think they see a way to make an easy buck," he declares. "They have no contacts and no idea of what it really takes to make it in modeling. But I had the know-how and the contacts. I joined Wagner as their first employee, so I was forced to do a little bit of everything. That was in 1959. I was later promoted to agency manager. When I left Wagner to open my own place in 1970, I had a well-rounded career. That's what you need to make it."

Although Zoli has never challenged Ford or Willy for the top ranking, he has built a successful business with a good stable of models and a reputable image in the industry. He has also managed to steer clear of the more bitter inter-agency legal battles, in spite of the fact that he lost models to Casablancas. A slight, quiet man with delicately chiseled features, Zoli is the least charismatic of the Big Four agents. His comments are always controlled, even-tempered, as if every word is carefully analyzed before it is permitted to pass from his lips. The electricity, the dynamics that flow from the others is absent here. Some say this is his hidden asset—that he appeals to models and clients more comfortable with a subdued personality. Perhaps this is the reason his agency continues to grow and prosper.

"Eileen Ford loves the catalog end of the modeling business," Zoli says. "That requires getting lots of all-American girls out to do routine, day-after-day work for Sears, Penney's, and the like. Covering that end of the market has been her key to success. Wilhelmina focuses on the Hollywood image, on getting girls to do the real high fashion work. That's her route to success. For me, success has meant letting the model do what she wants and then carefully managing her career so it goes as far as possible. You have to pay attention to details to build a career and that's what we do here."

In some ways, jealousy and competition have proved beneficial to all of the Big Four. The cutthroat atmosphere has had the effect of expanding the market and has made the agents pay more attention to financial management. Most have instituted tight cost controls and sound accounting procedures, so that the cash flow crises that crippled earlier agencies are less likely to occur now. As for the models, competition has both helped and hindered them. It has forced the agencies to make a show of personal service, even though this is mostly superficial. While some agents are turning on the charm in the reception room, they are also huddling with their attorneys to tighten up the loopholes in models' contracts. There is no doubt that agents still have the upper hand—they can make or break models' careers more readily than models can damage them.

"There are still very few important agencies in this town," says a noted fashion photographer. "An awful lot of power is still concentrated in very few hands. You don't want to get on the agencies' bad side because they have more clout and more resources than anyone else. Competition has made them somewhat more responsive, but not much. They all control some star models; to get them you have to do things the agencies' way."

Knowledgeable observers say that only one thing will unleash the full force of competition in the model industry: a decisive high court decision outlawing long-term exclusive contracts. This would open the floodgates, allowing models to bargain more effectively for lower commissions and for the highest standards of personal service.

"That's probably what should happen to make things more equitable, but I don't know if I could take it," says an executive with a top advertising agency. "The modeling agents are terrible monsters—no doubt about it. But the models are worse,

much worse. Can you just imagine a thousand demanding bitches running around Manhattan armed with all the power they
want? I'd pull my hair out of my head. No, better yet, I'd cash
in my chips, give up this job, and go out and sell aluminum
siding."

6

THE PHOTOGRAPHERS
Artists of the Industry

"People in the model business are mad at one another
because they all expect great glamour, but there is no glamour
there. We make up for the image of glamour, but it doesn't
exist. The successful ones build the best houses and have the
best clothes but can't find the glamour. There is no such thing
in this business."
—Frances Grill, photographers' agent

In the war between the agencies—the battle that pits models,
agents, and lawyers against one another—one force remains
neutral, moving freely between both sides in modeling's equivalent of the DMZ. It is the photographers—the technicians and,
in some cases, the artists of the industry. They are a diverse
group, positioned somewhere between the established power of
the agencies and the fleeting fame of the models. They manage
to retain neutrality not because they get along with both sides
but because they are loved and hated by both sides with equal
intensity. And the feeling is mutual.

Just how individual photographers relate to models and
agents depends to some degree on their rank in the system. But
the vast majority are forced into neutrality because they cannot
afford to make enemies on either side. They have much in common with the young models who will do virtually anything for
the chance to get public and professional exposure. They are
struggling to be discovered, to get that first break that can gain
them stature and recognition. To gain this, many will gladly
prostitute themselves in any way their profession seems to
demand: bidding for favors from established pros, hustling for

bargain basement jobs at one-third the going fees, and—if all else fails—doing nude shootings for the smut books.

"I grew up with one hero—Avedon," says Rick, a twenty-year-old high school dropout from Framingham, Massachusetts, who is struggling to get started as a New York fashion photographer. "When my friends were cheering Carl Yazstremski as the greatest baseball player in the world, I was following Richard Avedon, the greatest photographer. I'd buy *Vogue* just to clip out his works, hang them in my room, and study the style and technique. I've been practicing with a camera for as long as I can remember, and when I came to New York I thought I'd get a job right away. Nothing big, of course, but something. Hell, no way. First, Avedon wouldn't even answer my calls—and I must have tried about thirty times. The same is true all around the horn: the dream that some big name is going to take you under his wing and make you a star is a lot of horseshit—pure horseshit.

"I think the trick is to keep working on your own, to try to get one super photograph published in a big magazine and get some recognition. It's all a matter of being in the right place at the right time. Like I go to film openings and fashion previews on the chance I'll get a real good candid shot of Cheryl Tiegs or Cher. I've snared a couple of great shots that I submitted to the magazines, but so far no luck. I came close a few times, but unfortunately, the best shot I had was unpublishable. It was a candid of a famous model agent—who I won't name 'cause I may have to work for him someday—trying ever so discreetly to fix his toupee while standing in the lobby of Avery Fisher Hall.

"I know I'll strike it sooner or later, but until then I do have to eat. Not that I need much. My lover owns a smashing duplex off Central Park West and 73rd Street, so I live quite comfortably rent free. But for food, entertainment, and the like, I'm on my own and I do the only kind of work I seem able to get in the business. That's nude photography.

"How did I get involved in this? I don't really know. You look hard for a job in fashion photography—tap all the sources—and your name gets around. The only offers that come in are the ones you don't want. But the porno people have sensitive antennae: they seem to know who's out there looking for work, they get to you first and they make an offer you can't refuse. I do about one assigned nude spread every other month for a cheap sex book that runs a regular two-page feature on New York girls. They make the contacts with the models and I just shoot them, usually at the crummy Roosevelt Hotel. The money's okay—$1,100 a pop—but I hate it like poison. First, I don't enjoy looking at a nude woman for hours on end—there's nothing in it for me. Second, I love clothing, fabrics, patterns. That's one reason I was so attracted to the fashion business. So with nude photography, I get all of what I hate and none of what I love. But I do it 'cause it pays the bills and it keeps me working with a camera. As long as I can do that, there's a chance, if you'll pardon the pun, that big things will click. My childhood goal is still the one I live for: to be a famous, highly paid, and powerful fashion photographer who can exert some influence on both the art of photography and of fashion. Right now, I'm stuck shooting, as Monty Python says, 'naughty bits,' but I'll get where I'm going. I'll get there."

Rick is not at all unusual. Thousands of young photographers subvert their talents and forego their personal standards (much the way some would-be models do) because the desire to make it in the world of high fashion is so strong. To aspiring fashion photographers, life at the top of the heap appears to be rosy indeed. Their heroes—the famous photographers—earn tremendous sums of money, enjoy international prestige, exercise great power in the modeling industry, and are the darlings of the chic social sets that cluster around the world's fashion communities. Less than a dozen fashion photographers breathe this rarified air, but hordes of imitators are vying to be among them.

The fame, wealth, and prestige of the great photographers are not, however, their most valuable assets. The real source of their power is their ability to launch successful modeling careers, to propel previously unknown faces to international stardom, and to influence the world's standards of beauty, style, and design. Although there will always be a debate as to just who are the most powerful people in modeling—top agents, legendary photographers, or superstar models—in some ways the photography greats have no rivals. Only their power can bridge the gap between the image and the substance of the fashion business; only they are responsible for translating an attractive face into a marketing tool. Most important, only the photographers work with all the other elements of the business —models, agents, designers, art directors, marketers, and merchandisers—and tie them all together into a cohesive unit working for a single overriding objective: to sell something.

Fashion photographers live in two worlds: the artistic and the blatantly commercial. First and foremost, they are called on to provide an imaginative vision or concept that will add excitement, cachet, and sales appeal to an article of clothing, a bottle of perfume, or a piece of jewelry. Much like top film directors, talented photographers are the masters of their medium. They must select the ideal model, choose the most appropriate location, check the lighting, elicit the best performance from the model, and then edit the finished product so that only the best prints ever come into public view. In addition to all of this, they must never lose track of the fact that they are, in the final analysis, in the business of advertising—that their aesthetic impulses must be tempered by the hard-sell demands of the fashion industry. In a field where a single losing season can spell doom to an apparel designer or manufacturer, art must always share the stage with salesmanship.

The photographer's function, in the broadest terms, is to compose and produce a picture. In most cases, it is a picture that will be reproduced hundreds of thousands, perhaps millions of times. The photographer's canvas is a roll of film, his gallery a fashion magazine or daily newspaper. His works are rarely of lasting value; they have only fleeting significance, and are cast aside and forgotten after a brief commercial life. For this reason, fashion photography is very much a "what have you done for us lately" business. It's the rare professional indeed who produces a body of work and then is free to rest on his laurels, confident that his reputation will remain intact.

The closest fashion photography has come to producing a

classic artist is Richard Avedon. Only Avedon could lay down his camera now and be certain of a place in the annals of his art. His photographs have been featured in every prestige fashion publication in the world and in widely acclaimed exhibitions at leading art museums. Today, Avedon does little assigned fashion work, but instead circles the globe photographing the people and the places that turn him on. No other fashion photographer enjoys this status.

In this fickle and trendy business, the more famous the photographer, the greater the pressure to break new ground, to keep working, and to retain the leadership position. Top fashion photographers must produce their profession's equivalent of a new *Guernica* or *Ulysses* every season. Failing that, they may quickly sink into second-class ranking regardless of their former accomplishments. This is the photographers' dilemma. Most come into the business for the fame, the money, and the glamour. Those who achieve these objectives then yearn for more: to be taken seriously as artists. But most critics and museum directors do not take fashion photography seriously enough to equate it with fine art. As a result, many fashion photographers are poor little rich boys who get everything the world has to offer except what they seem to want most—recognition as great artists.

One of today's most famous fashion photographers is Francesco Scavullo. Attracted to photography before the age of ten, Scavullo nearly wore out the first camera he used—an old boxlike Kodak Brownie—taking endless pictures of his friends, parents, and siblings around the family home. His first models were his older sisters, whom he photographed incessantly, studying their movements, facial expressions, and the changes in their appearance brought on by changes in hairstyle and clothing.

His ideas about beauty expanded when, as a young boy, he began going to the movies. Scavullo was captivated by the beauty and glamour of screen star Dorothy Lamour, who now seemed much more of an exciting photographic subject than his sisters. The contrast spurred his creativity and challenged him to do more with the camera than he'd ever thought possible. He realized that the major difference between Lamour and his sisters was the star's more sophisticated use of makeup, a wilder hairstyle, and more exotic clothing (the famous Lamour sarong). Scavullo proceeded to transform his sisters' looks. He put some panchromatic makeup on their faces, ran his fingers through their hair, and dressed them up in sexy gowns for the camera. Before long his sisters' friends, all done up in prom dresses, were begging to be photographed in similar fashion.

The young photographer enjoyed the exercise immensely and, more importantly, he learned a lesson that has stayed with him and that remains a driving force in his career. Although his sisters never became mirror images of Dorothy Lamour, he had awakened them to ways in which they could become much more attractive, exciting, and photogenic. Scavullo realized that by careful analysis of a subject's appearance—by accentuating the strengths, hiding the weaknesses, and adding some dramatic touches—he could reveal a hidden beauty that had never before come to the surface. To this day, Scavullo is convinced that he can make any woman look and feel better than ever. He attributes this to his skill as a photographer and to his taste in the selection of cosmetics, hairstyles, and fashions. Scavullo also insists that working with loved ones so early in his career had a potent and lasting influence on his work: it taught him to use the camera as a loving instrument rather than as a device that merely records things as they are.

After graduation from high school, young Francesco was skilled enough to land a prized job as assistant to legendary *Vogue* photographer Horst. At age nineteen, he did his first cover for *Seventeen* magazine, won plaudits for this and other work, and two years later opened his own studio. Scavullo soon began to be invited to photograph covers for many of the nation's major magazines. The most important of these was *Cosmopolitan*. For more than ten years, he photographed every *Cosmo* cover girl, at a time when the magazine, under Helen Gurley Brown's direction, was becoming the most dynamic woman's publication in the world. As *Cosmo* grew rich and influential—and its cover girls became the symbol of an emerging female sexuality in America—Scavullo, the photographer most responsible for establishing the *Cosmo* look, shared in its success.

As his fame spread, and his business grew, Scavullo moved away from the pedestrian demands of routine fashion photography and increasingly concentrated on portrait work alone. Today he does cover portraits of top models for leading magazines, portraits of celebrities for record album covers, and portraits of young models he believes have the talent and the beauty to go directly to the top of their field. For his skills, he now commands a fee of up to $10,000 a day.

In spite of his success—or perhaps because of it—Scavullo is a controversial figure in the model industry. When it comes to opinions about Scavullo, few sit on the fence: most either love or hate him. Although his critics do make some legitimate points, most of the anti-Scavullo chatter that flows through the fashion industry appears to be motivated by jealousy and by envy of the man's power, influence, and sky-high fees. For there is simply no arguing that Scavullo is a superb craftsman, a gifted artist, and a man blessed with a highly refined sense of style. His greatness is in his eye: he is endowed with the unique ability to see those elements of an individual's appearance that are striking, sexy, or beautiful and to then present them on film with great taste and skill. His files of photographs showing some of the world's top models and show business celebrities before and after they were subjected to the "Scavullo experience" prove beyond question that the man—with the aid of his makeup experts and hairstylists—can literally transform pretty, plain, ordinary, and even ugly faces into striking beauties.

What is the "Scavullo experience"? The photographer himself equates it with a psychoanalytic session, whereby the person's hidden beauty is discovered by probing into the personality. Thus the subject's power, sensitivity, grace, sensuality, vulnerability, toughness, hostility, confidence, and the like become as important to the photograph as bone structure and hairstyle.

Scavullo believes that even women who are natural beauties make many errors in personal grooming—errors that detract from their inherent assets. That is why models who are subjected to the Scavullo experience for the first time undergo dramatic changes in their physical appearance. The process is basically a stripping down or cleansing of the woman to reveal her raw features. Scavullo is, in fact, obsessed with this cleansing process. He likes to march his subjects through a sort of human car wash, removing the cosmetics, clothing, and other ornaments that he believes cover rather than enhance their beauty. Scavullo insists that a woman must rid herself of her old preconceptions of what beauty is all about and give herself up to a fresher, simpler approach based on her actual physical attributes. In short, women must learn to deal skillfully with what they have—not with what they wish they had.

Scavullo preaches endlessly about excess makeup, contrived hairdos, and the showy use of jewelry. He detests excesses of any kind, will not allow them to come before his camera. To Scavullo's famous eye, most women look like clowns, painted with gaudy colorings and dressed in tacky costumes. He refers to them with the kind of elitist disdain Julia Child has for McDonald's. Scavullo's distaste for the made-up look is not only a matter of personal aesthetics, but also a professional observation of what will photograph best. In Scavullo's austere black and white style, that which is most basic comes across as most beautiful.

Scavullo's photographic technique involves more than consideration of proper camera angles, shutter speed, lighting, and makeup. Equally important to a successful shooting is the model's camera presence—her ability to use body movement, facial expressions, and eye contact to bring a sense of excitement, sexuality, or youthful energy to the photograph. Camera presence doesn't come naturally and it is not easily learned. Good photographers, like film directors coaching their actors, know how to draw it out from those models who have the natural instincts but simply need direction in how to release it. Here too Scavullo shines: the man's utter fascination with beauty gives him the patience and the will to draw out the best work his models can deliver. His first step is to build their self-confidence. He does this by convincing them that they are beautiful—and that his camera will flatter them and make them even more glamorous and desirable. Because he instills pride and confidence in them, they respond with a strong camera presence.

Scavullo tries to calm the models at his shootings by talking with them before the camera is even loaded. If it is the first time they are working together, he'll start off with a cup of coffee and quiet conversation. The idea is to relax the model and to give Scavullo himself some insight into the personality he's dealing with. He tries to develop an immediate rapport with his subjects, to get a good chemistry going and to fuse a bond between them. This encourages the models to open themselves up, to feel free and to trust.

Scavullo has to work especially hard for this. Women often become tense in his company because as one of the world's renowned experts on beauty, he is known to have a highly developed sense of taste as well as strong opinions about what is and is not attractive. Even the most beautiful and self-confident women fear that he will judge them adversely, that they can never measure up to his lofty ideals. Even his friends go to great lengths to groom and prepare themselves for meetings with him.

Typical is the story of a luncheon date he had with Bianca Jagger. It was to be a simple affair, just a light snack at an East Side yogurt shop. Scavullo called on Bianca at her apartment. When he rang her doorbell, he heard Bianca scamper into her bedroom and quickly close the door. A friend who was staying at Bianca's place was forced to remain in the living room and entertain Francesco while Bianca allegedly fussed with her makeup and hairdo for half an hour.

In his coaching role, Scavullo exhorts models to strive for the unposed look. He tries to make them familiar with the camera and so completely trusting of it that they are not at all intimidated. He wants them to play up to the camera but not to fixate on it. Scavullo demands movement—at all times movement. Because still photography catches subjects and freezes them in time, it can exaggerate flaws that motion hides. That is why Scavullo insists on motion. Also, he wants to get things right from the start. He dislikes going back to the studio to correct errors in the shooting. He retouches his photographs only to remove minor flaws in the composition—things like a stray hair. The rest remains as it is.

Scavullo's studio on Manhattan's East 63rd Street (housed in a million-dollar townhouse duplex where he also resides) is typical of many others. A small waiting room—crammed with telephones, a desk, a Mr. Coffee machine, and bulletin boards displaying his works—leads to the all-white room in which the actual photography is done. It is just a bare space equipped with lights and photographic gear. The physical setup is much the same as that found in thousands of photographers' studios. But that's where the similarity ends. With Scavullo, it is the process that differs. Nothing is rushed; nothing is left to chance. Before the shutter is snapped, the model is carefully prepared by a team of beauty experts who work closely with Scavullo on his assignments.* This association with leading beauty specialists is one of Scavullo's great strengths and is responsible, in part, for the superior quality of his portraits.

"When I go to Scavullo's studio I am completely relaxed," says Christina Ferrare. "That's because I know it's all first class there. He uses the most talented haircutters, the finest cosmeticians, the best of everything. This is very important to a model because poor treatment by these beauty experts can really damage the way you wind up looking in a photo."

Scavullo's detractors hold that he gets far too much of the credit for his photographs—that his makeup and hair people, in fact, accomplish the transformations Scavullo is famous for. Scavullo denies these complaints vehemently, claiming that other photographers use the same hairstylists and cosmeticians but turn out only second-rate work. He is right. His gift is his unusually perceptive eye and his almost flawless instinct for what is beautiful, elegant, and stylish. He is smart enough to surround himself with the best associates money can buy, but the top billing belongs to Scavullo himself.

In addition to their assertions that Scavullo takes too much

*The most sought after cosmetician in the world, Way Bandy, is often part of this team, along with the gifted hairstylist Harry King.

credit for what his staff accomplishes, Scavullo's critics also deplore his so-called transformations. The most common barb is that his style is sterile, boring, plastic—that when models are "Scavulloized," they all end by looking alike.

"Scavullo's models never look the way they really are, but rather the way Scavullo thinks they should look," says a Big Four booker who agreed to talk about the powerful photographer only if her name were withheld. "The problem is Scavullo thinks everyone should look the same. You can tell one of his photographs instantly: the model's hair is always blown back by a fan—Scavullo loves the windswept look—her eyes are wide, her head tilted playfully. Scavullo treats subjects as totally different as Barbara Walters and Marisa Berenson in the same manner—both with that blown-in-the-wind silliness. They have nothing at all in common—not in appearance, intelligence, or personality—so why should they be made to look the same?"

It must be said, however, that professional fashion models, for the most part, have nothing but admiration for Scavullo. They don't seem to mind that his technique is easily identifiable; they like to work with the man because he makes them look their best and, more important, he makes them commercially attractive. He has an unerring instinct for what the magazines and the ad agencies want and he provides it, some say, better than anyone else. Model after model who has worked with Francesco has only the most complimentary things to say about the man. And there is no doubt that Scavullo's work is, quite often, simply extraordinary. His celebrated photograph of top black model Iman—her glistening hair brushed back and her fine, elegant arms wrapped around her neck—resembles a carved ebony sculpture. It is a dazzling work of art.

Respect his talent or not, Scavullo is a superstar and a real lion of the modeling industry. He is also one of the very few photographers who is as famous as his subjects, makes more money than most of them, and will probably endure long after they have faded from memory.

"I'm no great fan of Scavullo's work, but I admire and respect him for knowing how to keep his name in the spotlight," says photographer Bob Stone, a casual and candid man who is unusual in this uptight business in that he says what he believes and lets the chips fall where they may. "He's an expert at public relations and let me tell you, that's very important in this crazy line of work. You have to keep getting attention— making news—and Scavullo knows how to do it. It's in his blood; it's instinctual. This, more than any special talent, is what keeps him working, attracting the media coverage and the big fees."

Scavullo is preoccupied with his public image. He is typical of so many in the modeling business in that, despite his accomplishments and success, he appears to be extremely insecure. To be in his company is to witness a nonstop show of braggadocio. Every word, every move, every gesture seems designed to impress one with his wealth, power, talent, fame, and —perhaps most important—membership in an inner circle of top artists, celebrities, and politicians.

Scavullo is an inveterate name dropper, spewing out a list of "close personal friends" that might make Truman Capote blush. Not only does he boast endlessly about his social connections, but he intimates that many stars would be reduced to a state of helplessness were he not around to help them with grooming, selecting wardrobes, and furnishing their homes. Scavullo rails endlessly against bad taste, against the double-knit hicks of the world, while simultaneously flattering himself as the foremost authority on what is in and what is not. He seems to believe that when it comes to a sense of taste, he has few equals; that Barbra Streisand and Donna Summer trust no one else to photograph them and to package their public images; that Liza Minelli consults with him before she cuts her hair or buys clothing; and that Barbara Walters applies her makeup precisely the way he has instructed her to.

Nevertheless, for a man whose friendships are supposedly ironclad, Scavullo takes extraordinary precautions to make certain that he doesn't ruffle anyone's feathers or say anything negative about anyone in the model business. Before consenting to an interview for this book he insisted that he have the right to approve every direct quote attributed to him prior to publication. And he wanted this agreement in writing. The interview could not commence until his secretary dutifully typed out a carefully worded statement to this effect, to be signed by the author.* This kind of action, which reveals a Nixonian distrust of the press, is unusual for public figures. Most are sufficiently self-confident to censor their own remarks and to trust that they will be treated fairly and accurately. Not Scavullo. What does he fear? Why is the man who proclaims himself to be the most powerful figure in the modeling industry so fearful of being misquoted? According to Scavullo himself, it is because his comments may be taken out of context, may be unflattering to his friends, and may jeopardize some of his treasured relationships. Asked why a simple phone call could not straighten out these misunderstandings—why close personal friends would choose to believe the press rather than him—Scavullo just shrugs and refuses to discuss it.

What is life like as a "superstar" photographer? What does all the fame, power, and money buy?

"Not as much as you might think," says Frances Grill, a successful agent representing fashion photographers. "They make lots of dough, but so what? To stay hot in this business, you have to spend big, throw lavish parties, have several residences. You have to spread the cash around—live big, act flashy.

"The whole success trip doesn't turn out to be what the photographers imagined when they were climbing to the top. They expected to find some sort of fantasy world which, sadly enough, doesn't exist. Whatever problems, fears, and phobias they had all along don't go away. They have more things, but there's no magic in their lives. They want you to think there is, but it's not true. The smiles on their faces are there partly to fool themselves into feeling happy and partly to fool everyone else into thinking that they are."

This portrayal seems to be accurate. In spite of Scavullo's regal possessions and his lavish life-style, for example, some-

---

*Scavullo subsequently refused to approve the use of any direct quotes of his originally included in the manuscript for this book. No reasons were given.

thing seems to be missing for him. One gets the feeling that he is trying too hard—trying to convince himself and others that his life is perfect. Over and over again, in the course of an interview, he flaunts his earnings, his social ties, his accomplishments. He boasts that the world is banging at his door: film producers, directors, book publishers, agents, models, editors—all are bidding, pleading for his talents. Scavullo does not want you to leave his company until you are duly impressed.

To understand Scavullo, finally, is to recognize that he is really a small-town boy (he was born and raised in a working-class community on rural Staten Island) who made it in the Big Apple and is still awed by how far he's come and by his lofty position in the dazzling world of modeling's superstars. In spite of his name and his Continental flair, Scavullo is thoroughly American. He is, in fact, a classic example of the American dream—the young man who through talent, hustle, and hard work rises from humble beginnings to a position of money and privilege.

When he occasionally drops his guard and allows this sense of excitement to emerge, Scavullo can be an engaging and thoroughly amusing man. Stories of the stars he's met—the leading models and show business personalities—are chock full of spicy tidbits, inside secrets, and hot rumors (much of which he demands remain off the record). And he has certainly had some interesting encounters. The story is told of a visit to his studio by the late rock star Janis Joplin, whom Scavullo found to be as outrageous in person as her press notices claimed she was. Apparently when she spotted a nude poster of an actor who has starred in a number of Andy Warhol films, Joplin pointed to his penis and said, "Now that's something I could spend a few days with."

Scavullo's supercharged world is a special place most fashion photographers view only from a distance. Even for the highly successful photographers who are just a notch or two below the top, the rewards and the requirements of the profession are very different. These professionals are not household names; they have to keep hustling for business, and despite the fact that they make exceptionally good money by most standards, their fees pale in comparison to those earned by Avedon and Scavullo. What's more, their assignments are usually routine affairs with the thousands of anonymous models based in New York, although most have worked at one time or another with the stars of the business. A look at the men and women at this level of photography is instructive in that it provides an inside view of the role many photographers play in the modeling industry.

Bob Stone is indicative of the breed. He came to the profession not with a burning childhood passion but through a rather indirect path. Raised in Los Angeles, Stone first set his career sights on engineering and enrolled at UCLA to begin his formal education. After dropping out, he knocked around a bit trying his hand at assorted jobs. Because he had some artistic leanings, he managed to get work doing photo layouts. Then, in one of those unexpected turn of events that can radically change a person's life, Stone ran into a former classmate who was trying to help a girlfriend break into modeling. She needed sample photographs to send to the modeling agencies. Bob had a camera. One thing led to another, and he was doing his first shooting.

"I had absolutely no experience photographing models," Stone recalls, "but I just jumped into it anyway. I did have some ideas about how the model should be posed and, surprise of surprises, it came out quite well. From that day on I was hooked; somehow I just kept photographing models and never stopped. I've never had any formal training. What I know comes from trial and error. I worked and learned, worked and learned, and finally made it."

After bumming around L.A. for a few more years, slowly learning his craft, Stone came to New York in 1967.

"Again my good luck came through a friend. A guy I knew learned of an opportunity at *Vogue* and managed to wangle the assignment for me. For the magazine it was just a routine fashion spread, but for me it was the chance of a lifetime—a chance to show my stuff and get some badly needed recognition. Well, that's just the way it worked. I got twelve color pages in *Vogue,* all of which came out great, and I was on the map from that moment on. Suddenly, everything started going right for me."

Of course, it wasn't just luck. The mechanics of building a photography career are similar to those in modeling in that both demand tearsheets to prove the individual's talents and to open doors. In addition, photographers and models benefit greatly by coming under the auspices of top agents. Armed with his *Vogue* tearsheets, Stone was able to make two great strides: to gain the support and confidence of a prominent agent and to impress prospective clients. Almost as soon as he finished the *Vogue* assignment, Stone won over Stogo & Bernstein, one of the leading photographers' representative firms in the city. This helped Stone reach his current standing as a very successful and highly regarded photographer.

Skilled reps play a major role in building their clients' careers. The photographer/agent relationship is much more intense than that between models and their agents. For one, photographers' reps generally limit themselves to handling less than a dozen clients, sometimes as few as two. In return, they command high commissions, a whopping 25 percent of the photographer's billings. Most do an extraordinary amount of work to earn it. Many are almost extensions of the photographers they represent. The rep's job, in the simplest terms, is to go into the marketplace, promote the photographer's talent, and win him bookings. This means making the rounds with the photographer's book, visiting advertising agencies and fashion magazines. Agents are also instrumental in setting fees and negotiating contracts. All of this involves a thorough knowledge of the photographer: his needs, preferences, strengths, and limitations.

"For a photographer working in New York—where the competition and the pressures are intense—having an agent is not a luxury, it's a necessity," Stone explains. "You simply cannot concentrate on your work, I mean really give it your best shot, if you have to spend half your time trying to bring in new business. The way I look at it, either you are a salesman or a photographer. It's hard to do both well.

"Of course, just having an agent is not the end-all, cure-all. It has to be a good agent. Some aren't worth a dime. They can't get out of their own way. I mean, they go out with your book, day after day, and their batting average in getting you jobs is very low—strictly bush league. Top agents have excellent contacts, a sharp eye for good photography, and a rapport with their clients. They understand both their clients and their customers and are thus able to bridge the gap between the two beautifully. The trouble is, when you are first starting out and looking for a skilled agent you have to deal with the old Catch-22 problem. The best reps won't take you on unless you have some good work to show, but you often can't get that calibre of work until you have a rep."

"The challenge of agenting for gifted photographers is to take their enormous talent and to fit it into what is a very commercial business without destroying that talent," says Frances Grill, who has been a top agent for more than twenty years and counts among her half-dozen clients Oliviero Toscani and Barbra Walz. "This requires a close, sensitive relationship. I have no contracts with my photographers. We're together because we like, admire, and respect one another. I intentionally limit myself to no more than six clients because with any more I'd lose touch with my people and their work. I am inundated with young photographers just starting out who want me to represent them, but unless I have an opening, I just have to say no.

"I'm in touch with my people every day. Our lives are intertwined. Agenting for photographers is more complex than dealing with models because photographers have artistic considerations. Ours is much less of a meat market. We're not simply matching up a face with the first available job. My clients and I make decisions together. It's never a one-sided process. Agents must know their photographers' strengths and weaknesses. You must channel their talent into commercial objectives rather than letting commercial objectives determine the photographer's work. You must let the photographer's talent find expression. As you can see, money is not the only consideration here."

Just how an agent goes about piecing together a photographer's career and how their relationship can become close and interdependent is best seen by Grill's handling of Barbra Walz, one of her newest clients.

A graduate of Pratt Institute, Walz landed her first photography job right out of college, working for *Fashion Week*, a West Coast trade newspaper. As New York correspondent, Walz earned a mere $15 per published shot, but she had a unique opportunity to meet and photograph the nation's fashion designers—Bill Blass, Ralph Lauren, and the like. Walz loved her association with the fashion world, enjoyed chronicling the work of the great designers, and became an active proponent of their efforts to make America a fashion leader and innovator. With this in mind, Walz came up with the idea for a book of photos and brief essays on the work and the personalities of America's leading apparel designers. The concept rang a bell at Random House, which contracted for the project and published it under the title *The Fashion Makers*. Though it turned out to be a modest publishing success, it was a real turning point in Walz's career.

"The book really blew my career wide open," Walz notes. "It lifted me out of obscurity. It gave me a name, a presence in the industry. Even though I'd made contact with a lot of powerful people before the book was published, I was still considered just a newspaper photographer. Also, the people I knew—mostly fashion designers—are not the ones who hire photographers. You have to come to the attention of art directors, fashion editors, and agents. *The Fashion Makers* did that, and in the process it raised my professional standing several notches as soon as it was published."

Enter Frances Grill. Greatly impressed with *The Fashion Makers*, Grill believed that she could turn Walz's newfound fame into choice photographic assignments by using the book as a marketing tool. She agreed to represent Barbra and made the rounds, book in hand, to the offices of leading editors and art directors—but not in the U.S. Adopting a practice that is used throughout the modeling industry, Grill decided to sell her new client to the European community first.

"If the Europeans accepted Barbra, I knew the Americans would embrace her," Grill explains, "and that's what happened, although not as quickly or as strongly as we would have liked. The Europeans were very much taken with *The Fashion Makers*. It opened their eyes to the American fashion community and made them take a new look at its skills and talents. The French and the Italians had always dismissed American designers as second-rate, but Barbra's book helped to change their minds. That's why I was able to land Barbra assignments with some of the top magazines on the Continent."

In a major coup of her career, Walz was assigned in 1979 by Bergdorf Goodman to shoot the collection of Aldo Ferrante, the store's choice as "Designer of the Year." Walz went to Italy and returned with a stunning collection of photographs that made news in the *New York Times,* were featured in Bergdorf's windows, and were the subject of a show at the International Photography Center in New York.

"The IPC show was great exposure for me and I know I'll keep moving up in this business," Barbra says. "I keep working at it and so does Frances. It's important to know that you have a dedicated agent in there pitching for you—and that's what I'm fortunate enough to have. I'm confident that I'll get into more and more of the top fashion magazines in due time." The excellence of her work should guarantee that.

Most of the leading fashion photographers have made the "magazine connection"—that is, they have established a solid relationship with one of the leading fashion publications. This is a key factor in their success and something they do not take lightly. Once a savvy photographer breaks into a major publication, he does everything possible to stay there, to keep getting assignments. This is done not for the money but for the excellent publicity it provides—the "showcase." Magazines like *Glamour* are important because they are widely read by everyone who is anyone in the fashion business. Models, apparel and cosmetics marketers, agents, and editors devour the leading publications to keep abreast of industry developments: to see who's modeling for Max Factor or Gloria Vanderbilt, which

John Casablancas has earned a reputation as a high roller, a man-about-town, and an agent the models love to love most. Although Casablancas claims to dislike this image, there is no denying that the man has flair and an instinct for generating favorable publicity.

Alain Walch

Models Danielle Guerra and Appolonia sporting the military look while perched on a rooftop above lower Manhattan. Good photographers, in this case Bob Stone, are always looking for some unique approach to make a shot interesting or dramatic.

Bob Stone—Zoli Management Inc.

Playboy publisher Hugh Hefner and photo editor Gary Cole reviewing pictures of candidates for the 25th Anniversary Playmate.

Candy Loving, the 25th Anniversary Playmate, posing in the grand ballroom of *Playboy*'s luxurious Chicago mansion.

Derek Burton—*Gallery Magazine*'s "Girl Next Door of the Month," December 1979.

Gallery magazine's popular feature "The Girl Next Door" publishes nude photos of nonprofessional models. Most of the pictures are submitted by husbands and boyfriends. Judyannah M. of New Jersey was Girl Next Door for the December 1979 issue.

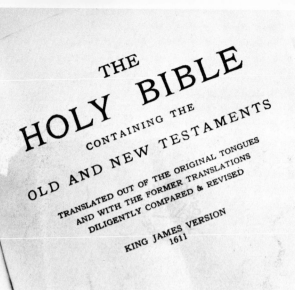

Pages from the now-famous "model wars"
Bible sent to Elite and addressed to the first
two defectors from the Ford camp.

said unto them: and they made ready

t *day,* the passover.

ple.   17 And in the evening he cometh with
house   the twelve.

meat,   18 And as they sat and did eat, Jesus
aster   said, Verily I say unto you, One of you
pre-   which eateth with me shall betray me.
and   19 And they began to be sorrowful, and
           to say unto him one by one, *Is* it I? and
indig-   another *said, Is* it I?
said,   20 And he answered and said unto

him, Lord, is it I?

23 And he answered and said, He that
dippeth *his* hand with me in the dish,
the same shall betray me.

24 The Son of man goeth as it is written of him: but woe unto that man by
whom the Son of man is betrayed! it had
been good for that man if he had not
been born.

25 Then Judas, which betrayed him,
answered and said, Master, is it I? He
said unto him, Thou hast said.

26 ❡ And as they were eating, Jesus

The late Wilhelmina always prided herself on maintaining excellent relationships with her models.

Pompeo Posar, *Playboy* staff photographer, at work on one of his many Playmate assignments.

colors *Vogue* is hyping for the coming season, who is doing Barbara Minty's hair, and which photographer is responsible for this month's cover shot. Fashion magazines are big on credits: virtually every major photo has, in small print along the side border, the name of the model's makeup artist, hairstylist, and photographer. Informed readers—those in the business—pay close attention to these credits. It's the best way to learn who is doing what.

"This is what the 'showcase' concept is all about," Bob Stone explains. "The magazines don't pay well—you work for a fraction of what you get elsewhere—but they give you that all-important window to the rest of the industry. You can do some exceptionally inventive work, get ten or twelve pages in *Harper's Bazaar,* and everyone knows instantly that you're as fresh as ever and doing really terrific stuff. This is the kind of exposure that keeps your agent's phone ringing—keeps the assignments coming in. I like doing magazine work."

Adds Barbra Walz: "I wouldn't trade some of the showcase work for anything. It's so spontaneous, so alive. For example, I was hired by the *New York Times* to shoot the fashions used in the movie version of *The Wiz.* The cast members, a real zany bunch, came up to my studio and they brought the house down. I put on rock music and they danced and jumped and flew through the air. Once they got started and the energy started pouring out, there was no stopping them. It was pure magic—a photographer's dream. The shots came out terrific—I was very proud of this work."

If magazines provide the photographers' showcase, advertising agencies serve up the bread and butter. The lucrative photo assignments are dished out by agency art directors, who are paid to produce advertising for clients such as Revlon, Estée Lauder, Ralph Lauren, and Calvin Klein. Here too photographers must handle complex and demanding relationships. That's because art directors—in fact, most ad agency people—tend to be a fickle bunch. Madison Avenue is quick to adopt the latest fad and then to drop it a month or two later when something newer comes along. An agency will suddenly be anointed the "hot shop of the year," simply because it has won a single new account or launched a new campaign. But the campaign may fail and the account leave, and in the meantime another agency has been crowned the "hot shop to beat." Advertising careers follow similar patterns. As one agency executive puts it, "In this business, when you're hot, you're hot as hell; but when you're cold, you're dead. You can go from one extreme to the other in less time than it takes to piss." Young copywriters just out of school can become stars overnight, simply on the strength of a single three-word headline. On Madison Avenue, slogans like "Coke Adds Life," "Melts in Your Mouth, Not in Your Hands," and "The One Beer to Have When You're Having More Than One" are considered English-language classics. Hot jingle writers are avidly sought after by the big agencies for as long as their pens keep churning out winners. In most cases, this all comes to a halt—the career burns out and the star becomes just another so-so copywriter—in a year or two. Advertising executives judge photographers by these trendy standards: all want to work with photographers who are currently hot, in demand, and commercially successful. Any sign that the photographer is slowing down or being upstaged by some brash new talent is enough to cause the photographer to be given the brush-off. That translates into fewer assignments and a significant drop in income. For this reason successful photographers and their agents devote considerable time and effort to cultivating good agency relationships—by maintaining that all-important showcase in the fashion magazines, by treating neurotic art directors to frequent liquid lunches, by just plain kissing ass.

"Some of the agency guys are real groupies," says a leading photographer. "I mean, if you know a top model—a real beautiful and famous woman—you can win Brownie points by introducing her to your agency contacts. They'll often ask to come to the shooting, and even though I prefer not to have an audience, I usually oblige. They really enjoy it.

"Sometimes, however, I wind up regretting my act of good will. That's because having a novice at a shooting can really fuck things up. They have a disrupting effect on the model and myself. Just recently an art director knew that I was shooting Lauren Hutton and asked if he could come over to meet her. The guy arrived before Lauren and he was full of nervous anticipation waiting for her. He paced back and forth. When she finally showed up, I noticed that his face turned white—you know that real sick, pale color people get when they're deeply upset. I couldn't imagine what was wrong, but he blurted it all out when Lauren went into the dressing room to get ready. He was terribly disappointed with her looks. Professionals in this business know that most models don't look nearly as good in person as they do on film. The makeup, the camera, the lighting—all give them an element of excitement and glamour that they lack face to face. This is especially true of Lauren. She's a beautiful woman, don't get me wrong, but she's very natural and casual and walks around looking like the girl next door—no makeup, a simple hairdo, and ordinary clothes. So when the advertising guy met her, he went into shock. 'When's the last time you saw her?' he asked. 'What happened to her? Has she been ill?' He was really carrying on. What he didn't realize, until he saw it happen, is that great pros like Lauren Hutton can walk into a dressing room looking like the housewife in a Tide commercial and then with the aid of a makeup kit and a hairbrush can exit half an hour later looking like the essence of glamour and style. When Lauren, the model, stepped out, the guy was floored. She was everything he expected—and more."

Nevertheless, photographers claim that regardless of how good they are at their work, and how well they butter up clients, the fickle nature of the advertising business is something they just have to learn to live with. "You think you have a super relationship with an art director—the two of you are close socially as well as in business—and then all of a sudden he just stops calling, stops requesting your services," says one photographer. "I've tried to find out why this happens, but all I can come up with is that these advertising people are so insecure, so afraid of being considered passé, that they dump you just because they've been dealing with you for a long time. Somehow, they equate a lasting relationship with a tired one. . . . The more I think about it, the angrier I get. These agency people

think they're so hot-shit sophisticated—that they can sell ciga-
rettes to cancer patients—but you know something, they're
really the dumbest bastards in the country. Anyone who has to
chase their tail to keep up with what's new is a sorry case, and
there are a lot of sorry cases on Madison Avenue. My curse to
bear is that I have to work with them and make like I enjoy it.
No one wins in this rat race."

Despite all their complaining about art directors, account
executives, and fashion editors, photographers' most intense
love/hate relationship is with models. It colors virtually everything they do and is in many ways even more complex and
demanding than their marriages or close friendships. One reason for this is purely quantitative: photographers and models
spend a lot of time together. Photographers can start working
as early as 8 A.M. and keep clicking away, with only a break for
lunch, until midnight. Sometimes it's with the same model for
the whole day or perhaps with a procession of girls marching
in and out of the studio for hourly bookings. They may be in the
studio, at a nearby location, or off in some secluded setting
working with a model for a week or more on a single assignment. Whatever the circumstances, the nature of the business
makes for an intense one-to-one relationship. Models and photographers rely on each other to do their jobs well, to make each
other look good. It is this emotional factor that is the most
crucial element in their relationship.

Leading photographers can do more than anyone else to
make stars of new or relatively obscure models. They have
power. Top models, by the same token, can throw their weight
around too, deciding which photographer will have the privilege
of shooting them. They too have power. What's more, both
sides have very definite opinions about the others' professional
standards. Models are certain that they know what makes a
good photographer, while photographers insist that only they
can tell a talented model from a dog. Add to this explosive
mixture the fact that photographers and models rarely see eye
to eye, that they tend to be sensitive and high-strung, that they
are usually engaged in a bitter battle over pride, power, and
money—and you don't need a match to ignite this one.

Most models want to work with a take-charge professional who has a proven track record not only in the techniques of photography but also in making women look beautiful. He should be able to suggest the perfect shade of makeup, correct an unflattering flip of the hair, and know precisely which camera angle will best capture the model's most striking features.

"Every once in a while you work with a photographer who is sloppy about his work," superstar Christina Ferrare says. "He wants to get it all over with as quickly as possible, collect his checks, and the hell with the quality of the photos. . . . The photographer who is in a rush is playing havoc with your career. If you are the kind of model who never accepts second best from yourself, why accept it from others? You can make all the right career moves except the way you handle photographers, and that one mistake can have a devastating effect. If I don't believe that the photographer is approaching me as a true professional, taking the time to do the job right, I'll leave the shooting. I'll just tell him my gripe and get up and leave. I'd rather lose the pay than be part of a second-rate performance. Some photographers can perform miracles. I once had to do a shooting in a swimming pool. The only problem was that I had a broken leg and was wearing a full cast. Well, the photographer positioned me so expertly, half in the pool and half out, that when the photograph was published, no one ever knew that anything was wrong. I looked great, like I was floating for hours in the water."

Models also talk a lot about sensitivity. They want the photographer to be strong and confident of his craft, but not overbearing. Best liked are those photographers who are willing to listen to the model's opinions and who do not carry on simply because she makes a request or expresses herself. It must be said, however, that this breed of photographer is rare. Most play the super-macho role, snapping orders and expecting total, unquestioned compliance. Any protest on the model's part is viewed as an attempt to usurp his power, a silly and ignorant intrusion on his work. Most photographers dismiss models as dumb, neurotic, drugged out hicks from nowhere USA; they are thought of as props, or perhaps as lovers, but rarely as intelligent human beings.

Photographers, for their part, don't deny that they are strong-willed—a characteristic many hold is crucial to success. As they see it, demanding that the models follow their instructions is not a macho power play but a professional action that protects their reputation and serves as a quality control for the shooting. In many cases, photographers, like film directors, are responsible for an entire project. If the shooting goes awry or for one reason or another turns out poorly, the photographer is held to blame—not the model, the agent, or the art director.

"All the pressure is on us," says Bob Stone. "We can't shift the blame when something turns out poorly even if we didn't do a damn thing wrong. All that anyone ever cares to know is that this or that picture is bad, Bob Stone is the photographer, Bob Stone fucked up. They don't ask questions to determine the real source of the problem. You're guilty by association. That's why you have to exert your authority at the shooting. You are the expert there, you know much more about the photographic process than the model. You have to take command and do things your way because you can bet your ass that you'll be the one to hear the bitching if something gets screwed up."

Says another photographer, "A model came into this studio recently sporting a bad sunburn. Her skin looked blotchy; she was in no condition to do an important shooting. I told her this and made her leave. There was no way I was going to put my reputation on the line and work with an ill-prepared model simply to please her. She believed she could use makeup to hide the burns and called me a hard ass for not letting her try. But let me tell you, if the photos were developed and then after seeing how bad they were the art director threw them in my face, that model wouldn't be around to share the blame. I'd be held fully responsible and I'd be the one they wouldn't hire again. I owe it to the client and the agency to be thoroughly professional."

One mistaken notion is that sex is often part of the model/photographer relationship. The casting couch syndrome, reported to be so popular in Hollywood, is not at all prevalent in modeling. The unwritten laws of the industry dictate against it. Nothing can so quickly wreck a career—that of a model, photographer, or agent—than for it to be tainted by sexual misconduct. The eager young model who tries to win bookings by sleeping around soon finds that she has ruined her professional reputation. She may well find some willing partners (rarely among the industry's more prominent names), but for sex only. She will be used—viewed as little more than a whore. And she will not be taken seriously as a model.

Most models never even try this route. They learn early on that it is simply not acceptable. Eileen Ford deserves much of the credit for this. As modeling's ruling monarch for more than two decades, Eileen established many of the customs and mores that still apply today. She detested the thought of young women being sexually manipulated or abused, and she laid down the law against it. Loose sexual behavior clashed entirely with her conservative middle-American values. Her standards have prevailed because they are shared by leading national advertisers—and they're the people who pay the bills.

The widespread misconception about the role of sex in modeling may stem partly from the fact that models and photographers are often paired romantically. In spite of frequent antagonism, there is a considerable amount of dating and living together among them. The closeness of their professional contact encourages this, and for the most part, these are legitimate, multidimensional relationships. Few reputable photographers are in it just for the sex. They refrain for the same reason as the girls—to protect their professional reputations. Photographers who come on strong with every model are simply not viewed as serious artists by the agencies and advertisers. Still, rumors about their sexual exploits persist. How do they start?

"A friend I grew up with in Brooklyn—he's a fireman today—once said to me, 'Boy, day in day out—models coming out of your ears,'" says Jerry Della Femina, head of the New York advertising agency Della Femina, Travisano, & Partners. "'You must be killing yourself,' my friend said. 'I've been up to your office and I've seen the girls. I mean, there really must be a lot of fooling around in that business. Can I come up and see? I just want to walk around and see . . .'"

Della Femina continues, "The only people who wind up sleeping with models are photographers. And photographers are monkeys. I mean they're really monkeys. You know, most photographers are very short and have very long arms. I guess the long arms come from carrying those bags around—that's a lot of equipment they haul around. Some photographers' arms scrape the ground, they're so long. The funny bit is that they make out as far as models are concerned. I may be projecting now, which is what my fireman friend is doing. The fireman's decided that I'm making it with every model in town and I've decided that the photographers are the ones who are really making it with the models."*

"If we learn that a photographer uses models for sex, he won't work in the business again," Eileen Ford declares, stabbing a finger in the air. "The word goes out immediately to all the agencies never to provide girls for that photographer again. And obviously, without models to work for him, he'll never be able to handle assignments."

How does the industry learn about a photographer's misbehavior? How does the word get out? "It's very simple," adds Eileen, with the steely confidence of a woman who knows how to exercise power. "We just get on the telephone and call up all the other agents . . . and make it clear that this photographer is not professional and should not be trusted with any models."

Eileen Ford's description of the industry's moral defense system is probably somewhat exaggerated. The agents' intense dislike of one another, prompted by their tough competitive battles throughout the 1970s, has led to a near total breakdown in communications. The feuding among agency principals is so bitter that Eileen is not likely to pick up the phone to warn Bruce Cooper of a lecherous photographer. In reality, the models themselves usually pass the word on to their colleagues and to their agents that a photographer is disreputable. The agents are likely to communicate only if the industry's very reputation is at stake, if a major scandal might erupt.

*From Those Wonderful Folks Who Gave You Pearl Harbor (Simon & Schuster, 1970).

"Every once in a while we get some nuts who set up studios and pretend to be professional photographers," Zoli explains, "but they're really just sex perverts. They call up to have girls sent over for testings, but the real purpose is to try to use them sexually. When nuts like this are on the loose, agents do alert one another.

"In more normal circumstances, if a reputable photographer has sexual interests in a girl, he'll usually keep it controlled, unless, of course, they develop a true relationship. But just jumping into bed together all the time is not acceptable. Modeling is work—there is no time for playing around at a shooting. The casting couch does not exist in this business."

What *is* the perfect relationship between photographer and model? What kinds of women do they like to work with? Where do they draw the line between a model's right to self-expression and their own need to retain artistic control? Which models get the highest marks for natural beauty, camera presence, and professionalism?

Certainly, all photographers have their own standards. They do not agree, uniformly, on what makes a model great. Still, they do hold many views in common, and there is a consensus about certain basic traits that are absolutely essential to the making of a successful model. At the top of the list is the elusive and somewhat mysterious quality of camera presence. Photographers know that a woman's beauty means nothing in a professional sense unless she can bring that beauty to life before the camera. Models with superb camera presence dig down deep within themselves to tap a source of energy that somehow makes the way they pose especially dramatic, alluring, or sensual. How this actually happens is impossible to say. Photographers equate good modeling with acting, asserting that both professions demand similar skills. The word they use most when describing a good modeling performance is "giving." The model must determine precisely what the photographer wants—be it a look of innocence, anger, mischief, or passion—must search within herself for the appropriate qualities, and must make the illusion work.

Top photographers recognize that this may not happen spontaneously—that they must act as catalysts in the process. Scavullo does this with his coffee-and-conversation routine. By interviewing the model and thus showing interest in her as a woman, Scavullo builds a rapport between subject and photographer. But this human approach doesn't always work: a growing number of models (more than the industry establishment will admit) are inveterate pill poppers who rely on a virtual drugstore of capsules to get them to sleep, to wake them up, to make them feel happy.

"In this business, time is money," says one photographer who gave up a staff position with a fashion magazine to open a studio of his own. "If a girl comes in here all bent out of shape psychologically, I don't have the time to do the analyst's couch routine. My job is to get her loosened up and in condition to work. Unless she's feeling free and easy, there's no way she can respond to the camera. I don't use drugs myself—in fact, I think they are poisonous, but I have no compunction whatsoever about keeping a good supply on hand for my girls. Once I learned that it could make the difference between a terrible shooting and a superb one, I put my morals on vacation and bought enough stuff to turn on the whole state of Maine.

"Is taking drugs unprofessional? No, not at all. A model must know what she needs to perform, to do her job well. If she does that—no matter what it takes—she's a pro in my book. There's one teenager who I've been working with for a year now—a sweet-looking little thing from Arizona who looks like a contestant in a Pillsbury bakeoff—who needs tequila to get going. Tequila at ten in the morning. Disgusting, right? But she drinks it, does her thing, is a great model, and what the hell happens when she leaves here doesn't concern me. If she's throwing up on the sidewalk after the shooting, well so what? The work is over."

This attitude is not universal. Many photographers will not provide drugs. They prefer to set the mood for a good modeling performance by more conventional means. Barbra Walz does it with music. Even before the model arrives, Walz fills her studio with music carefully chosen to get her subject in the right frame of mind and to establish an atmosphere that will comple-ment the shooting. She encourages her models to dance—to go with the music. Those who do so often feel as if they are alone on a dance floor, at one with the music and with their bodies.

"To me, a good model is one who can abandon herself to this process," Walz says. "She knows how to role-play. I ask her to be a dancer and she thinks she's doing her thing at a disco. When this happens it's great because the self-consciousness that can get in the way of great, spontaneous posing is gone. Also, when she's caught up in the flow and the energy of the music, the model is more likely to stretch herself, to try new movements, to do things she's never done before.

"I have a piano in my studio that serves as a great back-ground prop," Walz adds. "Models aren't used to working around a piano, so when I tell them to pose by it, I introduce an element of surprise and novelty. Here's where you can sepa-rate the great models from the duds. Some will approach the piano but remain detached from it. They stand beside it as if they too are inanimate objects. There's no interaction with the prop. But talented models, those who really give of themselves and really understand their jobs, seem to fuse with the piano. They immediately see all the possibilities. They lie on it, drape themselves over it, dominate it, or let it dominate them. Imagi-nation and movement take over, and the results are usually super."

Top models who get high marks from photographers are Lauren Hutton, Christina Ferrare, Iman, Roseanne Vela, Patti Hanson, Barbara Minty, and Barbara Rucker. These women are highly regarded for their thoroughly professional conduct and considerateness as well as for their beauty and camera presence. They are pleasant to work with, are punctual, rarely cancel bookings, call ahead when they are running late, keep themselves healthy and well groomed, and allow the photogra-pher to run the show. They don't pull prima donna routines, don't scream and shout with every frustration, and don't expect the rest of the world to put up with childish behavior.

Still, when the topic of models comes up, photographers

usually turn nasty and bitter. The truth is that there is a growing rift between models and photographers and that both sides are becoming increasingly caught up in an "us versus them" mentality. The reason has to do with a very emotional issue: money. Once the masters of the modeling business, photographers have seen much of their power shift to the new breed of aggressive agents and to the emerging class of superstar models. Much of their decline can be traced to changes in financial procedures. In the early days, photographers controlled the purse strings—they were paid by clients and in turn paid the models who posed for them—but today model fees are paid directly to the agencies.

"When photographers handled the money, some of them would make the models dangle on a rope until they got paid," says Jerry Ford. "It gave them great manipulative power. Some of the girls literally had to beg to get paid and others never got their money at all. Just being in the position to have to beg was degrading and insulting. It gave the photographers a lot of artificial power, power some of them abused. Most would like to retain control of the finances, but that will never happen again."

What rankles photographers is that they have lost not only their position as the industry's paymasters, but also become second-class citizens in terms of earnings. Except for the likes of Avedon and Scavullo, the men behind the camera make less money than the women they photograph. When it comes to raw earning power, models have bypassed photographers by a comfortable margin—and the losers are very unhappy about that.

One problem for photographers is that agents' commissions are particularly high, taking 25 percent of their fees right off the top. Second, photographers often have to wait months to get paid. Advertising agencies (notoriously slow payers) send checks directly to the agents, who subtract their own commissions first and then pay their clients, the photographers. Third, and most important, photographers have substantial overhead. Cameras, lights, studio rent, film, utilities, messengers, insurance, staff salaries, business lunches—all must come out of gross income. With the high costs of doing business in

New York, it is easy to understand how the $250,000 or more they earn a year shrinks considerably once expenses are subtracted. Because payments—sometimes even for major assignments—often come in late, cash flow is disrupted and photographers are forced to occasionally take loans or to dip into personal reserves to keep the studio humming. The photographers argue they have businesses to run—with all the costs and risks that entails—and are therefore entitled to more, not less, money than models.

Although savvy clients and their agencies appreciate quality photography, there is a widespread belief that quality can be bought for less than premium rates. Many competent and enthusiastic photographers are on the sidelines of the model industry, doing everything they can to break into the big leagues. They include the young, the new in town, and the seasoned pros who've never been discovered. Most have one thing in common: the willingness to accept $750 or $1,000 for the same assignments top names won't do for less than $1,500. Their very willingness to work for lower rates moderates the fee structure throughout their profession. When agencies are up against the wall working with a tight budget, they will often spend the most money on a top model but cut corners on photography. This is done by going to the farm league photographers or by threatening to do so. The latter approach is often more than enough to get the big names to compromise—to accept the job for less rather than to lose it entirely.

"The models never have to take a cut—heaven forbid," one photographer snarls. "They just get more and more and more, and their fees gradually eat up bigger and bigger pieces of the agency budgets. That means we often get stuck working for less. I do it sometimes. If I'm not heavily booked and a job comes along, I'll take less of a fee if it means that or nothing at all. I have a studio to run here; I can't sit on my high horse. Put too much of an emphasis on pride and principles and you'll wind up starving to death. It's important to be practical too. What makes it so hard to swallow is that the models never have to give an inch in terms of money. I don't know why that should be so, but it is."

Models are categorized as "talent," whereas photographers are considered providers of a service. Many models are celebrities, highly identifiable characters who cannot easily be substituted for one another. When Cheryl Tiegs's face became a marketing symbol for Cover Girl makeup, she could not easily be replaced by another tall, leggy blond from the West Coast. Only Tiegs would do. The public knows the face and identifies the product with it. Changing the model who represents it can be as drastic a move as changing a product's label. Advertisers don't like to do either without good reason. Photographers, on the other hand, rarely get the kind of public exposure that makes them so popular that they become virtually indispensable to a client. They can be replaced with hardly anyone knowing; the product, its advertising and positioning, are not altered a bit. This explains why photographers often earn less money than models: they bring less power to the bargaining table.

Most knowledgeable observers believe that photographers have become their own worst enemies. By openly competing with one another on fees—by accepting jobs that do not meet their standard rates—they play into the hands of Madison Avenue's bargain hunters. The very knowledge that some highly qualified pros will accept lower fees when they need work encourages art directors to reject higher rates and forces photographers to bear the burden of tight production budgets. Although photographers like to shift the blame for this onto the models, it seems clear that they just use models as scapegoats for the dilemma they have created themselves. If they simply refused to compromise on fees, they would effectively remove themselves from the bargaining process and would force the advertising agencies to increase their budgets and give them a bigger slice of the pie.

Photographers are a very competitive bunch. There is a great deal of hostility among them that reveals itself not only in financial bickering, but also in terms of professional conduct. It is standard operating procedure to steal each other's assignments, to discredit one another's work, to spread ugly rumors, and to be generally unflattering about their colleagues.

"I once learned from a party who shall remain anonymous that my book was being circulated in a major advertising agency," says one photographer. "The executives there were looking it over, along with a lot of other books, before handing out what was to be a major assignment. Everyone wanted the job, so there was a real competitive battle to get it. But it wasn't professional, civilized competition. It was real dirty tricks. My source informed me that an agent for another photographer was up at the ad agency, saw my book on the art director's desk, and made a snide comment about my work. What a cheap shot. Some people in this business are out to knock you down and build themselves up."

Just what photographers really think of each other's work is hard to say. They are too caught up in the jealousy and the paranoia of the business to be objective. Getting one photographer to compliment another is like pulling teeth. They seem to feel that saying something nice about a colleague will detract from themselves, will be taken to mean that the colleague is better than they are, and will ultimately lead to a competitive disadvantage. It is all very childish.

Mediocre photographers love to dismiss the greats of the business as nothing more than PR hype. "Darling, darling Francesco—if he's a great photographer, I'm Da Vinci," says one staff photographer at a fashion magazine. "A super salesman yes, but a great photographer—no, no. All he's good at is selling himself. Scavullo's secret is that he recognized that ordinary people like to see celebrities with their tits showing."

This self-styled critic declined to comment on the fact that Scavullo won plaudits for his photography long before he ever shot celebrity nudes. But such backstabbing is not unusual. Many photographers are more than willing to boldly denounce each other just as long as they don't have to face the music and accept responsibility for the insult. Even the photography greats are petty in this regard. Of all the men and women who have ever worked in fashion photography, Scavullo refuses to name a single one whom he respects or admires. When he is questioned about Avedon—the fashion photographer who has been treated to more critical praise than any other—Scavullo clams up, refusing to comment on the subject. To an impartial observer, however, he appears to be plainly jealous. New York's prestigious Metropolitan Museum of Art honored Avedon in 1978 with a major exhibition of his portraits. (No mean coup for a man who started out in photography as a merchant marine taking identification photos of new recruits.) The show reflected Avedon's preeminent position in the field and caused his competitors to grind their teeth with envy. Ever since his large one-man exhibition (1975) at New York's Marlborough Gallery, Avedon has enjoyed the ultimate tribute of being associated with fine art. At the Marlborough showing, his photographs sold, in limited editions, at prices of up to $20,000. "Suddenly photography is the great event in art," he said at the time, "and painting is standing aside." Avedon obviously relished this—an exaggeration, to be sure—but he also worried about his elevated stature. "I must be held responsible for what you are seeing here. I can't blame the images on a magazine editor or a bad reproduction. You're seeing the original print. I'm naked." Scavullo hints that he cares little about museum presentations, but considering the man's apparent ego, that is hard to believe.

Just what the competition, the petty jealousies, and the rigors of the business do to fashion photographers is probably best summed up by Bob Stone's telling comment: "I never want to know what assignment I'm being considered for, or what kind of awards my work may get, until I have it in the bag. Unless it's a sure thing, I don't want to think about it. My agent knows not to whisper a word until it's sealed. I can't take the pressure of wanting, waiting, and being disappointed. The best strategy is to think you don't want something, say you don't want it, try to forget about it, and then act surprised if you get it. In this business, that's the secret to sanity."

7

THE SNOB SISTERS
Inside the Fashion Magazines

"The glory days of fashion publishing are over—dead and gone. I mean, I've been sitting here watching my power slip away like sand through an hourglass. And there's nothing I can do about it—that's what really galls me. We used to be able to cut the models down to size, but it's not so easy anymore. The new breed of girls are more aware of their rights and they have tougher, stronger agents. Good for them; bad for us. Real bad. What fun is it if we can't come to work in the morning and be the baddest bitches in the world? If we can't push the little prima donnas around? Might as well stay home."
—A prominent editor at one of America's leading fashion magazines

It is a fact of life in the modeling business that everyone caught up in its crazy ways—the photographers, models, agents, editors, and admen—is under intense pressure. The volatile mix of egos, power, fame, and money that makes the business so appealing also makes it a veritable snake pit of anxiety and fear. The gambles are great, the deadlines constant, and there is always so much to gain and so much to lose. Everyone is afraid —afraid of aging, of fat cells, of split ends, of pimples, of competition, of failing, of losing bookings, of losing clients, of losing assignments. The pressures are inescapable.

Except at the fashion magazines. These are the only major institutions in the modeling industry where the pressures are invented, manufactured. Here, there are no superstars, no million-dollar contracts, no famous faces. Both the risks and the rewards are minimal. The editors, writers, art directors, and their assorted assistants are all corporate employees who do a

129

job, earn modest salaries, and live relatively routine workaday lives. Though the fashion magazines and the people who work for them are part of the modeling business—some are important powers in it—they are not members of the inner circle. In many ways, they remain on the sidelines, watching the parade go by. The magazine staffers are separated from the business they cover by invisible barriers of money and life-style. In a world of big bucks, stunning townhouses, lavish beach homes, and extravagant automobiles, magazine editors are the poor relations who can only watch with their noses pressed against the windows. They are relegated to a middle-class position that others in the industry despise.

Fashion editors are often drawn to the business because they seek glamour, excitement, and high style. Yet the contrast in life-styles between forty-year-old career editors earning $25,-000 annually and twenty-year-old millionaire models is glaring. By and large, editors resent and envy the models, who seem to have so much more of everything. Most editors (except for the real creative forces like *Cosmopolitan*'s Helen Gurley Brown and *Vogue*'s former editor Diana Vreeland) who may have fueled the models' careers and propelled them to fame never share in their wealth. They remain where they were from the start—working long hours for low pay, surrounded by a glittering world they can see and touch, but can rarely penetrate. Even the photographers and agents outstrip them in earning power and in their degree of involvement with the more glamorous side of the business.

A visit to any of the major fashion magazines quickly dispels any expectations of glamour. The facilities, usually in old, second-rate office buildings, are uniformly drab and poorly furnished. Staffers are crammed into closet-sized offices called bullpens. The lowest ranking assistants, those fresh out of college, may share an office with three or four colleagues. Even senior personnel—including those responsible for editorial departments (fashion, food, entertainment, etc.)—most often share space with an associate. Only the top executives, from art directors and managing editors on up, are generally accorded a place of their own. And even here the digs are nothing to get excited about. What passes for an executive suite at a fashion magazine would often be considered an insult to a routine middle manager at any one of the Fortune 500 companies.

"You can never even hear yourself think, what with the clack of typewriters, the sounds of dictating machines, and the din of a hundred different conversations going on all at once," says a young feature editor for one of the leading publications. "Even if you have your own office, the walls are paper-thin, so it sounds as if the girl in the next room is sitting right on your lap.

"When I first came to work here, I thought this would be an advantage because of all the juicy gossip I'd pick up. The back wall of my bullpen is adjacent to the managing editor's office, so I thought I'd be in a great position to get some inside dirt. The second day on the job I got more than I could have dreamed of. The M.E. was on vacation, but an associate publisher who I'll call Roger got drunk at a luncheon with a photographer's rep, brought her up to the office, and balled her on the managing editor's desk. Everyone knew because you could hear the moaning and groaning all the way to the Statue of Liberty. Roger couldn't use his office because his wife was supposed to stop by that afternoon to meet him for cocktails. She wouldn't have been impressed with his work habits.

"I had fun eavesdropping that day (I even used the old glass-against-the-wall trick), but it's been downhill ever since. The juicy gossip I thought I'd hear never materialized. All I ever pick up is bits and snatches of the M.E. talking about her dental work, her nose job, her lonely Saturday nights, and how sexy her analyst is. She's really a crashing bore. I wish the walls here were made of lead. At least I could have more privacy and could get my work done."

Office accommodations are not the only insult. Starting salaries for junior staffers range between $9,000 and $11,000, often for honor graduates from top colleges and universities. The magazines can get away with pinchpenny wages because there is great competition for the few jobs that become available every year. A certain breed of Seven Sisters women gravitate toward the well-known fashion magazines in the mistaken notion that they are glamorous, literate, and prestigious places to work. Most of the candidates are Waspy, prep-school types from upper-middle-class and even wealthy families. Many have always spent lavishly on clothing and have had an abiding interest in fashion, designers, and the finer points of personal grooming. As a group, they are exceptionally bright, articulate, well-read, and often blessed with a strong sense of taste and style.

"The kind of young woman who comes out of school hungry for a job with the fashion magazines hasn't changed much in the twenty years that I've been in the business," says a New York personnel officer who specializes in the fashion field. "They are brainy and ambitious, but they know nothing about the world. Money was never a concern when they were under Mommy and Daddy's roof, and they've never been taught to think in terms of making money. Nice girls don't do that. All they know is that they want to work somewhere or do something that separates them from the great unwashed. They want to work and be successful, but they don't want to get their hands dirty. To this kind of snob the prestige fashion magazines seem to be the perfect haven.

"But the bloom comes off the rose very quickly. The same Radcliffe graduates who kiss my feet for pointing them to the right people at *Vogue* often call me from a phone booth a year later pleading for help to get them the hell out. It doesn't take long to realize that there's no glamour there, that they're packed like sardines into tiny offices, and that once Mom and Dad aren't paying the bills, money does count."

Most of the girls who want to move out of their entry-level jobs nevertheless refuse to give up the idea that fashion magazines are the only suitable places of employment. They tell themselves that the low salaries, mundane duties, and dreary working conditions are unique to the particular publication they are with, that things will be better elsewhere. They cling to the notion that the glamour is real—that all it takes to find it is a change to another magazine and a move up the editorial ladder. To leave the mags is out of the question. Most are not trained for anything else and, even more important, they view the rest of the business world as pedestrian.

Those who do manage to rise to important posts admit that there's little glamour and even less pay in the fashion magazine field: "My work is a job—nothing more and nothing less," says an editor at *Cosmopolitan*. "It's certainly better than being a secretary, and I like what I do, but there's little power in it and no glamour in selecting models. I do get to meet a lot of interesting people, but the pay is very low. That's the trade-off and you have to be willing to accept it."

Adds an editor at *Harper's Bazaar:* "This is not a glamour business, it's a bitchy business. At one time the magazines could sit back and exercise a great deal of power. That was our golden age. But things are different now. Agents and models are very powerful in their own right, and everyone is throwing their weight around. The climate is hostile. Magazines have suffered most because a lot of our power has dwindled. Although I think we are on the rise again, we're not at the level we used to be. Much of the problems have to do with money. The magazines have traditionally paid models at low rates and this has hurt us in recent years. Models and agents are less tolerant of our fees than they used to be. Now the models walk away from our offers if something better comes along."

Editors don't have that luxury. They have no viable options, no easy way out. Senior editors (or department editors, as they are often called) rarely earn more than $30,000 annually, and this is often the culmination of years of hard work and persistent climbing up the corporate ladder. The models they work with, often many years their junior, may earn and spend in a single month nearly as much as the editors make in a year. Add to this the editors' feelings of intellectual superiority and it's clear that their frustrations are intense. To compensate for their poor status vis-à-vis top models, many editors assume a haughty air reminiscent of sales clerks at Tiffany's or waiters at Lutèce. They attempt to bolster their pride by taking themselves quite seriously and acting far more important than they are. The atmosphere at most of the fashion magazines is strikingly similar: dozens of women rush hurriedly from one office to another clutching pages of copy or files of photos. Their movements, even their manner of speaking, are fast if not frantic. No one laughs, few smile. Everyone, it appears, is just too busy and their work too serious to have a little fun. One gets the impression that they must convince both themselves and the rest of the world that they are, in fact, powerful and influential.

It would appear, in fact, that some editors believe there is a direct correlation between power and arrogance. As a result, their manners are often atrocious. It seems to be a common practice for them to cancel appointments with little or no warning, to discard written correspondence without a reply, and to leave telephone messages unanswered. Although no one is immune from this treatment, fledgling models come in for the worst abuse. The fresh, hopeful faces busily traveling Manhattan's testing circuit need the magazines badly. Good tearsheets can dress up a skimpy book, impress people, open doors, and get their careers moving. Models are told from the minute they arrive in New York that the magazines can make or break them in the early stages. Agents drum it into their heads to knock on doors, to meet editors, to do everything possible to get that all-important "showcase" the magazines can provide. There is method to this madness: by featuring newcomers, the top magazines really can turn unknowns into hot properties overnight. It happened to Wilhelmina, Beverly Johnson, Kathy Spiers, and Christina Ferrare, to name a few. And of course every would-be model who comes to New York hopes that lightning will strike again.

"When I first entered this business in the 1950s, the magazines used to make all the stars," says another editor at *Harper's Bazaar.* "Even Lauren Bacall got her first dose of fame this way. The fashion magazines really opened the doors for her in Hollywood. Although we're not that potent anymore, we can still make unknown faces famous and can still do much to help that one model out of a thousand reach the very top of her field. Our reputation with the newcomers is as strong as ever. Most still approach us with great awe."

Herein lies the last vestige of power wielded by the fashion magazines. They can still pull the strings of aspiring models trying desperately to establish themselves in the business. Faced with a roomful of girls trying out for a sixteen-page pictorial, editors can play the role of power broker. Who will make it and who will not? The choice is in their hands.

"The cattle calls at the magazines are the pits," says one young model. "There are as many as a hundred other girls there, all hoping to get picked, so the chances of any one person succeeding are small. You wait for hours, the editors give you a few minutes of their time, and you usually never hear a word from them on how it went."

Adds a well-known photographer, "I was recently on location for a fashion magazine. The editor I was traveling with—who I happen to be very fond of—thought that she needed another model for a particular shooting. One of the agencies was notified to send along another girl on a rush basis. A young model flew 3,000 miles to join us, but when she arrived the editor decided she was too tall in the clothes. The girl was sent home without a second thought. This can be a very insensitive business."

The top American fashion magazines are *Vogue, Glamour, Seventeen, Mademoiselle, Harper's Bazaar,* and *Gentlemen's Quarterly.* (*Cosmopolitan,* which is not strictly a fashion magazine, is similar to the others in some ways but differs markedly in its editorial approach.)

Vogue positions itself as the most elegant and worldly of the group. Although its standards have declined over recent years, it is still the best of its genre. *Glamour, Harper's Bazaar,* and *Mademoiselle* look virtually identical; each appeals to fashionable young women of average means from the late teens to the late thirties. *Seventeen* does the same for younger readers, mostly high school girls.

All of the fashion magazines serve up a steady and predictable diet of bland articles on romance, fashion, self-help beauty programs, travel, careers, food, and entertainment. But mostly they are chock full of ads, ads, ads: for Ultima cosmetics, Catalina swimwear, Saks Fifth Avenue, Norell perfume, Ciani jewelry, Olga negligees, Albert Nipon fashions, Neutrogena soap, Leslie Fay resort wear, Burlington hosiery, Cie cologne, Lancôme skin cream, Piaget watches, Famolare shoes, Maidenform bras and panties, Clinique sunscreen, Virginia Slims, Ciga Hotels, Air Canada, Stretch and Sew Fabric Centers, Sahadi's rugs, DeBeers diamonds, Calvin Klein dresses, and hundreds of others. If nothing else, the fashion magazines are very profitable. Yet just what profits they earn is hard to tell because all the publications are extremely secretive about their operations. There is general agreement, however, that some are money machines.

The richest of all are the Condé Nast publications (part of the Newhouse newspaper empire), which gross more than $100 million annually. Among its fashion holdings, Condé Nast lists *Vogue, Glamour, Mademoiselle,* and *Gentlemen's Quarterly* in the U.S.; British, French, and Italian editions of *Vogue;* and Italy's most influential men's magazine, *L'Uomo Vogue.* Based in its own building at 350 Madison Avenue in New York, the company has enjoyed a long and illustrious history. Founded by publisher Condé Nast, the corporation came into its own in 1909 with the purchase of *Vogue,* then a struggling twenty-four-page weekly. Nast upgraded the magazine by changing from cheap, uncoated pulp paper to a glossy coated stock and by emphasizing a strong identification between fashion and the arts. From 1913 to 1935 Nast also published *Vanity Fair,* which eventually merged with *Vogue.* (In its heyday, *Vanity Fair* boasted a staff of gifted editorial assistants and contributors, including Robert Benchley, P. G. Wodehouse, Dorothy Parker, and Robert Sherwood.)

With the purchase of old-line publishers Street and Smith in 1959, Condé Nast added *Mademoiselle* to its stable of fashion publications. This magazine, launched in 1935 by Street and Smith, has always been identified with younger women. To its credit, *Mademoiselle* has published some excellent fiction and has encouraged young writers (among them Truman Capote and Joyce Carol Oates, who were first published in its pages).

A recent Condé Nast publicity piece reveals the seriousness with which the publisher takes its magazines: *"Vogue* reports trend-setting fashions, beauty news, views on art, the theatre, decorating and entertaining. It also publishes photographs of women internationally known for taste and beauty. *Vogue* is a quality magazine, edited for and read by women who are the recognized leaders of their communities. These *Vogue* families influence thousands of others so that *Vogue*'s influence reaches far beyond the subscribers and the people who buy it on the newsstands.

"*Mademoiselle*'s overall point of view presents its discriminating readers with the best of the news in every field from fashion and beauty to home decorating, food, travel, entertaining, careers, books, movies, and health."

But at least this observer believes that the Condé Nast publications are now trading on past glories. Whatever fine qualities the magazines once featured have been stripped away by modern managers who are far more concerned with advertising revenues than with quality art work or high literary standards. The Condé Nast magazines, much like the other fashion books, are advertising vehicles slapped together with a minimal investment of time, talent, and money.

Condé Nast's editorial director Alexander Liberman admits what most publishers and editors will not: "It's a mistake to consider fashion journalism an art. True art doesn't belong in this medium anymore. I say this to my friends, to writers and photographers: 'Do what I do in my life! Do what is necessary. Take the pictures, write the articles I need for my magazine, and then use the money you make for your private, creative purposes. Don't put your deepest soul into this kind of work.' "*

A Condé Nast power for nearly forty years, Liberman was responsible for *Vogue*'s association with some of the nation's most respected photographers, including Irving Penn and Richard Avedon. He also supported the work of famed *Vogue* editor Diana Vreeland, who gave the magazine an elegant, dreamlike appearance during her reign from 1963 to 1971. It was only when the magazine fell on hard times, suffering a decline in

---

*Marie Winn, "Liberman: Staying in Vogue," *New York Times Magazine*, May 13, 1979.

advertising revenues, that Liberman hired current editor Grace Mirabella and supervised the shift from a class book to what some now consider a work of popular trash. The accent on great photography and on superb graphics has given way to an editorial approach that is more concerned with pleasing the lowest common denominator than with assuming a position of leadership. Indicative of this is the fact that *Vogue*'s and all other Condé Nast covers must now get final approval from circulation executives—not the art director. That is because newsstand sales are crucial to the magazines' appeal to advertisers.

The change in the Condé Nast magazines—especially *Vogue*, which has suffered the greatest decline in terms of artistic standards—has, however, had a positive effect on the company's finances. In the past five years, big monthly circulation gains have been registered by *Vogue* (from 580,000 to 1,000,000), *Glamour* (1.7 to 1.9 million), and *Mademoiselle* (850,000 to 1 million). Liberman says he has accomplished this by replacing "the visions of loveliness" with "the excitement of the streets." Others think differently. Says Irving Penn, "There was once a possibility that one's work at *Vogue* could be an artistic fulfillment, but *Vogue* has changed. It has a different public. Nowadays my best work doesn't get into the magazine."*

Most people at Condé Nast are tight-lipped about all of this. The company's policies of dealing with the press are firmly rooted in the nineteenth century. Secrecy is the byword: from the lowliest assistants to the top editors, there is an apparent effort to avoid "serious" reporters. Grace Mirabella, for example, refused to acknowledge nine requests by this author (three written and six by telephone) for an interview; her rejections were funneled through various assistants. Condé Nast's managing officers do not want journalists probing around, asking questions, or filing firsthand accounts of the company's operations. Although contacts with fashion, gossip, society, and women's page reporters are carefully cultivated, there seems

---

*Marie Winn, "Liberman: Staying in Vogue," *New York Times Magazine*, May 13, 1979.

to be an aversion to hard news journalists—those interested in more than fluffy chitchat about who wore what to Bill Blass's cocktail party. In a tactic that is considered archaic for any business—especially one involved in communications and owned by a newspaper enterprise—Condé Nast asks that questions for interviews be submitted in writing, in advance, and holds that they will be answered the same way. This procedure is of course completely unacceptable to responsible journalists.

Why this fear of direct contact with the press, this reluctance to speak openly and candidly about their work? For one thing, fashion magazines are in the image business. They sell the illusions of glamour, elegance, youth, beauty, excitement. Their message is that life is fun-in-the-sun, drinks-at-the-ski-lodge, dancing-at-the-disco, lucky-at-love-and-successful-at-the-office. Everyone looks wonderful in clothes. Everyone is beautiful. Everything has a happy ending. In both their editorial layouts and their advertising the fashion mags portray a world in which models are always smiling, honored to be chosen by editors to adorn their books. This image is essential to the magazines' survival. It is what keeps the young women of America gobbling up issue after issue and it is what keeps the advertisers shelling out ever-greater sums to share in the action.

But the image is bubble-thin. It is an illusion that survives because it is carefully nurtured, protected, and secured. That is why anyone who may probe into the reasons why models gripe about the magazines, who may reveal the industry's miserly pay scales, and who may report on the editors' declining power is viewed as a threat to the corporate honchos. Here the fashion magazines are no different from the rest of the fashion world. Trendy department stores, big-time model agents, top clothing designers, and giant cosmetics firms do everything possible to manage the news—to keep it upbeat and positive. Another reason for all the secrecy surrounding the fashion world is that so many of the characters in it take themselves and their work too seriously. Often it is the underlings who are the most pretentious. They equate their refusal to discuss the hype of a new toilet water with a diplomat's silence on sensitive political issues. It is as if divulging secret information on the "Charlie" girl would ignite World War III. Nowhere is this self-aggrandizing attitude more evident than at the fashion magazines. Star models and top designers agree that the magazines exaggerate their importance in the order of things.

Harry Coulianos, the talented art director of *Gentlemen's Quarterly*, admits: "The business takes itself too seriously. Fashion is not that serious. There's more to life than fashion."

Coulianos is well respected throughout the industry. He gets high marks from models, agents, and clothing designers, all of whom label him a talented innovator. A graduate of New York's Pratt Institute, Coulianos was appointed *GQ*'s art director in 1970 and has been largely responsible for maintaining the magazine's high standard of quality ever since. *GQ*'s pictorials are inventive and eye-catching, reflecting Coulianos's personal philosophy that readers should look to fashion magazines for enjoyable, escapist entertainment rather than for ironclad statements on how they must dress. There are those in the business who believe that *GQ*'s acquisition by Condé Nast in 1979 will lead to a gradual cheapening of the magazine, but Coulianos insists that he has seen no sign of this yet. Meanwhile, many male models still consider it a real plus to be selected for a *GQ* feature.

"I love it," says Paul Palermo, a successful Elite model who has branched out into television commercial work (for Gimbel's) and acting (Off Broadway). "I'm a model who takes risks. Let's say a photographer is stuck; he can't decide what to do. So I'll bend down and tie my shoes. He'll say great. With magazines you can be liberal and creative. There is no selling involved . In editorial, you sell a look, a concept, or an energy. I was named in *GQ* special issue as one of the top male models of the seventies. I did my first *GQ* cover in Paris. When I came back here, people already knew me. People see you on the cover and ask what agency he's with. It gives you great publicity."

GQ is atypical of fashion magazines in many ways. It has a virtual monopoly on its end of the business (male fashion), but has kept its standards high; it is respected by models and agents alike; and its art director (whose responsibilities include the selection of models for the magazines) works hard to retain a cordial, friendly working environment.

"*GQ* is a warm place, almost like a family," Palermo adds. "No one does a number on you there. You're treated with respect and that makes it easier to perform well—to do your best work. Coulianos is great that way."

"It takes just as much energy to be nasty as to be nice," Coulianos says. "I'd rather be the latter. I like models as people and as professionals, so why should I treat them poorly?"

Coulianos is also different from many of his colleagues in that he does not tour the party circuit. The fashion industry is addicted to parties. The showing of a designer's collection, the announcement of an award, the opening of a new office is bound to be feted at an Orsini's luncheon, a late night bash at Xenon, or a cocktail party at Bloomingdale's. Fashion editors are expected to attend these affairs, ostensibly to keep up with current activities, to spot new trends, and to discover new talent. Most, however, go simply to be seen and to rub elbows with the real stars of the industry. Just how important the parties are to an editor's work is a matter of opinion.

"This is very much a social business," says one editor. "At parties you get some of the inside information that you don't get anywhere else. You have to attend your share of parties in order to keep abreast of things. You can't devote your life to the parties by any means, but you do have to put them in perspective and go to those that you believe will be valuable from a professional standpoint."

Another editor thinks differently: "It's absurd to say, as many people do, that partying is a prerequisite for success in this business. The trouble with parties is that they invariably interfere with your work. If I have a choice between paying close attention to the quality of color separations or going to a big luncheon in so-and-so's honor, I'll stay in my office and work. I avoid almost all business luncheons. I prefer to spend half an hour walking along Fifth Avenue, watching New Yorkers go by and soaking up the energy of the city. I find that to be far more valuable than sipping cocktails with the same crowd day after day. I don't think partying has much to do with a magazine's success in life."

Just what is a fashion magazine's "mission?" What are its objectives? What goes on behind the scenes? What impact do the magazines actually have on modeling, fashion, and lifestyles?

First and foremost, the magazines are the vehicles of Seventh Avenue, the publicity organs for the nation's apparel industry. Although the publishers deny this—or try to couch the truth in more subtle terms—it is clear that the fashion magazines, especially the women's books, are in business to sell the products of their advertisers. And this extends beyond the confines of paid advertising space; all of the top magazines devote a major share of their editorial coverage to promoting the suits, sweaters, and scents of the companies and designers that buy the paid space. At times there is said to be an actual deal made with the space salesmen—something like one editorial page for every five ad pages. More often, however, the obligation is an unwritten one: editors know without being told that they must cater to advertisers, that advertising is the magazines' bread and butter, and that officers of the corporation view it as far more important than editorial independence or any such lofty ideals.

Notes one editor, "We all try to please our advertisers, especially the big cosmetics companies. If we leave someone important out of a feature, or forget to cover them for some time, we'll get a call from the advertising director reminding us of what to do. Sometimes a minor or emerging designer who might not warrant coverage on the merits of his work alone gets featured because he is an advertiser. The advertising department will ask us to give him some play and we usually do. After all, advertisers pay the bills."

The magazines like to say that they are in business to identify and popularize fashion trends—to isolate what the editors believe are exciting and tasteful innovations in apparel, cosmetics, and hair design and to bring them to the attention of readers. But with the constant efforts to satisfy advertisers, and the resulting commercial pressures on editors, this role gets distorted. The editorial features, which may cover anything from the new look on college campuses to a preview of ski apparel, are often advertising sections in disguise (some call them "advertorials"). The skirts, shirts, ski caps, parkas, gloves, and boots highlighted ostensibly for their design qualities are often featured due to commercial considerations relating to the magazine's sale of advertising space.

Magazines also arrange most of their location shooting on a tie-in basis, with advertisers uppermost in their minds. Typically, a deal is made with the tourist board of a tropical island or a resort to get free food and accommodations for staffers in return for publicity. If a shooting is done at a hotel in the Bahamas, for example, the island will be touted as an ideal vacation spot and the hotel will be pictured as the ultimate in luxury accommodations. There is no mention that the hype is a form of payment by the magazine for the hotel's hospitality.

"I worked for an advertising agency when I graduated college—I was a media buyer—and it was there that I learned of the connection between the magazines' editorials and their advertising," says business writer Carol Bloom. "It really perturbed me. Throughout my teenage years, when I took the magazines to heart and believed that their recommendations were based on high standards of beauty and fashion, I was being misled. The most deceptive advertising is that which is presented as editorial. It should be labeled for what it is."

The apparel manufacturers feel differently. They applaud the magazines because they are influential with many readers, are widely circulated, and reach the kinds of consumers who spend lavishly on clothing and cosmetics. "The magazines are important because they provide a showcase for new designers, new looks, new concepts," says designer Ralph Lauren. "They are important because everyone reads them—consumers, store buyers, and manufacturers. You have to understand that fashion is a process of change. A forum is needed to bring that change to the attention of the public and to the fashion industry itself. The magazines do that."

This is in fact the prime function of the fashion books: to

generate, exploit, and popularize change. The advertising and the editorials work together to help designers establish a new look—to push out yesterday's fashions and make room for today's. The system has little to do with aesthetics. It functions almost exclusively to keep consumers buying, to assure a ready and waiting market for the millions of articles of clothing that come streaming out of the factory buildings in New York's garment center.

"We make fine quality sweaters that sell for more than $100," says a Seventh Avenue manufacturer who is licensed to produce designer apparel. "Some of the goods we sell could last twenty years. If we kept churning out the same style over and over again, year after year, our sales would drop precipitously. If the garment is in great shape and the styles don't change, why would our customers buy new clothes? They wouldn't.

"But, we're not dummies. We keep the shit moving, the people working, and the salesmen happy by changing styles every season—sometimes twice in a season. . . . We've gone from crew neck to boat neck to V necks to shawl collars to bulkies to tight-fitting to earth tones to pastels to iridescent to you name it. These designers know exactly what to do to generate demand.

"When the designers come up with a new look, we work with the magazines to present it to the public. The magazines do a great job at this. They know exactly how to feature a new style so that it makes everything that came before it look dated. No, let me go further than that: they make everything that came before it look silly and ridiculous. Just months after the designers stopped making cowl-neck sweaters and the magazines stopped featuring them, the same women who once loved the look wouldn't be caught dead in it. That's what keeps us in business."

A crucial factor in the selling of a new look is the use of attractive models photographed in exotic locales. A striking, long-haired beauty pictured rosy-cheeked and schussing down an Alpine run can do wonderful things for a Head ski outfit. And an elegant brunette bathed in the colorful glow of a Jamaican dusk can heighten the drama of a Halston evening gown.

Matching up products with the right models and the right locations is the major responsibility of fashion editors. Their job is to orchestrate all the elements of a shooting to make sure that everyone is on the job and ready to work at the scheduled time. This requires selecting a photographer, choosing a model, deciding on a locale, and getting permission to shoot there. The editor must use his or her skills, instincts, and experience to make the selections that will produce the best photographs and that will, in turn, present the featured products in the most attractive way. The job is definitely not glamorous; it can be difficult and demanding, and the responsible editor deserves full credit when a feature or pictorial comes out well.

"My job is to present new fashion ideas to our readers," explains a *Harper's Bazaar* staffer, "and to do it as attractively and dramatically as possible. The whole process starts three or four months before the issue is published. I'm always in touch with designers, cosmetics executives, and our own advertising department, and that's how I pick up on what to feature in the magazine. For example, I attended the first showing of Ralph Lauren's Western look. I liked what I saw and I took samples from the show. My next stop was a photographer's studio. I made arrangements to get a model and we held the shooting a few days later. I acted quickly because I wanted to feature the Western look before the other magazines went to press. As it happened, we came out with the collection before anyone else. There's a lot of competition to scoop the other fashion magazines because the more firsts you have to your credit, the more readers think of you as the best in the business —the leaders. You want to get known as an authoritative source.

"The Ralph Lauren shooting came out exceptionally well. The model looked great and so did the clothes. That's what we're in business to do. We enhanced the reputation of the magazine and we pleased an important designer. Everyone involved in the project added something special to it. That represents another part of my job: getting people to work together harmoniously."

Cathy Spellman comments: "There is a business behind the business, and that is the business of selling fashions. All the cosmetics and apparel makers are into marketing strategies these days. They're involved in the mechanics of product positioning. This means that they are no longer simply developing products, putting them up for sale, crossing their fingers, and hoping they'll be well received. Through positioning, they stake out a particular market in advance and then come up with a promotional strategy that will appeal to the market. Models are crucial to this process because they can be so effective in establishing the right image to make the product highly attractive. When fashion editors do their job well, they can set the stage for a product's positioning. They can really aid the marketing process. That's what sells goods and that's what we're all in business for."

The fashion magazines devour models. In their editorial sections alone, they can use up to fifty models in a single issue. Every suntan oil, eye shadow, lipstick, bikini, shawl, scarf, shoe, skirt, and slip needs a model to present it. Without models, the fashion magazines could not exist; without the magazines, fashion models would find their professional opportunities greatly diminished. The magazines are important to modeling because they provide so much employment and because they can publicize models widely.

One of the best examples of the magazines as star makers can be found in the story of Beverly Johnson. A leading black model ever since she broke into the business in 1970, Johnson has been a darling of the magazines throughout her career. Editors searching for an acceptable black woman to feature in their white-dominated publications found that Beverly fit the bill perfectly.

As a scholarship student and an athlete at Boston's Northeastern University, Johnson dreamed of modeling. But when she summoned up the courage to make the rounds at New York's top agencies, she found no takers. "They told me I was too fat, too thin, too tall, too short, too this or too that. When I went to see Eileen Ford, she said to come back when I lost ten pounds."

Undaunted, Johnson turned directly to the magazines, showing up at cattle calls and at any other interviews she could get. Her breakthrough came in 1971 when *Glamour* editors, who found her sitting in a waiting room, loved what they saw and gave her an eight-page spread in their magazine. With her *Glamour* tearsheets in tow, the young black girl found that she was suddenly in demand as a hot model.

Now that she was getting so much attention, the agents were out to recruit her. According to Beverly, Eileen Ford called and asked if she'd like to affiliate with her agency. Thinking she was the best in the business at the time, Johnson agreed. (She later moved to Casablancas's agency.) "Eileen's first words this time were 'You've lost so much weight.' But I hadn't lost an ounce."

Under Ford's tutelage, Johnson's star shone even brighter. Her earnings climbed steadily, reaching about $200,000 a year. She did more than a dozen *Glamour* covers, and in 1975 she became the first black woman to appear on the cover of *Vogue*. *

"The reason I've done fifteen *Glamour* covers is not because I'm pretty, but because I sell magazines," Johnson notes. "I've gotten new third-world girls to read the book."

Johnson, who has studied acting for seven years, is determined to establish a successful career in show business. She took a big step in that direction with her starring role in the 1979 film *Ashante*, a second-rate kidnapping drama that boasted an impressive cast including Michael Caine and Peter Ustinov. Beverly has also released her first record album, titled "Beverly Johnson."

"I always knew that it was important to establish myself as a personality and as a celebrity as well as model. Only then can you break into show business and keep your career going indefinitely. Here, the magazines are crucial. They can keep you in the spotlight, give you prestige, and make you a household name."

The knowledge that the magazines can be so influential in shaping careers makes them very much sought after by young models. Every beginner dreams of a big spread, or best

---

*"My breakthrough at the magazines can't hide the fact that blacks are still second-class citizens in this business," says Johnson. "We are major consumers of so many products, but we are not allowed to be the model for many of them."

of all a cover for the likes of *Vogue, Glamour,* or *Harper's Bazaar.* For a crack at this, they are willing to wait for hours at the cattle calls, hoping desperately to be selected from among the hundred others waiting anxiously for the same chance.

Fashion magazine editors boast that they know everything there is to know about selecting models. They fancy themselves as experts on what it takes to be a great model, how to spot hidden talent, how to pick the ideal model to wear a featured garment. Editors like to speak of the selection process as scientific, with established principles, concepts, and theories. But when asked to be specific, they cannot point to hard-and-fast rules for model selection. That is not surprising. The truth is that model selection at the magazines is a subjective process based on each editor's personal tastes and preferences. A girl who is rejected by one editor for looking too plain to appear in an evening gown may be viewed as perfect for the job by another editor at the same magazine. Models and agents know this; only the editors themselves deny it.

Whether the selection process is as simple as eenie, meenie, minie, moe, or if it takes, as the editors claim, a sixth sense, is not important. What really counts is that the editors have the authority to select, hire, showcase, and publicize so many models. This is their source of real power—and they milk it for all it's worth.

"The women's books can be quite mean," says a *GQ* staffer who asked to remain anonymous. "They love to manipulate the models, really wring them dry, physically and emotionally. Many times, for example, they audition a newcomer and select her for a shooting. The kid thinks it's the break of her life; she's on cloud ten and a half. She does the shooting marvelously. She works her cute little ass off, giving and giving and giving to that camera with all that she has. Everything inside that girl gets poured out into this one chance to make it in modeling, to get a head start.

"Well, what happens all too often is that the witches at the magazines decide that because they don't like the girl or because they don't need a redhead after all, they won't use her pictures. They never tell her. No, they just put the shots in the circular file and wait for the model to find out on her own that all that work she did and all of her great expectations are to no avail. It's a crashing disappointment to the kid, but the editors are totally unconcerned. Some of them secretly like it. They're so fucking brazen, so hard. It's the old chip on the shoulder syndrome."

Privately, some of the editors do admit that their mistreatment of models can backfire. With today's breed of strong and aggressive agents behind them, the girls have become tougher and more financially astute in their own right. The beginners still have to take what the magazines dish out because they are in no position to quibble, but the established faces keep their options open. They know that the magazines need top stars and that if one editor is hostile or nasty the others are more than likely to roll out the welcome mat.

When it comes to relations with the magazines, the established models now recognize that although the publicity showcase is important, they don't have to appear in every issue to get coverage. An occasional cover and a smattering of pictorials is enough to keep a face in the limelight. Thanks to intensive tutoring by agents, the girls know that they must parcel out their time for maximum profit. Every cheapie magazine booking means a loss of up to $600 to $2,000 a day, depending on the model's going rate for noneditorial work.

"The top girls are much wiser now about their finances," says one editor, "and that means we have a harder time getting them to work for us. That makes our lives a lot tougher. If I have a star model in mind that I think will be perfect for a shoot, I know I can get her only if nothing else is scheduled. Sometimes they even agree to work with me but then back out if a better booking comes along. You really can't blame them."

Adds Eileen Ford, "The magazines are important to us and we maintain close relationships with them. But still, I want my girls to earn as much as they possibly can. It's in their own interest to do so. That's why I balance editorial requests with the other bookings that come in. You can't make good money doing nothing but editorials."

The relationship between the magazines and the Big Four is strained and grows increasingly tense. It is a classic love/-hate affair. Agents recognize the important role the magazines play in publicizing new talent, but they complain endlessly about the low fees. Rarely, except when they are talking press-release style, do they have anything nice to say about the magazines. Fashion editors, for their part, rail against the Big Four for their poor service, understaffing, jammed telephone lines. They resent the fact that they are forced to compete with commercial clients for the models' time and that they are often on the losing end.

One word that crops up constantly when the talk turns to agent/editor relations is "credibility." Top agents know that the best way to stay in favor with the magazines is to send over only those girls with real potential. By limiting their introductions to worthy contenders, the agents maintain credibility with editors and are thus assured of getting a fair shake whenever a new face is sent by for inspection.

"The agents know what I like and they try to give me that," GQ's Coulianos explains. "They know it would be counterproductive to waste my time with mediocre models. If an agent was indiscriminate and sent me everyone on his headsheet, I'd probably turn off to that agency and would not give their models a close look. Fortunately, I haven't had that problem. Although I don't accept everyone who comes in here, most are legitimate candidates."

━ The relationship between the modeling industry and *Cosmopolitan* magazine is in a class by itself. That's because *Cosmo* has one foot in the fashion magazine business and one foot out. The range of *Cosmo* stories covers familiar turf, from "How to Improve Your Complexion" to "How to Spruce Up Your Wardrobe." The magazine runs features on love, fashion, travel, food, and all the other topics found in most fashion magazines. Where *Cosmo* differs from them, however, is in its willingness to be sexy, to talk about masturbation as well as mascara. The *Cosmo* girl is different from the *Glamour* gal in that she's a bit kinkier—she's more into men than fashion shows, she's a bit of an exhibitionist, she has an active libido and is not ashamed to admit it. The selection of cover girls alone reveals the striking difference between *Cosmo*'s editorial thrust and that of the more traditional fashion magazines. At *Cosmo,* the old-fashioned milk-fed cover girl has been replaced by a vivacious and alluring woman who flaunts her sex appeal and whose cleavage is more prominent than her cheekbones.

"You can get off on the *Cosmo* girl—she has sex appeal," says a photographer who has worked for three of the leading fashion magazines. "The other, more standard cover girls are plastic, lifeless creatures who appeal to the editors' dated notion of virginal beauty. You know, the cotillion ball type. Men can't relate to that; nor can many of today's women. There's no reason why fashionable females should have to hide their sex appeal. I know that some of the tight-asses at *Vogue* don't believe it, but you can look good in clothes and still enjoy a little sex now and then. It is possible. Please tell them it is."

As popular as *Cosmo* is with millions of men and women, it is not in good favor with the modeling establishment. Its revealing photographs and spicy stories have made it the *enfant terrible* of women's magazines. Some top agents are wary of *Cosmo* for fear that its racy image will rub off on their models and make them unacceptable to conservative advertisers. So they keep their distance in spite of the fact that *Cosmo* pays models only $10 less than full commercial rates (that's about five times more than they get at *Vogue, Glamour,* or *Bazaar*).

How do the models themselves feel about *Cosmo?* "The girls love to do our covers because it adds another dimension to their books," says a *Cosmo* editor. "With our tearsheets, they can show how sexy they can be. . . . Sometimes we cannot get a girl to work with us because the agent refuses to let her or because he has convinced her that a *Cosmo* appearance would be disastrous. . . . The truth is, however, that we are not all that sexy. We never show pubic hair; we just give the illusion of sex. We do show breast, but if an agent or a model stipulates that the girl's nipples must not be revealed, we'll honor that. We often get these restrictions written right on the model's vouchers—how much breast, how much ass, how much leg can be shown.

"The only time the girls themselves are hesitant to work with us is if they are flat-chested. Some of the models think that in order to work with *Cosmo* you have to have big boobs. One top model, for example, won't work with us because one of our top photographers told her she's too flat for our look. Well, that's not true. Boobs are the stars of our covers, but here again it's the illusion that counts. A lot of the girls we've featured have small tits. We make them look bigger by pushing the breasts up in the blouse and running tape across the bottom. This makes their tits stand up and out and gives the girl a much deeper cleavage."

Cosmo's art director Linda Cox adds an ironic note about the magazine's relationship with the agencies: "To tell you the truth, their fears of ruining the girls' images are completely unfounded. The same cosmetics companies that the agents are afraid of losing often call us to ask for the name of a *Cosmo* girl so that they can use her in their advertisements."

It was a *Cosmo* cover, in fact, that helped propel Christina Ferrare into the big leagues. Her agent, Eileen Ford, arranged a meeting with Scavullo when Ferrare was still an unknown quantity in the business. At the time she was kicking around New York and Los Angeles, contemplating dropping out of modeling completely. The date with Scavullo changed that. A successful shooting led to the cover of *Cosmo* and then the first of many *Vogue* covers. "Before long," Ferrare recalls, "I had a major contract with Max Factor guaranteeing me a hefty income from cosmetics alone. I did fourteen print ads and eight television commercials for them."

Yet despite such positive evidence of its influence, *Cosmo* remains the black sheep of the fashion magazines. As Linda Cox sums it up: "The agents are scared. Some of them simply have a closed mind when it comes to *Cosmo*. They think we're just too hot to touch. I'm convinced that they sit around worrying that one of their darling little girls will wind up in our magazine smack in the middle of an article on 'Sixteen Ways to a Better Orgasm' or 'My Life as a Prostitute.' "

8

NUDE MODELING
From Playmate
to the Girl Next Door

"A lot of men envy my job, and I must say it does have
some unique fringe benefits. It's not unusual for beautiful
young women to come into my office and offer to open their
blouses and show me their breasts. All I have to do is nod and
the pants would come down too. My problem is getting women
to keep their clothes on."
—the editor and publisher of a leading men's magazine

Another potentially lucrative market agencies prefer to tiptoe
around is the one that trades in nude models. A highly visible
part of the modeling scene, nude modeling is also highly controversial. Yet, in spite of the excesses, and the deep-seated inferi-
ority complexes of many nude models, it is viewed as exciting
and appealing by a broad cross section of the public. Part of the
reason for this is that nude models seem more human than their
high fashion counterparts: they appear to be alive and real, and
they jump from the pages of the magazines with sexual impact.
Like expensive call girls, they are exotic figures who live outside the establishment. Even if many people don't respect nude
models, they still want to peer into their lives, to know and to
touch them.

Lingering taboos notwithstanding, nude modeling is on the
rise. The growing appetite for nudity is evidenced by the prolif-
eration of nude magazines on the newsstands (including *Play-
girl,* which features nude males), the boom in home videotape
porno films, the swelling ranks of men and women vying for
nude modeling jobs, and the increasing displays of nudity in
such public places as beaches and discos. What's more, even the

major commercial advertisers are now using the illusion of nudity in ever more daring poses, including unclothed models carefully turned from the camera to reveal tantalizing profiles and hints of flesh. Products and services have always been sold on the basis of sex appeal; today, however, the sex is becoming more blatant and more explicit.

"Fragrance advertising makes considerable use of nude models," says Cathy Spellman. "There's often no better way to communicate the image of raw sex appeal than to have a beautiful woman photographed in dark, sensuous shadows, wearing nothing but her favorite perfume. The impact is powerful and immediate. If the product's positioning calls for this kind of image, the use of nude visuals can be more effective than 10,000 words of copy. People are excited, and motivated, by properly photographed presentations of nudity."

Playboy's associate photo editor, Janice Moses, who has been working with nude models for more than sixteen years, says: "Our Playmates are in great demand by advertisers for everything from musk oils to furs. They want the girls to do tasteful nude ads, featuring their silhouettes and similar sensuous presentations. This part of our business which services advertisers has been growing very rapidly and it keeps Playmates busy for months after their actual centerfold is published. Advertisers call us and we help to set them up with the appropriate girls. This kind of work for commercial products is one of the few kinds of nude modeling Playmates are allowed to do for the first year after their centerfold appearance. That's stipulated in their contracts with us."

However, the great majority of nude models have nothing at all to do with commercial advertising. Most appear only in erotic or out-and-out porno magazines. They are hired on the basis of their raw sex appeal, for how strongly they can turn people on. It is their breasts, legs, and derrieres—not their silhouettes, cheekbones, or hair—that are the star attractions. To some they are objects of great natural beauty; to others they are cheap sluts, sex objects in a world that caters to the prurient.

Whatever the truth, the fact is that tens of thousands of

women are now knocking down doors for the chance to strip to the nude and to reveal themselves to the world. The desire to become a nude model is widespread and apparently knows no social or economic barriers: housewives, college girls, teenagers, grandmothers, rich, poor, professional and clerical women are among the growing ranks of applicants competing against one another for the opportunity to be photographed in the raw. "We featured a fifty-three-year-old, dynamite-looking grandmother as the centerfold in one of our issues and the response was overwhelming," says Nils Shapiro, editor and publisher of *Gallery* magazine. "We heard great things from our readers, who thought she was sexy as all hell, and we also got tons of requests from other mature women who wanted to be nude models."

The backlog of unsolicited nude pictures is so great at *Playboy* magazine that candidates must wait more than two months for a decision on their entries.* And when the magazine advertised for Playmate candidates at some of the nation's leading universities, staff photographers were inundated by applications from hundreds of Ivy League coeds. Future geologists, lawyers, physicians, and bankers waited on line for hours for the opportunity to strip down to the buff before *Playboy* photographers.

"Being a sex object—a nude model—is a powerful fantasy that lies just below the surface of most women's consciousness," says one New York psychiatrist who prefers to remain anonymous for fear his opinions will antagonize female patients. "To many, it's a very appealing fantasy, but one they can't act on unless there is an illusion of legitimacy, of respectability. Doing it for *Playboy* gives them just that. It's a prestige magazine, known for its top writers and presidential interviews as well as for its cheesecake. So while a woman may have a secret desire to strip nude and be admired by the men in her office, she needs the excuse of doing it for *Playboy* to bring the fantasy to consciousness and to get her to act on it."

*It's alleged that not all the pictures get there. Many photos sent to *Playboy* without a registered mail return receipt are thought to be stolen.

With the market for nude models expanding rapidly, why are the fashion model agencies off to the sidelines, reluctant to share in the action? The answer goes to the very heart of the nude modeling business—to the reasons why it is considered a separate and distinct part of the modeling industry. Primarily, nude modeling is still viewed as essentially dirty in many quarters. To millions of conservative and religious people, it is a lewd and blasphemous activity that caters to perverse interests. Even those who are outspoken proponents of a free press, free sex, and the body beautiful are often embarrassed by it. No one understands this better than Hugh Hefner, *Playboy*'s founder and a man who has made millions selling nudity. By surrounding his magazine's erotic photography with thought-provoking articles and quality fiction, he made it possible for "respectable" people to purchase *Playboy* while claiming interest in its literary value alone. Many other major men's magazines have adopted the Hefner formula, finding that by positioning themselves as purveyors of "artistic sex," by appealing to more than libidinal instincts, they could overcome social taboos and achieve sustained financial success.

The fact is, however, that nude modeling, in spite of its large following, remains a controversial activity, a sensitive issue and a business that for the most part operates somewhere between the commercial modeling establishment and the world of hard-core porn. In many cases, only a fine line separates legitimate nude modeling from outright smut. And to many people they are one and the same. This is precisely why the leading high fashion modeling agencies shy away from seeking a major interest in the field. Big-time modeling is geared not only to the relatively sophisticated New York community in which it makes its home, but to the more traditional middle-American markets elsewhere in the country. New York's Big Four rely for a substantial chunk of their billings on catalog work for the likes of Sears and Penney's. These straitlaced retailers want models who are as pure as homecoming queens. And so top fashion models, like politicians holding national office, must be careful not to offend those who control the purse strings.

"The fashion agencies lay down the law in no uncertain terms," says Derek Burton, *Gallery*'s design director and a man instrumental in the selection of hundreds of nude models. "Any of their girls found to be modeling nude for sex magazines are thrown out on their ears, no ifs, ands, or buts about it. It's considered an absolute breach of the rules. That's why there is such a small nude modeling community in New York. The girls and the photographers who do fashion work come to New York; the ones who do erotic stuff gravitate to the West Coast."

Not that the New York fashion agencies abstain completely. In our capitalist society, the most acceptable form of nude modeling is that which is directly related to selling a product or device. The growing use of nudity in superbly produced, tastefully designed advertisements for perfumes, suntan oils, resorts, and other luxury products has expanded the part of the nude market the agencies are willing to tap.

Agents flash the green light here for several reasons. One is that much of the impetus for this kind of nudity comes from renowned fashion photographers who have used it to weld a closer bond between art and advertising. What's more, although the model is frequently nude for an actual shooting, only the outline of her body or at most a blurred view of her breasts is seen in the final ad. Since the purpose of the nudity here is to sell products and not solely to provide sexual diversion, it is deemed acceptable by the agencies. Another reason they get involved in this aspect of nude modeling is that there is big money to be made here. When national advertisers are paying the bills, they are willing to spend top dollar to get the best models money can buy. And the agencies demand this. To get legitimate high fashion models to disrobe for even the most tasteful ads, clients must pay a premium over standard hourly rates.

To prove that they don't take nude modeling lightly, the agencies charge extraordinary fees (even by their lofty standards) when they are willing to provide girls for this service. This fee schedule from the Wilhelmina headsheet shows that modeling assignments with even the slightest sexual connotation command a premium; the more clothing the girl removes, the more the agency charges:

Nightgowns and peignoirs.......... $150 per hour
Slips.............................. $200 per hour
Bras, girdles, and pantyhose....... $250 per hour
Nude photography .... $500 per hour

Most nude magazines, on the other hand, are not as demanding or as particular as are national advertisers, and they are unwilling to come up with the high fees set by the big agencies. The vast majority of nude magazines prefer to get models through alternate means and to pay as little as possible for them. Because so many men and women are willing to pose nude—at any price—and because the nude magazines are less selective, it is easy for them to detour the agents and get freelance models to work on their terms. (This is another reason the big agencies largely avoid the nude magazine market: they refuse to compete for small potatoes and are determined not to venture where their power can be diluted and compromised.)

"We have nothing at all to do with the trashy nude scene, with the porno magazines and crap like that," says Bruce Cooper. "Representing centerfolds is not our business and I'm sure we'll never sink to that level. There's a sex business and a fashion business in this country and we're involved only in the latter. People often lump the two together because both employ attractive women, but they really have very little in common. Our girls have more class, poise, finesse, and beauty in their fingertips than centerfolds have in their whole bodies. High fashion models are trained professionals who must know about makeup, camera presence, acting, and dozens of other skills. Great fashion models don't rise to the top simply because they can give someone an erection. Wilhelmina, who was the greatest model that ever lived, never would have made it were she not highly intelligent as well as beautiful. Most centerfolds can't say that—they're just sex objects who never make much money and who never sustain long-term careers. The only nude assignments we'll handle is when one of our fashion models is hired for a legitimate and tasteful advertisement."

The high rates charged by the agencies for nude work are not the only departure they make from standard fashion modeling procedures. Agents take elaborate precautions to make certain that the shooting is legitimate, that the model is not abused, and that the photographer is not just looking for a way to get his rocks off playing around with a nude beauty. Their deep fear of a sex scandal makes the agents diligent in this regard. Before a girl's name even goes on the headsheet, she is questioned about her willingness to do "respectable" nude shootings. No bookings of this kind are made without the model's approval, and in spite of the big money to be made here, about 25 percent of the high fashion models flatly refuse to do nude ads; some even decline lingerie assignments as well. Any hint of exhibitionism flies in the face of their home-grown modesty and sense of virtue. Of the remaining 75 percent, less than half are ever called on to do nude work; the others simply do not project the image photographers and art directors want for nude assignments.

"Every big agency now has its share of 'womany' women," Cooper continues. "I mean the kind that's more bosomy, more rounded, and less like the classic ironing board that some models are said to look like. It's the well-endowed girls that are most in demand for nude work. Some will do it, some will not. In those cases where the model agrees, we as agents have to manage the shooting to protect the model physically, to protect her image, and to protect our reputation as well.

"Every request for a nude shooting is scrutinized closely. We check out the photographer's credentials and his reputation, determine precisely how the model will be asked to pose and, most important of all, how the photographs will be used. We make certain that the advertisement itself will be tasteful and that it will not use the model as a sex object. Also, it's the policy of this agency to insist that a female supervisor be on the set to assure proper handling of the model, and we demand that the set be closed to all but essential personnel. We'll never let one of our girls become the subject of a peep show."

How do the fashion models themselves feel about peeling off their clothes in front of strangers? About spending hours exposed to the camera and to one or more strangers? Do the taboos which prohibit sexual relations in routine fashion shootings collapse here? Are the temptations too great to resist?

"You find yourself going through a process of change," says a Big Four model from California. With her long legs, flowing black hair, dark skin, flashing eyes, and beautifully rounded breasts, she is a stunning woman. "I went from embarrassment to pride. I came to New York thinking that posing in the raw was wrong—you know, like a real sin or something. What would my mom think? My brothers? I worried about that. But then my booker had some requests for me to do nude ads and she tried to talk me into doing them. She almost convinced me to change my mind but, oh, I'm so mortified to say this, I would go home and practice getting undressed in front of the mirror. I'd take off each piece of clothing, one at a time, and would make believe the photographer was right there shooting me. Well, it would go all right until I had to remove my panties. I could rationalize showing my boobs, but my cunt seemed too private a thing to show to just anyone. Why, in high school I never even liked to have the lights on when I balled my boyfriends.

"But slowly, my mind changed. Don't ask me how or why —it just happened. The people at the agency put pressure on me because they said I was turning my back on good bookings, on big money. Also, they promised it would be very proper and everything—no monkey business. What finally tipped the scales and got me to do it was a major nude booking that paid more than $7,000 for one job. The money was too much to pass up. What's more, I was assured that although I'd be nude for the shooting, all that would appear in the ad was a side profile of my body and breasts.

"Anyway, it turned out to be fun—real fun. You know what, once I started peeling off my clothes, I relaxed. The photographer loved it, that was obvious, and I felt free, liberated, and more beautiful and feminine than ever before in my life. I've done it so many times since then that it's almost second nature now. The magic feeling is gone—I still do it for the money—but that first shooting has had one hell of a lasting effect in my life. I now live with the photographer, who, shall we say, initiated me into nude modeling. I love him more than I've ever loved anyone else in my life. I don't know if I'll ever get married, but if I do, it will be to him."

Insiders say that this kind of mating is common. The ban against sex between fashion models and photographers generally holds up, but there is a greater likelihood of romantic relationships developing in the intimate context of nude shootings.

"The girl often equates the nude modeling with sexual intercourse," says the New York psychiatrist previously quoted. "She is under the control of a man and she feels very vulnerable. He's turned on and she's turned on. Her clothes are off; he's touching her body—arranging her in different positions. All the elements of sex are there. When it's over, she often wants closeness with the man. She wants a personal involvement to legitimize the incident, to make it more than just a cold professional encounter. Above all, she doesn't want to feel like a prostitute. The man, if he's at all sensitive, senses this need in the woman and responds to it. He's been privy to something private, and he may feel special for it."

Adds a noted woman photographer: "The interaction between models and photographers can be very sensuous. You are physically close, looking into each other's eyes, playing up to one another. This is especially true with nude modeling. When there's a man and a woman involved, it's easy for both sides to be turned on and for romantic feelings to enter what is supposed to be a professional business relationship. That's why some girls want to do their nude work only with women photographers. They don't want to complicate their careers with emotional ties; they don't want to wind up falling in love with photographers."

The girls who do nude magazine work exclusively are far removed from the high fashion crowd, although some start out there. Often they are considered too short, too old, or too fat to satisfy fashion modeling's tough standards, and so they turn to nude magazines as a second choice. Others are simply compulsive exhibitionists who find every possible excuse to pose in the nude, be it in front of a camera or at home by an open window.

"I knew that I was an exhibitionist ever since I was eight years old," says nude model Suzi, who has appeared in more than eight men's magazines and in two porno films. "I got my early kicks showing my ass to my babysitter. I'd make believe I had a sore there and I'd pull down my pajamas and ask him to examine my boo-boo. Later, when I was about thirteen, a friend told me about a diet doctor her mother forced her to visit. She told me the guy was a dirty old man, that he made her get completely undressed, panties and all, just to be weighed, then he'd squeeze her tits for fifteen minutes to feel for fat cells. My girlfriend was disgusted, but little did she know that I was coming in my pants just hearing about it. I made an appointment, put on a real short skirt, and watched him drool when he looked me over in the waiting room. He had a great time taking my clothes off, he never knew that I enjoyed it even more. My doctor fad lasted for about a year; then I graduated to showing my pussy to the guys at school. My favorite thing was to go to the library, hide in the stacks, and then lift my skirt for some unsuspecting bookworms. I've always been excited about showing my body; it's the only thing that makes me come. Even when I'm making love, I think of exhibitionism rather than of the guy I'm with. To tell you the truth, I don't ever need men for sex. I'd much rather show my stuff, get worked up, and then go home and masturbate. I do nude modeling for a living, yes, but I'd do it just as much if they didn't give me a dime."

In a new twist, some husbands and boyfriends are persuading their mates these days to pose in the nude and then submitting their photographs to the sex magazines. Sometimes the women are willing participants; others play along in order to keep peace at home. In most cases, the men are amateur photographers who plan the poses and do the shootings. They're in it partly for the money—they hope the woman can become famous and make money as a nude model—but they do it mostly for the kicks. Interviews with such men reveal that a strong sexual impulse motivates their photography projects.

"Other men are always giving my wife Jackie the once-over," says Shane, who keeps two hundred full color nude photos of his spouse in an attaché case. "She's gorgeous—perfect ass, beautiful knockers, hairy cunt—as sexy as a woman can be. When other guys look, I don't blame them. No sir, I'm proud. One day I realized, shit, they're always looking up her dress when she sits down and trying to peek in her blouse and all. That turns them on plenty, but wouldn't it be something, I thought, if they could see the real McCoy—I mean the whole show. I got so hot thinking about it, I couldn't work. I didn't know how to go about doing what I wanted till I saw this magazine that had a contest for sending in pictures of your wife. Well, that was all I needed to see. I told Jackie I wanted to enter and after a little sweet talk, she agreed to do it.

"We did the shooting in a motel near the house. Let me tell you, I had the biggest erection of my life from the minute I woke up that morning. I posed Jackie just the way I knew other men dreamed about seeing her: with her legs wide open, her finger in her cunt, and standing on the bed with nothing on but a pair of high boots. After we were done, we fucked and fucked and fucked. I just couldn't get enough. She hasn't gotten into any magazines yet, but we'll keep trying different shots, different positions until she makes it as a nude model. I love it: it's made our sex life more exciting and it's a whole lot better way to spend time than going to the movies."

"A lot of men love to see their wives photographed in the raw," says *Gallery*'s Derek Burton. "The idea of being married to a nude model—even if she's only an amateur—really turns them on. It's erotic, it's kinky, and it's a matter of pride. They want to say to the world, 'Look, my woman has as good a body as anyone.' Don't think these people are weirdos or oddballs or anything. Most of the couples who send us pictures are from otherwise traditional backgrounds; they are insurance reps, real estate agents, teachers. The only difference is that they get turned on in offbeat ways."

Although the publishers of the nude magazines hem and haw when asked, most admit that some of the nude models they work with are also prostitutes. The fact is that top call girls are often ideally suited for nude modeling because they are attractive, erotic, and uninhibited.

"To be successful as a nude model, a woman must have no inhibitions about revealing her body," Nils Shapiro says.* "She must be able to take off her clothes in front of strangers without blinking an eye. As a matter of fact, she should be the kind of person who enjoys doing it. Any fear, embarrassment, or timidity will come across in the pictures and will have a negative effect. On the other hand, pride, joy, and aggressiveness add to the photography, making it more alive and exciting."

Why do some prostitutes, rejected fashion models, and would-be actresses turn to nude modeling? Partly for the money, but mostly for the hope it holds out of being discovered. In other words, for the same reason that motivates the would-be fashion model. Much of the appeal of modeling lies in the fact that it can provide broad exposure and the opportunity to go on to fame and wealth as an actress or stage performer. For those who cannot, for one reason or another, get public attention through the classier routes (fashion modeling, acting, singing), nude modeling often seems like the last chance. Many stunningly beautiful girls who can't act to save their lives and who walk away from scores of auditions without the smallest parts can still hope to make it to the silver screen via the sex connection—by appearing in the nudies and catching a producer's eye. The sex magazines do their best to keep this myth alive because it helps them to attract models and because it enhances their reputations.

Even industry leader *Playboy* is not above fostering this notion. In its twenty-fifth anniversary issue (January 1979), the magazine devoted a feature to famous women who allegedly won their first big break appearing on its famous pages:

- Marilyn Monroe. As Sweetheart of the Month, she helped make *Playboy*'s first issue a virtual sellout. MM became a generation's love goddess; said Clark Gable, her co-star in

*Before assuming the top spot at *Gallery*, Shapiro was associate publisher of *Penthouse* magazine.

The Misfits, which was the last film for both: "She made a man proud to be a man."

- Jayne Mansfield. Miss February 1955 was an unknown when we found her. *Playboy* . . . changed all that. Jayne starred in eleven films and six of our most popular pictorials.
- Mary and Madeline Collinson. Identical models from Malta, these spirited young ladies became our only twin playmates in October 1970. After that introduction, they moved right along into movies: e.g., *The Love Machine*.
- Claudia Jennings. Another Playmate of the Year, Claudia held the title in 1970 (after appearing as Miss November 1969). Since then she has become even better known as "Queen of the B movies." You saw her in the futuristic thriller *Deathsport*, opposite David Carradine, and *Fast Company*.
- Lillian Muller. An unforgettable blond, this Norwegian import was Miss August 1975, then Playmate of the Year for 1976. Not surprisingly, she caught the eye of directors: you may have seen her on TV ("The Night They Took Miss Beautiful").

"Our models really use us as a springboard," says *Playboy*'s Janice Moses. "They know we can do more than anyone else to launch them on fabulous careers. We have the readers and the prestige that can get them noticed in the right places. Many of the girls come in here with no experience or confidence and we whip them into shape, show them how to groom and dress, and how to parlay their natural assets into the career they've always dreamed about."

Nils Shapiro, who also promotes this myth, says, "Most of the best-looking models we use are found in California. That's no accident; they weren't all born there. L.A. is such a good source for models because so many of this country's best-looking girls go there to be stars. . . . When they find out that that won't happen—and they usually get the bad news in a matter of months—they need some other way to support themselves. So they become waitresses and secretaries. But they hate it. . . . So they look for some way out, some other route to the top, and they often find it. There's lots of photographers in L.A. looking for girls to do nude modeling. They can't promise them stardom, but they can promise a chance at the big time. And this is not just an idle promise. A number of film and television producers have called on us to help set up auditions for girls who have appeared nude in our magazine."

The claim that nude modeling is a training ground for grander things is nevertheless misleading—not because nude models never make it from centerfold to center stage, but because it happens so infrequently. The impression fostered by the magazines that this is commonplace is a gross exaggeration. For the most part, nude models,* as pawns of the nation's sex industry, ride a dead-end circuit that leads to nothing but abuse, disappointment, and depression. Most are poorly paid, sexually manipulated, and generally victimized by the powers that be—the smut editors, photographers, and assorted porno kings. Their careers are extremely brief and are at times more closely related to prostitution than to modeling.

— The strict code of behavior that forbids sexual favors in the high fashion world does not exist in nude modeling. Sex between model and photographer is common, and some nude models insist it is the only way they can get work. "There's no question about it, in this business, you either put up or shut up," says Vera, a twenty-six-year-old native Kentuckian who has appeared nude (under varying names and with varying hair colors) in more than ten sex magazines and has worked in the porno communities of New York, Chicago, and San Francisco. "The only difference between me and the prostitutes is that they make more money. The only way you can get some photographers to give you work as a nude model, and more important to get them to pay you for it, is to let them fuck you as often and as long as they want. I was at a shooting on Long Island last year. It was supposed to show nudity in Southampton Beach in the off season. Well, it turned out to be a gang bang and guess who entertained the gang? We arrived in Southampton at 9:30 one October morning. Nick, my photographer, thought it was too cold to go on the beach then. He suggested that we go to Silver's for some hot coffee and wait for the sun

---

*This does not apply to high fashion models who do some agency-approved commercial nude modeling.

to warm things up a bit. It turned out that we ran into two guys, neighbors of his from Manhattan, who almost choked on their coffee when Nick told them I was a nude model. Soon one of them took Nick aside for a whispering session and then Nick comes back at me that I have to put out for his buddies. I mean these were real creeps, 100 percent slobolas, but I needed the work so I gave them what they wanted. It's part of the game. When you have to kiss ass in this line of work you literally have to kiss ass. Say 'no' to a photographer and they'll just get someone else to take your place. All nude models are anonymous—we never get famous enough to pull a queen move. Try it and they'll throw you out the window. In most shootings I've been to, you spend more than half the time stroking the photographer. That's the way it is: you accept it or find a new line of work. It's too damn bad too because I'm gorgeous enough to be a fashion model, but I'm cursed with a slightly crooked nose. What a bummer.''

Just how are nude models selected? Why are they chosen over hundreds of other applicants? Who makes the decisions? The answers vary with the different sex magazines, which have their own standards and procedures. Still, one can get a general overview of the business by reviewing the model selection process at *Gallery*. This is a representative choice because, of the more than 150 sex magazines on the market, *Gallery*'s editorial style is at the midway point between the sophisticated eroticism of *Playboy* and the rank porno of *Hustler* and other lesser known smut books.

The first, and most common, selection method is the review of unsolicited photographs. Literally thousands of photographers around the world specialize in catering to the sex magazines. Free-lancers, they find their own models, plan and produce the photography themselves, and then submit the finished product directly to the publications or to a small group of photo agents who represent them. Much like free-lance magazine writers, photographers who work independently must know their market. What are the current fads? What are editors and publishers looking for? Are black models in? How about blacks and whites together? Should the models be classic beauties or are ethnic looks in vogue? What about fat girls, bald girls with tiny breasts? Should the scene be shot indoors or out? In the city or on a Caribbean island? Color film or black and white? Because the magazines differ in their tastes and standards, it is impossible to satisfy every publication with any single approach, but photographers try to determine, along broad lines, where the market is headed. Those who do not do their homework waste considerable time and money trying to peddle an unmarketable product. If they don't know what's in demand, they don't sell pictures and they don't get paid. In this line of business, it's easy to go broke. The most popular strategy, therefore, is to keep close tabs on a small group of magazines, to remain up-to-the-minute on their needs and requirements and to sell to them on a regular basis. This gives the photographer an "in" with a circle of editors who get to know him and who he hopes will get to like his work, thus greatly improving his chances of making a sale. Since few free-lancers gain 100 percent acceptance at their target publications —those considered by the photographer to be his best market —their work often makes the rounds at dozens of other publications in the "secondary" market. Here, the photos may circulate to up to fifty publications, most of which are new to the photographer. Although he is not entirely familiar with their needs or standards, the hope is that the bid will pay off, that someone will see the shots and want to use them.

Photographers who cater to the middle and lower ends of the men's magazine market work informally. They get together with models for a day or two of shooting at the beach, in a country setting, or, most frequently, at a local motel. There are no contracts, no weather-permitting clauses, no union guarantees. No one gets rich in the process, especially not the model: she will be paid only if and when the photos are sold. A single shooting will often yield up to 1,000 shots. The photos are then edited down to several hundred of the best shots—called "a set"—which are sent to the magazines for review. Experienced editors can determine, in a matter of minutes, if the set is at all appropriate for their publication. The vast majority of photos are rejected almost immediately; the more promising prospects are set aside for review by the publisher, key editors, and the art director. Rarely is the choice of a model a unilateral decision: more commonly it is the work of a committee or an editorial board. In the better publications—*Playboy*, *Penthouse*, *Oui*, and even *Gallery*—the selection is a careful, painstaking process, one considered crucial to the magazine's image and salability.

Just what makes one set superior to another is a function of the photographer's talent, the model's appearance, and the editor's personal aesthetics. A review of dozens of unsolicited sets reveals that many are very poorly produced and are instant rejects. They are marred by harsh lighting, fuzzy images, grainy reproduction, and sloppy composition. In one shot of a ravishing black woman wearing nothing but a flowing straw hat, the sexual image was damaged by the sight of an onlooker's foot accidentally included in the photograph. In another, a sandy-haired pixie was pictured with one enormous breast; the other was shielded by a strange dark shadow that crossed over her chest. In still more sets, some of the women were unkempt and dirty looking, with wrinkled skin, matted hair, and unsightly patches of gooey makeup. Many of these models—most of whom are amateurs photographed by amateurs—turn to sexual theatrics to gain attention: frankfurters up the ass, penises in the mouth, woman on woman. Usually, these attempts backfire: they are considered crass by all but the most vulgar porno rags. Rejecting the worst of the sets—the poorly produced and the grotesque—is the simplest part of the selection process. Much harder is sifting through the great bulk of photographs—about 75 percent of the total—that are submitted by capable free-lancers using attractive models. After an editor has spent several hours reviewing these quality submissions, one set seems to blend into the others: the women, the beach scenes, the garter belts—all appear to be identical. Choosing one over another is mostly a matter of personal taste or, even more likely, a matter of friendship with the photographer.

Exclusive shootings, considered real plums, are the second way sex magazines contract for nude models. In this case, photographers are hired on a project basis to shoot special spreads for upcoming issues. Let's say *Gallery* wants to do a big December issue featuring warm, sunny locations in Mexico or the Caribbean. Rather than gambling against the odds that a quality set of this type will come in over the transom, the editors hire a photographer they like and respect, one who has a good track record with the magazine and who does nice things with color film. He'll be told precisely where to shoot, how to shoot, and how much to shoot. Unlike unsolicited work, these photos are scheduled, in advance, for a guaranteed spread in the magazine. They must be technically good and they must fit a specific editorial theme.

With contract work, the photographer may be free to choose his own model, but it is quite common for him to be assigned the one selected by the magazine. In fact, these exclusive assignments are often ordered for the express purpose of highlighting what the editors believe to be an exciting new model—a "find" that may have been made accidentally when the publisher spotted a promising young woman in a restaurant, disco, or department store and invited her to audition. Since the pressure is always on to find and feature new faces, the magazine generally wants the model to sign a statement swearing she has never appeared nude before. (It appears, however, that many models lie about this.)

"I had one model in here recently who swore up and down that she was never in any other nude magazine," Shapiro says. "I questioned her hard because the face rang a bell, but no, she held fast that this was to be her first time. Then a month after she appeared in a *Gallery,* I was looking through a really trashy magazine—a vile competitor of ours—and found her in a cheap, explicit lesbian spread. I don't want models who do that kind of garbage to appear in our book, but what can I do after the fact? Nothing!"

Modeling for the vast majority of sex magazines (with the noticeable exception of *Oui, Penthouse,* and *Playboy*) is not a lucrative occupation. In most cases, the fee for the shooting is paid directly to the photographer, who in turn compensates the models (the way it used to be done in high fashion modeling before the new generation of aggressive agents put an end to the practice). Just how much the model gets depends for the most part on the photographer's sense of fair play or, more frequently, on his level of greed. For unsolicited spreads that do get published, the photographer will pull down between $800 and $2,000, depending on the quality of the photos and the number that are used. Exclusive assignments bring in more— between $2,000 and $3,000. In either case, the model may earn as little as $75 or as much as $300, but rarely more.

"Models are contributors to the magazines," says *Gallery*'s Shapiro, an experienced executive who claims to be eminently proud of his occupation. "Like writers, artists, and cartoonists, they simply provide the publication with a special service. They get paid less because we can get them for less. It's pure economics: if I could get a qualified art director for $10,000 a year rather than $50,000, then I'd do it; if I could get good writers for $200 rather than $2,000, I wouldn't hesitate. But nude models are the only ones who do come cheap, so they wind up getting paid the least. I'm a businessman, not a social worker. It's my job to get the best services at the least possible price and that's exactly what I do.

"Still, I must add that the nude models don't deserve any tears. There's no need to feel sorry for them. They do better than the millions of clerks working in so-called respectable offices all over the country. The nudes make in a day or two what a clerk makes in a week; they make it in cash and they have plenty of free time to take acting lessons, to go to theater auditions or to just lie on the beach. When a girl goes out to L.A. to be a movie star and finds that she needs some means of support until she makes it big, she's faced with a choice: slave away in an office from nine to five and never see the sun or model nude a couple of days a week and have the rest of her life to herself. Many opt for modeling and I think that's the wisest choice."

How does this view square with the experience of an actual nude model? Would-be high fashion model Cecily Williams was turned away by the Big Four because she fell two inches below the minimum height standard. A firm believer in modeling as a launching pad to stardom, Cecily was willing to try just about anything to get her picture published. After getting the door slammed in her face at Zoli, Wilhelmina, and Elite, she decided to put a backup plan into effect and to make a run for *Playboy* magazine. Cecily was sufficiently motivated to cast aside her inhibitions, to overcome her deep-seated modesty, and to pose in the nude. She seemed like a natural: a native New Yorker, Cecily combined sexy good looks with a dash of urban sophistication. A dark-skinned, dark-eyed, seductive brunette, she has the kind of softly contoured body and sensual expression that keep men gawking wherever she goes. In the nude her tight tan stomach, voluptuous breasts, and delicate arms make her at the same time dazzling and vulnerable looking.

A call to *Playboy*'s Chicago headquarters (assistant photo editor Michael Ann Sullivan answered the phone) brought the suggestion that Cecily submit a half dozen nude photos clearly revealing her face and her body from a variety of angles and positions. So Cecily found a photographer through a friend of a friend and nervously set a date for her first nude shooting. She tells it all in her own words: "I had, for years, a secret plan to someday try out for *Playboy*, but it's one of those things I never really thought I'd act on. Now it seemed like my best move. Perhaps I thought this type of modeling could lead to wonderful opportunities in the movies or on television. Maybe I would even have a chance of becoming a star like Suzanne Somers. She had done nude modeling and look what it did for her career. The more I thought about it, the better I liked the idea. I set an appointment with the photographer and began to prepare for the shooting.

"When the day finally came, I wanted everything to be perfect. Posing for *Playboy* meant that I had to check myself over from head to toe. Legs and underarms shaved, nails polished, my body had to be oiled and smoothed, makeup just right. You know. I also had to pick sexy, revealing things to wear like lace-trimmed bikini underwear, a short nightgown opened down the middle and ending just below my rear. Also a large black silky shirt belted but with the buttons open to my waist and nothing on underneath except pantyhose. Posing with clothes on is a very simple thing: you turn the collar on a coat, roll up the sleeves on a sweater, or open the slit on a skirt. The fashions do most of the work. But when you're posing in the nude, your body alone has to make the statement. To do this best, I thought it would be good to let my imagination run wild. The more excited I could get, the more erotic I'd look. I should put myself in the mind of the man opening the magazine, his temperature rising as he gets closer to the pages where the nude bodies are. Images of men thumbing through *Playboy* went through my brain. What could I do that hadn't been seen before—that would really get them going? After all, I wanted my pictures to stand out from the others. I practiced poses in front of the full-length mirror beside my bed. I began with my nightgown, dropping one shoulder strap and then the other. Then I opened it down the front to reveal my pussy. I began to spread my legs apart to get the best and most erotic view. Then I rolled over on my stomach and stuck my ass in the air. I ran through a whole series of poses so that I would be ready with ideas for the shooting.

"Well, the photographer finally arrived at my apartment. In order to be convincing, I knew I had to feel hot myself. After all, I was about to take my clothes off in front of a total stranger and parade around and pose in erotic positions. I'm smart enough to know that you can't do that well if you feel timid about it. I decided to start out in the first few pictures mostly clothed and then peel off a layer at a time until I was down to a pair of high heels and nothing else. Getting undressed slowly always made me feel sexy, so I figured it would do the trick. It did. . . . The photographer suggested that I stick my tongue out a little, that I take a breast out from my shirt and play with the nipple. This was the first time I really showed anything—and you know something, I didn't mind it at all. The whole thing was really like acting, and I always wanted to be an actress. . . .

"For the next series of shots I put on a short, black negligee. When I sat down on the couch and put my feet up on the coffee table, you could see between my legs in full view. Then I dropped the shoulder straps and slipped the negligee off. I rolled all over on the couch and the photographer shot me from every direction. He came really close: at times I felt as if the camera was inches from my body. . . . I was flying, really flying. . . .

"I had never been so turned on in my life, but it was different than any other experience I'd ever had. That's because after we were done I was embarrassed by it and felt partly like I'd done something wrong. . . . Still, the major reason for the session was to get the pictures to start my career, and that I thought went very well. I was confident that I'd make it as a nude model and, who knows, maybe go all the way to Hollywood. All sorts of dreams started filling my head. What I would buy once I was rich and famous. How I would build my all-glass dream house. How I'd get Bob Mackey, the guy who designs Cher's clothes, to make me a knockout wardrobe. One with feathers and diamonds. Why not?"

But her dreams had to wait. First, there was work to be done. The shooting produced 511 color slides. For a full week, Cecily edited them down to the dozen shots she believed were the most professionally produced and the most flattering to her face and figure. They were then developed into 6 × 9 glossy prints and were mailed, as instructed, to associate photography editor Janice Moses at *Playboy* in Chicago. Warned in advance by the magazine that *Playboy* was inundated with unsolicited photographs and that it would take about six weeks to hear from Ms. Moses, Cecily was prepared for a long wait. She was patient for the first two months, but became frustrated by the third and angry by the fourth.

"I called *Playboy*," she says, "to find out why it was taking so long to get a decision. I didn't know if no news was good or bad. But I never expected what they told me: Michael Ann Sullivan, my original contact, checked the files and said they never even received my shots. I was mad as hell. They refused to accept responsibility, told me it was my fault, and suggested I resubmit the photos by registered mail. I knew the screw-up was theirs. I'd heard from others that pictures of this kind often get clipped en route to *Playboy*. Some slobs probably steal them and then sell the pictures in the streets or use them to masturbate. But what could I do? I wasn't out to build a case, just to get into the magazine. So I developed the same slides and sent them along again, only this time by registered mail."

When the answer came, a full two months later, it was nothing to cheer about. Cecily Williams, the girl voted "Best Looking" by her New York high school graduating class, was crushed by her second big rejection in less than a year:

June 19, 1979

Dear Ms. Williams:

Your recent pictures to Michael Ann Sullivan have been referred to me for evaluation.

In this time of expanded Playmate layouts and critical demands on the Playmate in a photographic sense, our standards are extremely high. We understand that it is very difficult for young women such as yourself to realize what our needs are. We are very sorry we can't accept all the enthusiastic women who send us pictures.

Again, thank you for your continued interest in *Playboy* and for writing.

Respectfully,

Janice Moses
Associate Photography Editor

As Cecily and the tens of thousands of others like her have learned, getting into the pages of *Playboy* is no easy feat. Model selection at *Playboy* is never a casual affair—never a case, as the publisher of a lesser magazine puts it, "of getting by as cheaply as we can." Much time and care go into the process, with little expense spared to discover and present new faces. Witness the Great Playmate Hunt of 1978—a three-month coast-to-coast search (the most massive in its history) to find a special Playmate for *Playboy*'s twenty-fifth anniversary issue.

Advertisements in both daily and college newspapers in twenty-eight cities announced that *"Playboy* Is Searching for a Special Playmate. . . . The lucky lady will receive a $25,000 modeling fee and could represent *Playboy* on TV and in public appearances throughout our anniversary year!" The ads told when and where to find the *Playboy* photographers who were arriving in towns across the nation to shoot the candidates. They also offered a $2,500 finder's fee to any "connoisseurs of *Playboy* beauty" instrumental in discovering the anniversary lady. *Playboy* representatives moved into the selected cities, setting up makeshift studios in local hotels. Before clicking their shutters, they did two days of nonstop interviews on radio and television, alerting every available young woman of their mission and inviting them to audition as the Anniversary Playmate. When the calls started coming in—by the thousands—the *Playboy* teams set up ten-minute Polaroid photo sessions in the hotels. Contributing photographer Dwight Hooker, at his Drake Hotel suite in New York, photographed a steady procession of nude hopefuls—421 would-be sex queens—in less than a week's time. Other *Playboy* staffers, including associate photography editor Jeff Cohen and contributing photographer David Chan, did the same in Kansas City, Chicago, Los Angeles, Miami, Baton Rouge, San Antonio, Knoxville, Gainesville, Raleigh, and other target cities.

Says Louann Fernald, who went on to become the June 1979 Playmate, "I went to audition when the *Playboy* photographer came to town because I had nothing else exciting to do at the time. I was bored with school, bored with my social life, and also broke—I mean clean out of money. I needed some fun, some change of pace. The *Playboy* session seemed like just the thing, like my ticket out of a routine I wasn't really enjoying." Wherever they went, the *Playboy* teams and the young lovelies parading in and out of their suites attracted considerable attention. Office workers in a New York skyscraper who spotted Hooker and his models in their room on the Drake's twenty-fifth floor ran from their desks to watch the *Playboy* action across the street. "Business came to a standstill" is the way one television reporter put it. In another nearby building, a group of men made rating signs from one to twenty and raised one whenever a Playmate applicant came into view.

Although the prospect of traveling around the country photographing hundreds of nude women may sound like the ultimate fantasy to many men, the log of a *Playboy* photogra-

It is typical at the big agencies for the men's divisions to be crammed into small, tacky quarters. Here, Wilhelmina is seated in the agency's male booking room. The models' names and work schedules are posted on appointment cards above the telephones.

Nina Leen—*Life Magazine*, © 1948 by Time Inc.

Eileen and Jerry Ford, the queen and king of modeling, have aged along with the industry they helped to found. This early shot shows the Fords when their agency was located on Second Avenue and boasted seven telephones and $250,000 a year in billings. Now it rakes in more than $11 million and has ten times as many phones.

In a more recent shot, we see the legendary Eileen interviewing a Ford applicant. Many in modeling believe that Mama Ford has the best eye in the business for discovering new talent.

In her heyday as a model, Wilhelmina was a regular fixture on the covers of all the world's leading fashion magazines. Elegance was her trump card: she had more class and poise than any other model of her time.

Bob Stone

Top model Maggie Fahy pictured here in a rarely seen out take from a professional shooting. It often takes hundreds or thousands of shots to get one that is acceptable for publication.

A slight, quiet man, Zoli has managed to survive in the midst of New York's vicious model wars. He insists that his reputation for having racy models is not true and was simply invented by the media.

helly Smith, a top model, was reputed to be the highest noney-earning model in 1978. Of her success that year he said: "It's sort of like the tooth fairy—the checks just keep coming in."

Charles Tracy

One of the hottest models working today, Patti Hansen has what one observer calls "the sexy disco look." When she made the cover of *Esquire* magazine, her agency, Wilhelmina, shared the limelight.

pher is not all that glamorous or exciting. Staff photographers
work long, grueling hours (8 A.M. to 9 P.M. during the anniversary Playmate hunt) and earn considerably less than established fashion photographers. What's more, unlike the
free-lancers who provide photos for the lesser erotic magazines, *Playboy* men are not permitted to have sexual relations
with any of the models. To be sure, the rules are broken from
time to time, but opportunities are limited and sex cannot be
viewed as one of the fringe benefits of the job.

"Men will be men and women will be women, and when
you put them together in provocative situations, you'll always
have some playing around," says Janice Moses. "I'd be a
damn fool to make you believe the photographers never fuck
the girls, but it's much less common here than at other publications. The men don't consider it to be professional conduct.
Once, a few years ago, a model claimed she was sexually
harassed by one of our photographers and the others held a
sort of Salem witch hunt to determine his guilt. They pun-
ished him by ostracization."

In many cases, traveling *Playboy* photographers must
spend time with quite unattractive applicants who nevertheless deem themselves to be beautiful and must be granted all
the courtesies of a budding Suzanne Somers or Raquel Welch.
Asked what he would do if a 500-pound applicant came in for
a tryout, *Playboy* photographer Bill Arsenault answered, "I
figure she might have a 500-pound boyfriend at home who
thinks she's beautiful. Who am I to shatter her ego?" When
one 400-pound applicant, a local stripper named Baby Honda,
did show up for the Playmate Hunt in Toronto, David Chan
suggested, "Since you are already a performer, perhaps you
have a glossy you can hand over." But Baby Honda insisted
on original photography and 120-pound Chan, outweighed
more than three to one, politely obliged.

Why did so many candidates try out for the Hunt? This
project, like most casting calls for nude models, attracted its
share of thrill seekers, exhibitionists, and nature children. One
girl, interviewed by the *Seattle Record-Chronicle,* was asked:
"Why do you want to pose for *Playboy*?" "Because I like to

take my clothes off," she answered. "That's good?" "Of course. People are always nice to me when I take my clothes off."

But most applicants, even by *Playboy*'s own admission, were out for the money: the $25,000 fee, the chance to be discovered—that long-shot opportunity—and to make considerably more.

The Hunt for the twenty-fifth anniversary issue produced 10,000 Polaroid prints, all of which poured into *Playboy*'s headquarters for review by top photo editors and editor-in-chief Hugh Hefner. The prize went to twenty-two-year-old Candy Loving, a superbly endowed brunette from Norman, Oklahoma. Like many centerfolds before her, Candy had never done any previous nude modeling and had never even considered it. She is strikingly beautiful, wickedly sexy-looking, and yet full of the homegrown freshness and radiance one would expect from a native Oklahoman. Loving is typical of *Playboy* women in that she far outclasses the second-rate models who pose nude for the smut magazines that cater to the nation's hard-core fans.

Finding winners like Candy is not easy—as the complex logistics of the Playmate Hunt attest—but a similar process is repeated month after month at *Playboy*. Thousands of girls apply even when the prize is less auspicious than the title of Anniversary Playmate. Model selection is a major project even for routine issues. Every week, photo editor Janice Moses reviews the flood of unsolicited photographs to find that tiny minority worthy of a closer look by *Playboy* editors. "Right now I have seventeen wire baskets on my desk, all filled with as many as 1,000 photos each," Moses says. "From this I will select perhaps four girls who are good Playmate potential. They'll be flown to Chicago, worked on by our makeup and hair experts here, and photographed by a pro. If that test comes out good, we schedule a formal centerfold shooting, which takes from two to five days and is done with a special, highly sophisticated camera. Once the photo is developed, it is sent to all of our top editors who vote it either up or down. The results of the vote are sent along with the pictures to Mr. Hefner, who alone makes the final decision. After all, it's his magazine."

~ Selected Playmates must sign statements that they were

never before published in the nude and that they will not appear in any other publications (except for advertisements approved by *Playboy*) for one year after their Playmate issue. In return, they are paid $10,000 ($2,000 on completion of the photography, $2,000 on completion of the full layout, and $6,000 on publication). In addition, they have the opportunity to earn more money throughout the year by making *Playboy*-arranged personal appearances ($200 a day) at local businesses and trade shows and by doing nude modeling ($250 a day) for minor *Playboy* pictorials.

Playboy's standards, as we've noted, are extremely high. "We'll accept nothing less than perfection," says Moses. "No droopy boobs, no big asses, no fat thighs. Those with flaws won't make it here. That comes as a shock to many girls. All their lives their friends and parents told them they were gorgeous specimens and they believed it. When they walked into a room, everyone always noticed them. But what they failed to realize is that what people were reacting to was their clothing, jewelry, and perfume. When you're nude, you don't have these accessories to get you by. You have to be perfect through and through and few girls are. Those who meet that high standard qualify as Playmates. Bear in mind, we don't use any retouching. The only time we doctor up a photo at all is if the girl has a glaring birthmark or something like that. Otherwise, what she is is what you see. That's not the way most magazines operate; it's the exception to the rule."

Still, not all Playmates are completely happy with their experience at the magazine. Says Candy Loving, who is an intelligent and articulate young woman, "The photographers can really distort your image, distort what you really are. I hate when they do that. In my two major pictorials for *Playboy*, I've worked with what I consider to be a bad photographer and an excellent one. The former shot what he liked best with no regard for the model. He loved big tits, which I happen to have, so he focused on that part of my body exclusively. I came off looking like a walking tit. That's not what I am or how I want to appear. The other photographer, Arnie Freytag, however, was terrific. He noticed that I have beautiful hair, nice legs, and a good ass, and he captured all of that."

Playmates tend to be small-town lasses from conservative, often religious families. Former prostitutes, strippers, or those with any kind of questionable background at all are simply not accepted here. Sometimes, however, this emphasis on purity backfires on *Playboy* itself.

"We do occasionally get a girl in here who suddenly realizes, after we've gone through the time and expense of flying her to Chicago, that she just can't take her clothes off in front of our staff," Moses states. "It was okay to do it with a home-town photographer that she's known all her life, but not with strangers. She gets here, says 'Oh, what would Mom think?' and then insists on leaving without having her pictures taken. We feel very ripped off when that happens because we've wasted our time. But I guess it's the price we have to pay for dealing with fine, respectable young women who also happen to be beautiful. Some change their minds, but the majority are dying to appear in the magazine."

Says Louann Fernald, a 5'4", twenty-two-year-old student at the University of Miami who was the June 1979 Playmate, "I can't imagine anyone not wanting to appear in *Playboy*. They are so professional, and so courteous, that they make getting undressed in front of strangers seem so natural. I had never done it before my *Playboy* session, but I felt perfectly comfortable. I'm proud of my body. I've got no sexual hangups, and I enjoy being the center of attention."

That *Playboy* and its closest imitators, *Penthouse* and *Oui* (the latter is also published by *Playboy*), steer away from cheap smut, that they present a balanced editorial product combining lovely nudes with good writing and first-class art work, makes them acceptable to leading national advertisers. And for virtually any mass circulation magazine to prosper, it must attract the major liquor, cigarette, automobile, and travel advertisers who have the big bucks to invest issue after issue. This is publisher Hugh Hefner's true genius: he produced a sex magazine that unlike its predecessors did not have to rely on the tiny porno mail-order ads hawking dildos, vibrators, erection cremes, body oils, plastic vaginas, and stag films. Although some black-and-white cheapies still crowd *Playboy*'s back pages, they provide the magazine's pin money rather than the bulk of its revenues. The heavy hitters—the likes of Smirnoff, Seagram, Camel, Honda, BMW, and Panasonic—boast four-color ads up front in the choicest, high-rent districts of the magazine. Sewing up contracts with these biggies assures *Playboy* of the kind of robust cash flow publications need to stay vital and to afford the class touches that keep them at the head of the pack. It means they can spend large sums of money to find and compensate the most attractive nude models available.

Gallery magazine, by contrast, proves that the shortcuts often taken by the grade-B erotic publications result in worse rather than better conditions for nude models: lower standards, lower fees, and a general demeaning of the occupation. It is when such amateurism is allowed into the field that nude modeling becomes a tasteless business.

In its short but checkered history, *Gallery* has been toned down considerably from its early days, when it had a very explicit photographic style. Specifically, it has moved from raunchy "pink shots" of open vaginas and rectums to a slicker, softer look featuring sweeping views of the body. The emphasis, as in *Playboy*, is on breasts, pubic hair, and the rounded contours of hips and derriere. This change in direction is attributable to Nils Shapiro's arrival at the magazine. A savvy salesman, he recognized that *Gallery*'s image needed cleaning up before it could be made palatable to the large national advertisers.

"We made a conscious effort to change the editorial direction here—to clean up our act," Shapiro explains. "That meant positioning ourselves not with the bulk of the men's magazines that specialize in cheap photography, but with the milder and more artistic style of *Playboy*. I ordered the change so we could appeal to national advertisers and also because the hard pornographic stuff offends my sensibilities."

Shapiro's claims are accurate in terms of *Gallery*'s shift to a less explicit photographic style, but this is only half the story. To register circulation gains, the magazine instituted a novel editorial feature called "The Girl Next Door." For this section of the magazine, men are invited to submit nude pictures of their wives, girlfriends, and mistresses for possible publication in *Gallery*. The photos are published as submitted. There is no attempt to airbrush or retouch them. What's more, the photos are not necessarily chosen because the women are attractive or sensual but quite often because they make for kinky and unusual models. *Gallery*'s May 1979 issue, for example, featured among its Girls Next Door a bookkeeper who appeared to be in her late forties; a plain-looking woman with uneven breasts and stretch marks running across her stomach; a fat young woman wearing a jockey's cap; and an obese housewife slumped down in an armchair that was covered with tacky slipcovers. The backgrounds are generally sleazy (mostly cheap motel rooms and poorly furnished homes) and the technical quality is obviously amateurish, marked by shadows and very poor composition. The overall effect is one of tawdriness. Still, the feature is popular with readers because it has brought active nude modeling to the masses. This has helped the magazine boost its circulation considerably.

"*Gallery* has struck a real chord here," says our New York psychiatrist. "It has given men the ultimate in voyeurism. That is, the chance to see a great fantasy come true: to see their next-door neighbor or the office secretary in the nude. The unrehearsed look of the photography and the obviously amateur status of the models feeds this illusion and makes the experience even more real and exciting. To many men it's like peeping through the keyhole at women who are accessible—at models who can be fucked as well as looked at. That's the most erotic and exciting response nude modeling can generate. You don't get that feeling with *Playboy*."

9

MALE MODELS
Misfits in a Woman's World

"When I was working for Fuller, Smith, and Ross, I
happened to be on the agency basketball team. One night our
team had a game scheduled with a group of male models.
Invariably the word is out that all male models are fags. It's
not true that all of them are, but quite a few of them are a
little too cute for words. . . . The game gets started and pretty
soon I get a break and start dribbling toward their basket. I'm
going up for a layup and as I go up, one of these beautiful,
beautiful guys comes down on me with his elbow and catches
me across the top of the nose. Blood was gushing out of my
nose, all over me, the floor, everything. As I was bounding
around on the floor I remember I was shouting, 'My nose, my
nose,' and this beautiful guy just looks down at me and says,
'You call that a nose?' "
—Advertising agency president Jerry Della Femina *(From
Those Wonderful Folks Who Gave You Pearl Harbor,* Simon
& Schuster, 1970)

Daddy Warbucks is alive and well and living in the world of
big-time modeling. He's as rich and powerful as ever; he can
still turn scruffy urchins into pampered princesses. He's an
old-fashioned guy; he favors sweet little things who have nothing to do with sleazy magazines, sex, or nudity. To him, *Playboy, Gallery, Penthouse,* and *Hustler* are all the same, and he
avoids them like the plague. He wants no part of that world. It
doesn't go with his image or, more importantly, with the image
of his annointed princesses. Daddy Warbucks is modeling's
dream-come-truer, star-maker, fairy godfather. He forks up
multimillion-dollar contracts, markets posters by the truckload,
and hands out leading roles in "Charlie's Angels." He's a movie

mogul, a TV producer, a press lord, a cosmetics tycoon. He's all of these things and more: he is the money man, the investor, the power in the business behind the business. He bankrolls the big bucks that create modeling's legends—the stories of wealth and fame that keep the public fascinated and keep the models streaming out of America's heartland in record numbers.

The modeling business is full of such men. They are the powerful executives who control the huge promotional budgets at the likes of Revlon, Wella, Max Factor, Fabergé, and Estée Lauder and who pay models gargantuan sums to represent their products. All the Daddies have one thing in common: they like to shower their largesse on women—on beautiful, all-American women who can appeal to millions of consumers from coast to coast. Not only because these women are attractive, seductive, or charming, but because they are profitable. Modeling is a business like any other in that it attracts capital to its most promising investments—and in this business most investments are made in women. They reap most of the rewards that modeling has to offer because they are instrumental in selling products and services.

Where does that leave the men in modeling? Although there are powerful male figures throughout the modeling establishment, few males of any consequence are found in the ranks of the models themselves. Male models are clearly second-class citizens, the stepchildren of their profession—inferior to their female counterparts in status, income, and opportunity. Daddy Warbucks rarely ever smiles on them. In the business behind the business—a good indication of where modeling places its heavy bets—males are virtually ignored. They are not superstars, they rarely get lucrative contracts, they do not have shampoos named after them. And their problems are not limited to money alone: agents, editors, and photographers also view male models as the supporting players in a show dominated by leading ladies.

There is a general malaise in male modeling that goes deep into its core—into the minds and souls of the male models and into the industry's own confused vision of itself. What is this malaise and why does it exist? It starts with the widespread belief that there is something wrong with men serving as models. Just the words "male model" rub many people the wrong way. Visions arise of flighty queens getting paid to stand around with their hands on their hips. This challenges the macho notion that men should get by on brains or brawn, never on looks—that women can get paid to look pretty, but for men to do so is a disgrace.

Although people in the modeling business write this off as the petty prejudice of small minds, there is substantial evidence that such a parochial attitude actually extends throughout modeling, up to and including the male models themselves. Many male models judge themselves by the same harsh standards as the "small minds in middle America," often secretly believing that there is something wrong with what they do. This produces a tremendous internal conflict. And there's no doubt that most male models are an unhappy, brooding lot.

"I can't remember ever being really happy—never in my whole life," says Daniel, a model with the Wilhelmina agency's men's division. (Like most of his colleagues, Daniel refused to be quoted by his real name. Male models are terribly afraid of saying anything that may offend anyone in the business. They are too expendable.) "I was born and raised in Wheeling, West Virginia, and I hated the people, the houses, the school, the other kids. It seemed to me as if nature had dropped me down in the wrong place. It felt as if I were a square peg being jammed into a round hole. No matter how much my parents, my teachers, or even I tried, there was no getting me to fit in. I detested the place and I rebelled against everything. My only sanctuary was my room: there I'd read children's stories about glorious fantasy lands and magic kingdoms. I wanted to be a king in one of those places, all decked out in real velvet robes and a diamond crown. . . .

"I finally did break out the day after high school graduation and made a beeline straight for New York. Oh, New York, I thought: You are my salvation. Well, rats to that too. I mean I've done all that I ever dreamed of: met people of my own ilk, got accepted here at Wilhelmina, built up a little bank account. But I'm still miserable. I feel guilty as hell for saying this because you're supposed to be thankful when your dreams come true, but shit, I still feel empty. Something's missing. Something's wrong.

"I cry a lot. My letters to Mom say that all is fabulous, but I really cry a lot. It just comes over me. And I'm nervous. For the first time in my life I bite my nails. My hands look chewed up—so awful. I've tried to stop—I know it looks tacky—but I can't. I just don't seem to be in control of myself. I'm tired and sad and anxious and I'm not really sure why. I wonder if the little creeps back in Wheeling who went on to become barbers or miners and who married one of the townie pigs are happier than I am. I have a sneaking suspicion that they are, but—again I shouldn't say this—I hope to hell they're not."

On the surface, Daniel is the Hollywood version of the ideal American male. Tall, well-built, with sharp masculine features and an abundance of thick, glossy black hair. He is supremely good-looking. Outwardly, he exudes great strength and self-confidence. There is something of the quality of a dashing young military man. The shoulders are square and erect, the chin prominent. His clothes are rugged and decidedly masculine —heavy corduroy trousers, a flannel workshirt, worn riding boots, and a leather bomber jacket—and he carries his book and grooming aids in an Army surplus knapsack. When he stops by the agency to pick up his mail, to meet with his booker, or just to chat with colleagues, Daniel appears to be loose, cheerful, extroverted. The talk among the male models runs the gamut from news of a great boutique on Madison Avenue to a story about a new disco on the West Side and a run-in with a nasty photographer at *Gentlemen's Quarterly*. The conversations tend to be very brief, just a few words with one person and then on to the next. Daniel, like the others, acts very flip. Every comment is a joke, a wry one-liner. He gives the impression of a man who takes life as it comes, one who lives free and easy with no hangups, no concerns.

"What did you do yesterday, Daniel? Thought I'd see you at the *New York Times* shooting," says Kevin, a young fair-skinned model with knotted blond hair.

"Na. Thought I told you I begged out of that. I needed a

day to catch up on my shopping," Daniel answers. (Only ten minutes before he had revealed to the author that he had lost the *Times* booking at the last minute and was terribly depressed about it.)

"Food shopping?" Kevin teases. "Did you run out of sugar, poor dear?"

"I spent the whole day in Saks and it was great," Daniel retorts. "Really pampered myself. I ate lunch there and bought a suit, two pairs of shoes, and a great Polo sweater. The sweater was $115, but who cares about money!"

"A sweater for $115—that's a rip-off," Kevin replies. "Polo sweaters make you look like a farmer. They're too bulky."

"Yeah, Frank Perdue wears them," chimes in another model. "Frank Perdue and Daniel."

Everyone laughs, they pat each other on the back and then move on to another topic. Daniel gets in his measure of jabs and barbs and finally leaves after little more than two hours. Two hours of playing the role of happy-go-lucky model with a dozen or so young men who are all trying to do the same thing and who all see through each other as if they had laser vision. But no one talks about this; no one admits he knows exactly what the others are doing.

Agents at the men's divisions make a concerted effort to portray male models as better than their female counterparts in all the traditional ways men pride themselves on being superior. "The men are more serious-minded about their work," says a Big Four agency chief who demands anonymity on this subject. "The girls worry about how their profiles are captured on film, while the guys focus on more important things like personal finances and contract terms. And because there is less money on the male side of the business, the models are not as spoiled. They are less emotional and are not so caught up in playing ego games. This may sound corny, but the men genuinely like each other. If one guy is out on a go-see and doesn't get the booking because the client wants more of a European look, he may put in a good word for a fellow model who fits the bill. The men share; the women do not."

Adds Bob Newey, director of Elite Men, "The real bitchiness in female modeling is not a factor here. Everyone gets on much better in men's modeling. This is indicative even in the photographer/model relationships. When you have two men working together they're likely to have mutual interests like cars, sports, or the stock market. One of my models went on a shooting recently and he and the photographer spent the whole day talking about Porsches. When women are involved, they usually argue or talk about silly things like hairdos."

Newey's comments are absurd. The image that he and his fellow agents like to portray of male models as regular guys— as the kind of men who spend their spare time discussing the Super Bowl over a case of Budweiser—has no grounding in reality. The truth is that male models share many of the same concerns as the women. They are totally preoccupied with appearance, and they focus more on facial blemishes or split ends than on the Dow Jones averages. In addition—again contrary to the agents' hype—the men are viciously competitive, are determined to outdo rather than to help each other, and are rarely good friends. They spend their free time at the agencies together because they would like to be close, but there is more that divides than unites them.

"It's a shame, a damn shame," says Daniel. "We never admit it to each other—and very rarely even to ourselves—but we go up to Willy's place because we need the closeness with our kind of people. The only human beings in the world who really understand male models are other male models. So it's natural to want to be with those who speak your language and share your concerns. There's a great yearning to be with them —to embrace them emotionally and to give yourself the chance to open up.

"But it doesn't work that way. We wind up playing games with one another. The idea is to make everyone else think that you're the only really happy and together male model. It's okay for all the others to have hangups, but you want to come across as being very cool. You want to show that you're superior because then you might believe it yourself. Instead of letting your hair down and admitting that we all have some problems —problems we could help each other work out—we pretend that all is rosy and that nothing gets to us. So we wind up suffering inside. I guess we're all so accustomed to being put down and to putting up a false front against the rest of the world that we don't know how to drop the guard when we're together."

The defensiveness starts very early in life. Most male models come out of sleepy, rural towns that dot the Midwest, the Plains states, and the Southwest. Like the women who become models, most feel a compelling urge to break away at an early age, to head for New York or Hollywood. The urge arises for two reasons: First, stardom beckons. Budding male models cannot follow in their fathers' footsteps and go to work on a farm, in a coal mine, or an insurance office. Something in their chemistry says "no" to that. They yearn for glamour and therefore turn their attention to acting, singing, or modeling. Second, many male models are gay and most endure the very frustrating and even frightening ordeal of growing up in conservative, religious communities where everyone knows everyone's business and homosexuality must remain in the closet. Young gay men trapped in this stifling environment often try to hide their sexual impulses. Some try desperately to conform to accepted standards, to be like the other guys. It is a difficult lie to live: one that leads to loneliness, isolation, and depression. The pull of New York, with its large and active gay community, is therefore very strong.

Thus we have a major distinction between the men and women who flock to Manhattan to make it in big-time modeling. Both come for the glamour, the glitter, the excitement. But a good number of the men are also seeking a sanctuary; they have come through a difficult experience and have been scarred by it. For this reason, they want more, need more, and demand more from New York than do the women, and they are more dejected and disappointed when they don't get it.

Typically, males launch their modeling careers much the way women do—by writing to one of the major modeling agencies. All of the Big Four have separate men's divisions which are managed by male executives and are run as separate businesses. They are usually housed in the same building as their sister operations, but have their own suite of offices, switchboards, and bookers. It is no secret that the male side of the business is given short shrift by agency principals. The men's quarters are smaller and frequently shabbier than the women's, the staff is limited to a handful of people, and agency brochures and other promotional literature focus almost exclusively on the women. At Casablancas's agency, for example, all of the men are lumped together in a single division. There is no distinction, as there is on the women's side, between newcomers in Model Management and stars in Elite. In conversations with Casablancas, or for that matter with his competitors (Zoli is a notable exception), there is little or no talk about the males in the agency. Clearly, male modeling is not nearly as big or as profitable a business as the agencies' major line.

Still, the men's divisions are frantic with activity. They are besieged with far more applicants than they can possibly handle—almost as much as the women's division, even though there are many fewer opportunities. The Wilhelmina agency, for example, represents about 250 women and only 100 men. It gets 3,000 inquiries a year from prospective male models, mostly in the form of letters with accompanying photographs. Dan Deeley, the amiable director of the Wilhelmina men's division, sifts through this voluminous correspondence, weeding out the immediate rejects (the vast majority fall into this category) and selecting the few (perhaps 10 percent) who appear to have some potential. These candidates are encouraged to visit the agency for a formal audition, at which time Deeley carefully reviews the best prospects and their books. A few dozen usually get the green light and work their way onto the Wilhelmina headsheet. For that opportunity, thousands of applicants travel across the country just to get a five-minute interview with Deeley. Many come to New York solely because correspondence from Deeley or his counterparts at one of the other Big Four sounded promising and opened the door to a shot at the top.

"There are at least a dozen letters on my desk every morn-

ing from guys in Texas, Louisiana, Nebraska, Wyoming—
throughout the country—who want to break into the business,"
says Bob Newey, a bearded and bespectacled man whose office
is just a small open space in the Elite Men's booking room.
"They all want to be invited to audition here, but I am very
careful about handing out those invitations. I don't want to get
someone's hopes up too high, and prompt them to travel all the
way to New York, just to find out they are not really qualified.
Some will come anyway, no matter how much you discourage
them, but that's not my responsibility. I just want to be certain
that those I do encourage—the men who leave home and who
wind up spending all sorts of money traveling to New York
simply because my letter sounds hopeful—really have a chance
of making it here. You can get a good indication of that from
their pictures and their physical descriptions."

The men's division managers talk passionately about
their concern for model candidates, but this seems to be
mostly hot air. Many executives throughout the modeling industry play the same tune, loudly proclaiming a great respect
for male models' rights and feelings while at the same time
treating their applicants in a rude and high-handed manner. It
is said to be quite common for travel-weary young men, who
come to New York for a scheduled appointment, to be
stranded in an agency's reception area while the men's division chief chats on the phone, makes weekend plans, eats
lunch, or flips through *Gentlemen's Quarterly.*

"I had a three o'clock appointment with an agent, but I
didn't get to see him until 4:45 and he never even apologized for
the wait," says Curtis, a tall, prep-school type who looks like a
character in the movie *The Paper Chase.* "With the rides to and
from the airports and the two connecting flights from my home
town outside of New Orleans, I'd been en route since eight
o'clock that morning just to make the appointment on time. I
spoke to the agent on the phone before coming and he sounded
as if he really wanted to see me. I knew there were no guarantees, but I did feel important. I believed that the agency was as
excited about seeing me as I was about meeting them.

"But I was in for a rude shock. The receptionist didn't even know who I was and she said she had no record of my appointment. That was terribly exasperating. They said the agent would see me, but I'd have to be patient. At first I didn't mind the delay, thinking it would be brief, but as the minutes ticked by I felt powerless and humiliated. At least five people came into the agency, asked to see the agent, and were ushered right in. Every time I inquired as to when he'd see me, I was told ten more minutes, ten more minutes. I wanted to scream, but what was I to do? I knew that if I stood up and made a big stink about it, I wouldn't stand a chance. They'd write me off.

"When I finally got called in, the agent was on the phone. I had to wait fifteen more minutes while he talked, and he never even acknowledged my presence. Finally, I got my twelve-minute interview and I was back on the streets. They gave me no commitment, no encouragement, not even a 'thank you' for traveling all the way to get there. And you know what really irritates me terribly? When I was talking with the agent, I could see that my name was in fact on his calendar. I was reading it upside down, but I could see it clearly. I think they knew I had an appointment all along."

Agents deny that they treat applicants this way and Curtis's allegations may well be the comments of a bitter reject. Still, discussions with dozens of male applicants show that the disillusionment with their chosen profession begins almost as soon as they arrive in New York. Many come to Manhattan not primarily to model but to pursue show business careers, mostly stage acting. They turn to modeling only when they learn that Broadway is not waiting with open arms. Modeling can keep them going, paying the bills, until—and if—a big acting break comes through. Some are led to modeling by casting directors, agents, or fellow actors who know from experience that struggling performers need some form of steady income in order to survive in New York and to keep on the audition circuit. A letter (wet with coffee stains) found in a wastebasket at Zoli's office tells a familiar story:

April 21, 1979

Zoli
Zoli Models
121 E. 62nd Street
New York, New York 10021

Dear Zoli:

Just when you thought you had seen every beautiful guy in the world, another one has come along who is the most beautiful yet: me! Brash? Yes. Confident? Yes. But when you meet me, I'm sure you will agree.

I am an actor, living and working in New York for the past seven months. Broadway needs me badly, but the producers just haven't discovered that yet. Everyone tells me that my Shakespeare needs some polishing, but my looks are near perfect. (I have enclosed a picture. You be the judge.) I would love to model for your agency on the days when I am not "on the boards." My vital statistics are as follows:

Age: 20	Suit Size: 40 Regular
Height: 6'0"	Personality: Charming,
Weight: 160	Suave, Adorable

Please call me at your convenience. I will be happy to stop in at any time.

Your Best Discovery Yet,

Rance

Rance's playful approach did not land him an interview. Agents are put off by hot-shot kids who come off as too beautiful to resist. The only way to get a foot in the door of an agency is to come with hat in hand, humble as hell, pleading for a chance. Agents want to make discoveries; they don't want them thrown in their faces. Tell an agent that he needs you and he'll likely kick you out of his office on the spot.

What qualities do attract the big-time agents? What do male applicants need to gain entry at the Big Four? The physical prerequisites are simple enough: between 6' and 6'2" in height, 31–33 waist, size 40 regular suit. These proportions look best in photographs and correspond to the sample clothing sizes used at shootings.

Many of the facial characteristics that make for successful

female models also apply to the men: chiseled noses, high cheekbones, prominent eyes, and soft, tapered mouths. The term "camera presence," however, which is used so frequently when describing successful female models, is rarely mentioned in reference to men. Instead, editors and agents alike say that male models must have "style." The vast majority of handsome males who make it to the personal audition stage but are then rejected fail because they lack this all-important quality. Good looks are not enough. Male models must know how to carry themselves—how to walk, act, and pose—with a certain style or flair. This has more to do with body language than with facial expressions. The man must add something to the fashion he is modeling. Just what direction this takes depends on the particular fashion and on the theme of the advertisement. Good male models bring elements of grace, strength, poise, and confidence to their work. They can examine an article of clothing and know precisely how it should be worn.

"Most men don't wear clothes, they let clothes hang on them," says Bob Newey. "Go to a department store and watch the procession of average guys trying on suits by the fitting mirrors. The shoulders drop, the arms hang loose, the belly bulges. The clothes look awful, uninspired. You'd never be moved to buy them. But put the same suits on a talented male model and he'll take command of the clothes. He'll bring another dimension to the apparel. The models will hold their chests out, put their hands on their hips, tilt their heads gracefully, and generally make the garment look as the designer envisioned it.

"This is what we mean by having 'style' and it's what distinguishes top models from everyone else. Don't get me wrong, a lot of our guys don't have it when they first walk in here. Women learn as youngsters how to walk with style and sex appeal, but it is unacceptable for young boys to do that. That's a major difference between male and female models: the men haven't spent their whole lives learning how to look attractive. A girl's routine upbringing aids her modeling career while a man's often works against him. Men who want to model must learn to do the things that they've been brought up to believe are unmanly. We can tell who has the potential to develop 'style' but we usually have to see to it that they are taught. Very few hopefuls ever walk in here and are ready to go out to work the next day. They need weeks or months of coaching and polishing up. It's a matter of working on their technique."

Young model Tom, a Newey protégé, says, "When you first start posing, you feel very self-conscious. Nothing you've ever done before really prepares you for it, so you don't know exactly how to act. As a result, you wind up trying too hard to project a certain image or to look natural. But the pictures tell it all. The fear and the uncertainty come out on the prints. You look anything but natural or relaxed. Experience teaches you how to replace that frozen look with a graceful and stylish pose."

Unlike women models, men are usually typecast into one particular category of looks ranging from the all-American preppy to the brooding Latin lover. Male models are less flexible than women; they cannot transform themselves into a gallery of different faces. Photographers say this is because they have less to work with.

"Women can make great use of cosmetics and hairstyles to radically change their appearance," says photographer Barbra Walz, who has worked with both male and female models. "A girl can go to one shooting looking very elegant and European and then simply remove her makeup, let down her hair, and go to another job that requires the girl-next-door image. Men can't do that: they have one hairstyle and they use little makeup. They are what they are. They cannot fit into many different roles. This translates into fewer job opportunities."

Whatever the model's particular look, he must sharpen and refine it before going out on paid bookings. He must develop that all-important sense of style. Here photographers play a major role. The agencies do not give modeling instruction to men; pointers must be picked up on the outside. Much of this is done at fashion shows in France and Italy. Agencies ship out their young prospects to Europe to work at the major designer previews. June and September are prime times for this because that's when the men's clothing collections are introduced to the

trade. There are plenty of jobs available and the work is especially good for newcomers. By spending weeks walking up and
down the fashion show runways, wearing every conceivable
style of suit, resort and casual attire, the men learn to put it all
together: they develop a strong personal style. Fashion photographers attending the previews serve as catalysts in this process by coaching the models. For this reason, the previews are
widely regarded as crash courses in the finer points of male
modeling.

"Photographers help the boys develop an 'effect,' as I call
it," Newey adds. "They leave New York for their first European shows as green novices and come back with all the rough
edges polished. It's terrific. Very often, a boy who is not at all
ready to work here returns from only a few months in Italy and
is capable of handling any booking I send him on."

The European connection is also important in terms of
press coverage. Young males (again like the women) can break
into the fashion press much easier on the Continent and can
collect handsome and prestigious tearsheets for their New
York debut. In the States, *Gentlemen's Quarterly* is the only
major male fashion magazine, so the opportunities are very
limited. By crossing the Atlantic, emerging talents can model
for half a dozen or so quality books that do stunning photographic spreads and are open to working with newcomers.
What's more, European contacts remain important to male
models throughout their careers. Established pros who feel
that their look is tired or played out can return to Europe every
few years to experiment with new ideas, new fashions. Europe
is a hotbed of activity in fashion and modeling; designers, the
press, and photographers there tend to be more inventive, more
daring. This atmosphere can help to generate change in the
model, to update his style. In Europe, he can afford to try new
things, to take chances, to gamble. The model can rehearse, get
his act together, before returning to New York.

Some male models reverse the traditional process by first
earning a name for themselves in New York and then turning
to Europe when their popularity wanes. Such was the case with
Tom, a young man who came onto the Manhattan scene with a

splash in early 1979. A native of New Jersey, Tom graduated from high school and turned his attention to a career in acting. A photographer friend, positive of Tom's modeling potential, did some testings. Although the photographs turned out extremely well, Tom had never thought of himself as a model and did not pursue it. "I thought, no way am I going to be a model —no way," Tom recalls. "Acting was definitely on my mind, but not modeling. I just couldn't picture myself as a model."

But the seed was planted. Months later, while scanning a local newspaper, Tom noticed an advertisement for a small outfit that serviced would-be models by helping them assemble photographs, giving advice on personal appearance, and bringing them to the attention of top agents. Tom acted on the advertisement, and it was the turning point in his career. He learned what he had to do to be commercially acceptable. "They told me to lose ten pounds, cut my hair, and shave my mustache —and I did it all," Tom recalls. "I guess the prospect of being a model didn't seem so strange to me by then. I started to want to make it and I was ready to do whatever was required."

As his next step, Tom entered a male beauty pageant at New York's Biltmore Hotel. Here he modeled three different outfits and acted in a mock television commercial, all before a panel of judges. "The judges were influential people in the model business," Tom says. "That's why pageants are so important. You get instant recognition by the most important agents and you can get discovered right on the spot. That's exactly what happened to me. One of the pageant judges—an executive of Elite's women's division—thought I was terrific and immediately arranged for me to meet with Bob Newey. Bob also liked me and I was accepted into the agency. Everything moved quickly from there: my testings went very well, I put together a great book in about a month, and I was soon busy working almost every day of the week."

Timing is crucial in a model's career. Tom came along just when his brand of fresh, all-American looks were sought after by a number of major clients. Some of the big catalog producers were looking for a new face; Tom had the good fortune of being in the right place at the right time. For this reason, and because he has great instincts for what the business demands, Tom managed to achieve commercial success without first making the European connection. He is one of the few young males who come on the scene and just take off. Agents dream of models like this because they start producing income almost from day one and do not require up-front investments of time, training, or money.

Still, everyone involved knows that modeling is very much a here-today, gone-tomorrow business. In the same breath that Newey boasts of Tom's success, he cannot help but anticipate his rapid decline. He indicates that Tom has enjoyed a type of beginner's luck—that he has worked steadily from the start because he appeals to a small, exceptionally active group of clients. To be successful over the long run, however, Newey believes that Tom will have to be trained and polished to develop the kind of style that can attract a wider range of bookings. This will involve making the European connection not at the beginning of his career, but when his hot streak starts showing signs of cooling off.

Tom himself, although flushed with the glow of his instant success, knows better than to bank on modeling as a lifelong profession. He senses, even in his moment of triumph, that it is a fleeting high. What's more, he seems already to be restless and somewhat dissatisfied with his work. "I'm twenty years old and making great money all of a sudden," Tom says. "I'm getting a lot of attention. It's great, but I would like to make the transition to film. I will enroll in acting courses. I will start at HB."*

It is a common form of self-deception for male models to promise themselves more rewarding careers but to stay with modeling until they are forced out. Despite their dissatisfaction, they get hooked on modeling. Most are not qualified for any other work that even approaches the amount of money they earn as models. And even if they were otherwise trained or educated, few have the temperament to sit behind a desk or to sell insurance. What they don't realize at first, however, is that modeling does them long-term damage. It interferes with and

*The Herbert Berghof Studio, Inc., an acting school.

limits their opportunities in acting, ballet, singing, and the other fields they would really like to pursue.

How do they get derailed? Why do they tend to stay with modeling once they make a go of it? What happens is that most come to New York broke, spend months or years living slightly above the poverty level, and then if they turn to modeling and are successful at it, they start earning relatively good money very quickly. As soon as the first big checks come through, the guys trade up to luxury apartments, DeNoyer wardrobes, and dinners at Maxwell's Plum. They don't get rich, but those who hustle and plug away at it are able to live quite comfortably, and the old poverty days are forgotten. Having money is nice and no one wants to turn back. But herein lies the rub: modeling is the kind of business in which if you miss a day's work you lose a day's pay; there are no free rides. So, as the model develops a money habit—as he becomes addicted to an affluent life-style—he is less likely to pass up a lucrative booking in order to waste an entire day at an audition for a new Neil Simon play. What's more, he worries about disappointing good clients and angering his agent by showing more loyalty to acting than to modeling. As a result, he puts his most cherished career goals on the back burner and pursues modeling for every dollar he can get. All the while he keeps promising himself that things will be different soon—that he'll save enough money to abandon modeling and devote himself to his true love. But although a handful of male models do make the transition to show business, most simply keep on modeling and wishing they were doing something else.

Dan Deeley's description of what models encounter when they first get started in New York explains why this happens: "The guys go through what I call the shit-kicker syndrome. They're hicks, straight out of pathetic little towns no one ever heard of. They come here looking and sounding like the Marlboro Man—straight off the ranch. The only jobs they ever had before coming to New York earned them a fast hundred bucks a week. If they have the looks and the talent, however, they score big here in a few months and make maybe eight times that amount. Well, that's quite a change and it goes right to their heads. They start spending like crazy; every dime they make goes in the checking account and right out again. All the beautiful things in New York are so tempting—the shit-kickers, and I'm one of them, can't resist anything. We never had such great clothes, furniture, or restaurants back home, and now that we can have it there's no going back to the farm."

The problem is that the male models don't make enough to get rich. They soon get in debt over their heads and they have to hustle to pay for the things they've acquired. Many have to stay in modeling for this reason alone—to keep feeding the charge account—and they find that it just isn't enough to keep them happy. Once the novelty of modeling wears off, it's not that satisfying.

Even those models who say they like their work seem eager to find a way out. A case in point is Milos, a successful model with more than five years in the business. Milos came up through the traditional route: discovered by a photographer, he did successful testings and landed his first job with Fabergé. He soon went off to Europe, hooked up with Elite in Paris, traveled around the Continent, compiled an impressive book, and returned to the States for what has been an increasingly successful career. Still, there is apparent dissatisfaction.

"When I did that first Fabergé job, I was hooked," Milos recalls. "I loved the money, the excitement, the cameras, the people. But the thrill of it all, of seeing myself in the magazines, died after a few months. The job's not personally rewarding or fulfilling. There is good money to be made, but it's not satisfying."

In behavior typical of male models, Milos quickly tries to cover up his negative remarks with positive ones. No sooner does he find himself questioning his life-style than he changes gears and goes on the defensive: "I wouldn't be in this business if I didn't enjoy my work," he says. "I look at modeling as any other job. I sell myself. I sell my looks and my personality. Other people make money by selling their minds. What's the difference between their way of making money and mine?

"I plan to model for another three or four years—that's all. I'd like to do something else. I don't plan on modeling until I'm middle-aged. I am not sure what it will be, but I'll find something else to do to get me out of this."

Deny it as they will, much of the dissatisfaction in male

modeling stems from the fact that the men are ashamed of the way they make their living. It becomes evident, in bits and snatches of conversations, that they share society's negative view of their occupation. Something deep within haunts them with the feeling that it is inappropriate for a man to be paid just to stand around looking "pretty." Those who will talk on this subject with any candor express the fear that they may be wasting themselves. There is a common yearning to do something constructive—to write songs, paint works of art, or design buildings.

Many male models are intelligent, aggressive, and competitive people who sense that they have fallen into a rut and are no longer stretching or challenging themselves. In addition, like their female counterparts, they are saddled with the "dumb blond" image. Friends, lovers, and family members often view them as mannequins. Women can take great pride in boasting at a cocktail party that they are models; the men often mumble it under their breath.

"I know you're not supposed to care what other people think of you as long as you love yourself, but that sounds easier than it is," says Hugh, a former Big Four model who was dropped from the headsheet in 1977 because his billings had declined over a period of years. He now works in a wine shop in Soho. "The agents and the fashion editors all think you are hopelessly dumb, but they keep it to themselves. It's the photographers who really make you feel like shit. Some of them regard you as nothing more than props, as things to push around and drop clothing on. Once, a photographer requested me for a lawn care products ad. I thought he wanted me to stand with a mower and play the suburban homeowner type. But no, no. He wanted me to pose as a tree. He was doing a real way out ad. I was to raise my hands to the sky, wear a green hat, and look as much as possible like a towering oak. The photographer was going to put a price tag around my neck, showing how much the tree costs. I drew the line there, called my agent and screamed about how I wasn't going to do that. My agent agreed that it wouldn't be good for my image, so I left. But the photographer was perplexed. As far as he was concerned, a model is just an object and should do whatever he is told.

"I hated that attitude. I hated being thought of that way. It made me angry and depressed. I'm making less money now that I'm out of the modeling business, but I'm much, much happier. People don't look at me as if I'm some sort of flake and I personally feel a greater sense of accomplishment."

Dan Deeley admits that "many of the guys are embarrassed to say what they do. They're ashamed of it because they feel as if they are not really putting in an honest day's work. They feel guilty that they're making money on their looks."

Some feel guilty about their sexual involvements as well. Although going the casting couch route is not a prerequisite for success in male modeling, some photographers are said to ask for sex in return for testings, bookings, and general career guidance. It is not a widespread practice but it does occur, and those who start selling themselves for the sake of success usually live to regret it. There is a thread of sexuality that runs through the male side of the business that makes these encounters possible without professional repercussions. The code of conduct that prevails on the agents, models, and photographers in the women's divisions does not apply here. No one gets worked up if male models are casually jumping into bed with each other, with editors, or with anyone else for that matter. The men who engage in this activity have to worry more about their own personal values than about what the industry powers will think. Again, the old double standard applies. Men are freer to make their own decisions and accept the consequences; women have to live by the rules. In this case, however, the difference is based more on economics than on moral considerations. Women play for much bigger stakes. They can earn extraordinary sums of money, but they can also lose it all if their image is tarnished by a reputation for promiscuity.

Just what amount of money can male models expect to earn? The average Big Four male makes from $35,000 to $50,-000 annually; the big stars in the business draw up to $100,000. Hourly and daily fees are similar to the women's—about $100 and $750, respectively—but the men work less frequently, since the demand for male models is nowhere near as great as that for females. That is because modeling is a service business and its major clients—the apparel and cosmetics industries—cater mostly to women. For every brand of men's cologne on the market there are ten different types of perfume for women; for every page of men's fashions in the daily newspapers there are five pages of women's clothes; and most important, there are a half dozen women's fashion magazines and only one that features men.

Daniel, the model with Wilhelmina Men, notes: "I'm considered a success in this business. Everyone is pleased with my career progress, and my income has reached a comfortable level. But I don't spend most of my time modeling. Not at all. I'd like to, but there just isn't enough demand for my services. Typically, I'll model two days or so a week and spend the rest of my time either hanging around the agency or at the Central Park Zoo. There's something very tranquil about the zoo. It makes me feel like a child again. It's really a great place to go because it keeps me from going to Saks, where I wind up spending more money than I should, and because it isolates me from the workaday world. When I'm at the zoo, I don't have to confront all the other people who are busy at their jobs. It makes me feel guilty and depressed to see others at work when I'm on the bench.

"It's a shame that clients can use models just when they want and we have to sit and wait for them the rest of the time. Sometimes I feel like a pawn. It seems to me that the agencies should get us more contract work so that we can be associated with a product and get paid whether we work or not. A lot of women get that but then again, they get the best of everything."

It is widely acknowledged that black male models get the worst of everything. The modeling caste system has white women at the top, followed by white men, then black women—and, on the lowest rungs, black men. The opportunities for black male models are severely limited, and most of them earn less than $15,000 a year; the very best command $25,000. The problem stems from the overall system of advertising products and services in the U.S. Although black faces have become more evident in printed advertisements and TV commercials in recent years, they still have a long way to go before reaching parity with whites. Most marketing executives still believe that the presence of black models in an ad makes the product take on the image of being used mostly by blacks—and that is simply unacceptable for most promotional campaigns. Discrimination is built into the system, resulting in fewer bookings for black models. The modeling agencies recognize this and therefore keep only token black representatives on their headsheets: an average of one black man for every ten whites. This is just enough to avoid charges of racism and to have an adequate inventory of black faces to meet market demands. Most black models are extremely handsome men who, were they white, could be earning three or four times their current wages.

Ebony magazine described their plight this way: "They are sensitive and sensuous, resolute and egotistical. But primarily they are outrageously fine black men. They have to be. Their rent is dependent upon their bronze physiques and tantalizing smiles used to push everything from liquor to shorts.

"Whether they are smiling at you from a cigarette billboard, munching hamburgers in a television commercial, or modeling skin-tight jeans in a magazine, there is no denying that they are indeed a salable product.

"They are black male models and although they may look like a million bucks in idyllic advertisements, many are often broke and disillusioned."

Few will argue with this. One well-known black male model complains that he has to drive a cab to make ends meet; others are waiters, clothing salesmen, bartenders. They keep at modeling because, like so many others in the business, they hope that somehow it will lead to something better, that they will be "discovered." Modeling keeps their faces in the spotlight. As long as that happens, they imagine there is reason for hope.

The modeling establishment likes to boast that males enjoy a longer career span than women. This is supposed to compensate for the fact that they earn less and that they rarely achieve star status. Agents claim that the typical male will start out at age eighteen and, if he stays sharp and up-to-date, can remain active and well paid until reaching thirty-five or forty.

This is a gross exaggeration. A glance at any one of the Big Four headsheets reveals what the models themselves readily admit: that some of the men are still teenagers, the vast majority are in their mid-twenties, and a small sprinkling have managed to cross the thirty-year line and still hang in. There is a place in male fashion modeling for the salt-and-pepper "distinguished" look, but it accounts for only a small percentage of the billings. Clients requesting mature males to model apparel lines aimed at middle-aged consumers are outnumbered ten to one by the trendy, youth-oriented apparel houses. As a result, young models are the most marketable. Agencies continuously review their inventories to check for signs that older models are losing their appeal. When that is found to be the case, the aging pro is quickly replaced by one of the eager young Turks lined up outside the agency door waiting breathlessly for a shot at the big time. Of those who gain entry, most last for less than a year; their billings never take off and they are axed before their first anniversary.

"I accept about twenty new models a year," says Dan Deeley, seated in his narrow office lined with photos of beautiful men, sexy women, and the Incredible Hulk, "but only about five of them make it. A full 75 percent of the guys who start out as models can't cut the mustard and are asked to leave. Some never develop a sense of style, some simply don't catch on with clients, and others are lazy and irresponsible. But those who survive the first round usually have what it takes and are with us for quite some time."

Successful male models stay in the big leagues for about ten years. Typically, they enter the business during their late teens and exit before age thirty. The pink slip comes at a time when others their age are first starting to advance in the more traditional professions. Just when attorneys, physicians, and corporate executives are starting to hit their stride, male models are washed up, burned out, written off the books. Although a token few can stay with the Big Four up to and beyond age forty, most of the men in this age group manage to keep their hand in modeling only if they switch to commercial agencies (the same tactic favored by women who have passed their prime as high fashion models but want to stay in a related field).

"We are, in one sense, the dumping ground for models, male and female, who can no longer make it with the high fashion agencies," says Cye Perkins, owner of the Perkins commercial agency and himself a former model for Powers and Ford. "Our strong suit is in providing clients with models who look like average people, sort of character models. For example, we get a lot of requests for men who look like middle-aged business executives. A good many of the male models who can no longer qualify as glamour boys can fit the bill perfectly for this kind of booking. So they are able to extend their modeling careers by coming over to us once they are forced out of the high fashion shops. There are absolutely no age ceilings for commercial work; we can use male models even if they live to be one hundred. Advertisers ask us for grandfatherly types now and then and we are happy to oblige."

The drawback to commercial modeling is that it is even harder for a man to make a decent living at this than at high fashion modeling. The hourly rates are similar to those in high fashion, but there are even fewer opportunities here. Clients tend to request commercial models for one-shot deals. A luggage manufacturer, for example, may need an executive type for an advertisement to introduce a new attaché case. That one ad will likely run for a year or more. Unlike the high fashion field—with its voracious appetite for models to present breaking styles on a daily or weekly basis—industries that turn to commercial agencies are less promotion-oriented and use models far more sparingly. Thus few commercial models earn more than $25,000 a year and a good number make substantially less. For this reason, many supplement their modeling incomes with flexible part-time jobs that allow them to take off when a booking comes through.

"We also attract one type of male model that the high fashion agencies never see," Perkins adds. "That's the guy who is a successful business executive or professional and who models not for the money at all but just for the kicks. Many of these guys make plenty of dough in their regular occupations; modeling is just a fun thing, an ego trip for them. They like to see their pictures on billboards and in magazines.

"The men in this category are among the most pleasant and delightful people in the entire modeling business. It's a pleasure to work with them. They don't fancy themselves as prima donnas; they are not finicky or neurotic. I guess that's because they get satisfaction from their primary careers and because the quality of their lives doesn't depend so much on their appearance. That takes a lot of the pressure off."

One of the most common complaints among high fashion male models is that they are used as accessories in ads rather than as the main attraction. When an ad features both male and female models, the complaint goes, the men are invariably in the background, striking some silly pose, or they are made to lean against the women like inanimate props. The men are bitter about this because they believe that it adds to the women's star status while detracting from their own importance.

Although there is some validity to this complaint—many ads do relegate males to the position of background objects— the nature of the business is changing. Slowly but surely male models are gaining stature, the market for their services is growing, and the first group of male stars to be known beyond the confines of the modeling community is emerging. This development is a result of the increasing concern among American men with looking good, dressing well, and meticulous grooming. Ever since the so-called "peacock revolution" of the 1960s turned men on to trendy apparel and to longer, more individualistic hairstyles, there has been a steadily increasing demand for male designer fashions, fragrances, and how-to books on the dos and don'ts of personal appearance. All of this has led to a surge in male-oriented advertising, more bookings for male models, and more frequent use of the male models as central rather than as supporting figures. Though the change has not been sweeping, it has improved conditions for male models, and the trend is expected to continue.

The growing market for male models has brought with it a taste of the bitter inter-agency rivalry that has long characterized the women's side of the business. Until now, the Big Four model wars have raged almost exclusively over the pirating of prize female faces; there simply hasn't been enough money on the men's side to warrant major raids. Even John Casablancas, the acknowledged master at luring away top stars, has built his men's division mostly from scratch. Here, he has followed the slower but less controversial strategy of finding and cultivating new talent.

But the relative calm that has prevailed on the men's side appears to be ending. There are signs that as the stakes rise so too do the animosities. When Elite's men's division started a softball team, executives there say that they challenged Ford men to meet them on the diamond for their first game. Ford allegedly accepted the invitation, but then backed out without giving any explanation. "We tried to find out why they cancelled, but no one was talking," Elite's Bob Newey says. "Some of the other agencies are wary of us and they just don't want to be friendly. Not that it's all bad blood. I'm on cordial terms with Dan Deeley and with some of the other male model agents. But every now and then I get a clear signal of what's brewing beneath the surface. Recently, I was at a model's ball at Xenon, where I happened to bump into Jerry Ford. He saw me and instinctively raised his hand to shake mine. Then, in a flash, he realized what he was doing, let his hand drop back to his side and quickly passed me by."

Dan Deeley of Wilhelmina Men comments, "Everyone is just getting more serious about this end of the business. Before the peacock revolution, male modeling was really a poorly managed and poorly marketed enterprise. When I first took over at this agency ten years ago, the headsheet was very sloppy, very poor. Most of the guys on it were fillers—just faces with little style or appeal. I cleaned house and brought in men with a distinct flair and with a European look to coincide with the growing popularity of European fashion. The timing was right; the European look dominated male modeling until very recently."

The rising eminence of American fashion designers is now changing the look of male fashions and in turn is calling for a new breed of male models. The casual, masculine collections of Bill Blass and Ralph Lauren, for example, demand strong, athletic-looking models. For this reason, the skinny, supple European-type males are being nudged out. It is no longer unacceptable for male models to be hard and muscular; in fact, it is now a real plus. In line with this trend, many are now into body building, weight lifting, and vigorous, well-rounded physical fitness programs.

"I've gotten into working out a little and I like it because my body is important to me," says Daniel. "Physically, I look and feel better than ever before. But some of the guys are going overboard. I mean, they're building up these huge muscles even though they're never called on to lift anything heavier than a bottle of cologne. It's like driving around Manhattan in a Ferrari—there's no way to use all of that horsepower." Then, in that disillusioned tone that creeps into the talk of so many men in the modeling world, he adds, "Modeling's the same thing: it has a way of making everything you have or do—all of your best assets—seem wasted."

10

THE FUTURE
On to Tinsel Town

"If you think the craze over top models will soon peak
you're wrong—dead wrong. You're witnessing the birth of a
phenomenon that's still in the incubation stage. Models are not
only the hottest things in the fashion world; they're becoming
the biggest things in show business as well. There's no stopping
them and there's no stopping us: we're going to the top
together."

—Bruce Cooper

Just what the future holds for modeling is difficult to say. The festering lawsuits, the new breed of male models, the emergence of celebrity superstars among the women, and the challenge to the establishment by new agencies make anything possible. One thing, however, seems certain: the fate of this world will be tied more and more to that of another surreal community—Hollywood.

The latest and most significant development in modeling is that the agencies are moving slowly but inexorably toward full-talent representation, bringing them in competition with the likes of the William Morris agency in handling actors and actresses for television programs, theatrical films, and broadcast commercials. As increasing numbers of models become popular figures who can add immeasurably to advertising campaigns and to box office receipts, producers are vying for their talents and offering big money to get the cream of the crop. By letting others represent their girls in these deals, model agents recognize that they are cutting themselves out of an extremely lucrative market. What's more, they are in danger of developing a girl, guiding her to fame as a model, and then losing out when she goes on to stardom in the entertainment field. For this reason, the agencies are now focusing more of their efforts on the theatrical and broadcast commercial markets. Although most of the big agencies have had television departments for years, these were always considered secondary divisions. Now, management is paying close attention and is stretching its net over a wider and wider number of clients. Here, the Wilhelmina agency has taken the lead. It is extending beyond the traditional representation of its own models to such diverse show business groups as actors, screen writers, and directors. In addition, Wilhelmina has become the first of the New York modeling agencies to open a West Coast office devoted exclusively to talent.

Whether in New York or Los Angeles, talent is becoming an ever-more lucrative part of the model agency business. Typically, talent divisions handle all agency business that is not related to the print media. This includes television commercials, soap operas, theater, and trade shows.

"The old saying that models can't act is no longer believed by the people who make the casting decisions," says Joan Howse, director of Wilhelmina's talent division and a former casting director herself for the McCann Erickson advertising agency. "Our people are in demand for everything from selling perfume to acting in films. We're the ideal agents to service them in these pursuits because we know how to manage their total careers. You can't have an elegant model with a *Vogue* type image doing commercials for oven cleaners or playing prostitutes in the movies. If she does that, out the window goes the elegant image—and it's the image that print advertisers want her for. So although the girl may want to take the acting job for the money it can bring, we have to control her—teach her to turn down those offers that will damage rather than aid her career in the long run. That's why a knowledgeable agent is so important. We can balance her modeling and acting careers. We have an overview."

Models who can successfully combine acting and modeling careers make extraordinary amounts of money—and so, in turn, do their agents. A hot talent may work two or three days a week in soap operas, two more as a high fashion model, and then slip off for a week to do a "Charlie's Angels" segment. For this variety of assignments, she can easily pull down more than a half million dollars a year. A girl in this category will likely belong to three different unions: AFTRA (American Federation of Television and Radio Artists, for videotape and radio), SAG (Screen Actors Guild, for film and TV commercials), and Equity (for theater work). These unions protect actors by setting guidelines for their contracts with agents and by establishing minimum standards of compensation. For a television commercial, the model's daily starting fees are only $250 (1979 rate), but she is paid every time the commercial is broadcast. These residuals can often add up to more than $30,000—and that's for as little as a single day's work.

"The top talents make up to $200,000 a year just for their broadcast commercials," Howse says. "Add to that $150,000 a year for TV shows and another $200,000 for print modeling and you're talking about some very successful young women. Precisely how much the talent makes depends on her desirability. Union terms tell us the minimum we can get for their services. It's our job to negotiate for more when the girl can command it."

With the Wilhelmina agency branching out to represent film personalities, directors, and screen writers, the commission opportunities are enormous. Latching on to a superstar can produce agency revenues of several hundred thousand dollars for a single film role. That's more than agents earn for representing five successful fashion models for an entire year.

Does Eileen Ford want to follow Wilhelmina out to the West Coast, to move beyond TV commercials and to tap a wider market of show biz talent? "We don't believe we should do that," Eileen snaps. "It's stretching yourself too thin to be running a business on both coasts. You have to stick to what you do best rather than running off to look for new challenges all the time."

Sour grapes? Whatever her intentions, Eileen's comments are accurate in their assertion that modeling's new challenges will bring new problems as well as opportunities. As model agents move away from their primary field, they multiply their risks and force themselves to go through a new learning process.

It is an acknowledged principle of business management that companies of all kinds must carefully research and prepare for their forays into new markets. Time and time again, established corporations—even the giants of American industry, who can invest unlimited funds and talent in the effort—have fallen flat on their faces trying to branch out in new directions. Even if the fields they attempt to move into are related to their primary one, the obstacles are still enormous. In many cases, the diversifying enterprises have had to admit that they were not experts in the markets they coveted and that it would be wiser to stick to their areas of specialization.

Companies try to stretch their capabilities because the new markets are so lush, so rewarding, so profitable. This is the way both agents and models view Hollywood. As they have made minor inroads into Tinsel Town, their appetites have grown for a bigger and bigger piece of the action. But the question remains: do they have the talent, skills, and drive to make it in this very different, very demanding business? Although it is impossible to answer at this point, one thing is clear: they will be in for many surprises along the way.

"We've had to learn that what would-be actresses say is not always what they mean," Howse explains. "Many times, girls come up here in tears, crying their eyes out for a chance to audition. They say they can't live another day unless they become actresses. Well, quite a few times we've given girls like this a chance, even if they didn't exactly meet our standards. Our feeling was that their motivation might make up for what they lacked in other ways. But you know what? We'd set them up with auditions and they'd never show up. One cancelled out five times before we gave up on her. Then she went out to the Coast and cried to the agents out there that no one in New York ever gave her a chance. Her problem—and it's one many others share—is that she wants to be an actress but is so afraid of failing that she won't even try. People may think that talent agenting is the same as model agenting, but it's not. We have to play shrink a hell of a lot more on the talent side. But we're willing to do it—there's a lot of money to be made."

Welcome to Hollywood.

INDEX

215

Ford Models Inc. (*cont'd*)
  Casablancas and, 80, 84, 85, 87–88, 89
  contracts with, 89
  income of, 21–22, 27
  men's division of, 208
  parental approach of, 4–5, 47–48
  training of models by, 4–5, 47
  Wilhelmina on, 33, 36–37
Freytag, Arnie, 179

Gallery, 167, 169, 170, 181–82
Gentlemen's Quarterly (GQ), 140–41, 150
Glamour, 135, 136, 138, 147, 148
Glamour, search for, 7, 39, 94, 130, 132–33
Go-sees, 55–56
Graham, Karen, 2, 66
Griffin, Merv, 60
Grill, Frances, 69
  on agenting for photographers, 110
  on glamour, 94
  on photographers, 106
  Barbra Walz and, 111–12

Hanson, Patti, 123
Harper's Bazaar, 135
Hefner, Hugh, 156, 178, 180
Hemingway, Margaux, 67–68
Hollywood, modeling industry and, 210, 213
Hollywood Blvd., at Wilhelmina Models, 38
Home town
  leaving, 40
  return to, 44–45
Hooker, Dwight, 176
Howse, Joan, 43–44, 73, 211–13
Hugh (model), 201–2
Hutton, Lauren, 115, 123

Image
  creation of model's, 51–52
  fashion magazines and, 139
Iman, 88, 104, 123
Income (earnings)
  of fashion magazine editors, 131, 133
  of modeling agencies, 21–22, 212
  models', 68–69, 202
  photographers', 124–25, 126, 170–71
See also Fees

Jagger, Bianca, 102
Jealousy, 55–56, 92, 126–28

John Robert Powers agency, 7, 22, 24–26, 61
Johnson, Beverly, 146–47
Joplin, Janis, 107

Kenner Toy Company, 1–2
Kevin (model), 186–87
King, Harry, 103n

L'Agence agency. *See* Agence
Lana (fictitious name), 60–64
Lauren, Ralph, 143, 145
Levinson, Ira, 87–89
Liberman, Alexander, 137–38
Location shooting, 143, 144–45
Loving, Candy, 178–79
Lundgren, Christine, 87

Mademoiselle, 135–37, 138
Magazines, 5
  fashion. *See* Fashion magazines
  pornographic. *See* Nude modeling
Male models (male modeling), 4, 183–211
  as accessories rather than main attraction, 207
  ashamed of their occupation, 200–1, 202
  attitudes toward, 185, 186–87, 191, 200–201
  black, 203–4
  career span of, 204–6
  commercial agencies and, 206
  competition among, 188
  Dan Deeley's shit-kicker syndrome and, 199
  derailment of, from pursuit of other careers, 198–99
  disillusionment of, 192, 204, 209
  dissatisfaction of, 198–201
  earnings of, 202, 203
  European connection and, 196–98
  fees of, 202, 203
  gay, 189
  growing market for, 208, 209
  malaise in, 184–85
  model agencies and, 187–93, 195–96, 203–5, 208–9
  photographers and, 195–96, 202
  physical prerequisites for, 193
  pretense among, 186–89
  qualities essential for, 193–95
  style and, 194–95
  as underemployed, 202–3
  as unhappy, 185–89
Marketing of models, 52–55
Marketing products, strategies for, 145–46